BASIC SALES SKILLS
Business to Business

The Sales & Marketing Foundation Established in 1989, SMF's mission is to elevate the sales profession through education, training, testing, and professional accreditation.

The International Certified Sales Professional's Library
Basic Sales Skills: Business to Business
Basic Sales Skills: Retail Sales
Basic Sales Skills: Direct Sales
Advanced Sales Skills
Basic Sales Management Skills
Executive Sales Management Skills

BASIC SALES SKILLS
Business to Business

The Sales & Marketing Foundation

IRWIN
Professional Publishing
Burr Ridge, Illinois
New York, New York

3 2280 00515 3069

© SALES & MARKETING FOUNDATION, 1995

Individual chapters are copyrighted by the chapter author, © 1995.

Senior sponsoring editor: Cynthia A. Zigmund
Project editor: Jane Lightell
Designer: Mercedes Santos
Art coordinator: Mark Malloy
Compositor: BookMasters, Inc.
Typeface: 11/13 Palatino
Printer: Arcata Graphics-Fairfield

Library of Congress Cataloging-in-Publication Data

Sales & Marketing Foundation (U.S.)
    Basic sales skills—business to business / The Sales & Marketing
Foundation.
        p.   cm. — (The International certified sales professional's library)
    Includes index.
    ISBN 0-7863-0270-4
    1. Selling.   2. Industrial marketing.   I. Title.   II. Series.
HF5438.25.S252   1995
    658.8'1—dc20   94–15155

Printed in the United States of America
1 2 3 4 5 6 7 8 9 0 AG-F 1 0 9 8 7 6 5 4

The International Certified Sales Professional's Library

I would like to lay to rest two myths. One, salespeople are born. Two, "my type of selling is different."

Myth 1. People can be *trained* to sell. Good salespeople come in many sizes, shapes, colors, and genders. Some of the so-called born sales types have an initial advantage because of a more outgoing personality or better communication skills. However, we have all met quiet and well-organized types who are effective salespeople. Practical training can erase the so-called edge. However, no education or training works unless it is put into practice. Since selling is doing, it is imperative that the training is put into use. The concept: on the job!

Myth 2. "My type of selling is different." "I am a computer salesperson." "I am in insurance sales." The list goes on. I would like to make an analogy. Doctors get a degree in medicine, then become a pediatrician or orthopedic surgeon. Lawyers become proficient in the law, then specialize in real estate, criminal, or patent law. Salespeople have to master the fundamentals of selling first. There are skills common to all types of selling. All salespeople have to learn prospecting. They all have to present their products or services. It is usually a matter of degree. Some salespeople have to use some fundamentals more and some less. Only when these fundamentals have been mastered can they specialize in computer sales or insurance sales.

The International Association of Sales Professionals (IASP) (formerly Sales and Marketing Executives of Greater New York) was founded in 1932 by a group of sales executives led by the legendary Thomas J. Watson, Sr., of IBM. It is the largest professional group of

The Certified Sales Professional's Library

its kind in the country, and we have been a keen observer of our profession for the past 62 years.

Three years ago, the IASP held a series of focus meetings to ascertain why the skills of salespeople appeared to have eroded. Sales executives, sales trainers, human resource managers, academic leaders, sales reps, and consultants attended.

The conclusions of these focus groups were that:

1. Large multinational down to smaller fast-track corporations had moved away from training their salespeople in the fundamentals of selling.
2. Most of the "training" was in product knowledge and applications (40 to 45 percent); corporate culture, that is, how we at the XYZ Company operate (40 percent); and the remainder in some form of sales training.
3. For financial and increased productivity reasons, salespeople were being put into the field sooner (average 90 days).
4. Mentoring and coaching by managers in the field was almost nonexistent.
5. The training they did receive was not very good. It was usually a "one-shot deal" with no real follow up.

Based on these conclusions, we set out to develop a list of the generic skills that these groups felt were common to most salespeople and were essential for initial success in selling. We then called on a group of professionals (members of IASP) to translate these skills into 12 fundamental sales training modules including ethics, business writing, and handling stress, which the focus groups said were also important.

We then asked this same group to join together and teach these modules to salespeople. We conducted these workshops over one and a half years. Each class had an average of 10 to 12 salespeople with experience of from zero to 10 years. The program was a resounding success. The students found the diversities in experience, style, and presentation by the faculty simulating and very practical. We also had each salesperson's manager observe the salesperson putting the skills taught to use on the job. Remember, selling is doing!

By this book on *Basic Sales Skills: Business to Business*, our faculty shares with you the fundamentals of selling. As you will see, each chapter author has a slightly different style and a different approach to the material. If you are new to sales, you will find it extremely helpful in laying the foundation for the selling process. If you are more experienced, it will serve as a solid refresher. You will also pick up more practical techniques and ideas to increase your present productivity.

Today, more sales organizations are moving to a consultative selling and partnering relationship with their customers. There is also an increase in team selling. Technology will provide more tools to help the process. However, before any salesperson or sales organization can adopt these concepts, they have to have a solid grounding in the fundamentals of selling which is what this book is all about. It has not been written as a panacea, but as a tool to help you be more skilled; To start you off on the right foot or to continue the process of being a sales professional. Good salespeople are not born; they can be trained. Learn what selling is all about first, then specialize!

This book is the first volume in a series that will become the International Certified Sales Professional's Library. Books on advanced sales skills, basic sales management skills, and executive sales management skills and retail/direct sales will follow. This book will be used as the text for the Basic Sales Skills course which will be offered by selected universities, schools of continuing education, and sales training firms as partners in a National Sales Certification Program which we also sponsor. See the next page for more details.

Edward B. Flanagan
President, International Association of Sales
Professionals and President, Sales and
Marketing Foundation

National Sales Certification Program

The National Sales Competency Evaluation Test reveals the profile of success. Success in sales has specific quantifiable and qualifiable characteristics, and IASP is now prepared to prove it. In cooperation with Professional Examination Services (PES), a leader in testing measurement and research, and Hofstra University, IASP is making history with the creation of the National Sales Competency Evaluation Test.

This test will serve as an important measurement tool in the certification program leading to the professional designation, International Certified Sales Professional (ICSP). Entirely performance-based and structured to mirror sales in real life, the test will measure not only sales professionals' skills, but how they apply those skills in a variety of situations. Participating companies and individuals will receive a powerful diagnostic analysis that clearly delineates which areas need to be developed.

Reality-based tests weigh performance authentically. Since the measure of success in sales is far too complex for traditional multiple-choice paper and pencil testing, PES has structured the National Sales Competency Evaluation Test to mirror reality. This sophisticated test objectively analyzes salespeople and sales managers' skills in three distinct ways: in-basket problems, case study simulations, and an oral sales presentation. Open-ended responses allow for the individuality of decision making.

Specifically, the three-hour in-basket test will measure decision-making skills as the salesperson sorts through a confusing pile of notes, memos, reports, faxes, phone messages, and mail. The materials, some of which are interrelated, vary in urgency, complexity, and impact on the salesperson and the company. Test participants will be required to organize the materials, analyze a wide range of problems, develop appropriate solutions, and communicate their decisions in writing to other staff members.

The three-hour case study simulation, with audio and video stimuli, gives salespeople real-world scenarios to dissect. Tested are listening, observation, assessing, and comprehension skills. The participants must interpret a myriad of details and provide specific solutions to the problems presented. They must analyze what they are hearing and seeing and report on it. Incorporated are interruptions that mirror the chaotic environments most salespeople face in their work.

Finally, the three- to five-minute videotaped oral sales presentation will test the communication skills that are essential for success in sales. For fairness, the participants will be able to select a topic familiar to them such as their company or product. For development purposes they will be given their videotapes, as well as feedback on their performances, after the test.

Comprehensive diagnostic feedback of the participants' performance, with pragmatic remedial strategies, will be delivered to the candidate or sponsoring company in a timely fashion.

CERTIFICATION ELIGIBILITY REQUIREMENTS

Candidates for the International Certified Sales Professional designation must meet the following requirements.

- A 4-year degree plus 2 years' experience, or a 2-year AAS degree plus 2 years' experience, or 4 years of experience.
- 5 letters of recommendation.
- Passing the National Sales Competency Evaluation Test.
- Signing a Code of Ethics.
- Approval by ICSP Review Committee.

The National Sales Certification Program has as its goals to:

- Increase the skill levels of salespeople.
- Increase their productivity.
- Focus training where it is needed, thus reducing training costs and time.
- Raise the image of sales as a career.
- Promote the concept of lifelong learning for salespeople.
- Establish the first national measure of sales skills abilities.

- Promote the teaching of sales and accessibility to it through universities, schools of continuing education, and training companies nationwide.
- Create the first Bachelor of Science in Sales degree program nationwide.

For more information, please call IASP at (212) 683-9755.

The National Sales Hall of Fame Awards Program

Sponsored annually by the International Association of Sales Professionals since 1989, this awards program recognizes the men and women, who by their special sales, communications, and leadership skills have helped to build and shape America's businesses. It recognizes these achievements in industry, commerce, the arts, government, sports, and entertainment. It also promotes the profession of selling as a career, for those already a part of it and for those yet to come. A prestigious Board of Trustees annually votes for the nominees selected for induction. Nominations are open. It is the "Oscar night" for the sales profession.

Some of the prior inductees are: Sam Walton (Wal-Mart); Stanley Gault (Rubbermaid/Goodyear Tire); James Burke (Johnson & Johnson); J. W. "Bill" Marriott (Marriott Corp.); Daniel Tully (Merrill Lynch); Mary Kay Ash (Mary Kay Cosmetics); William Howell (J.C. Penney); Kathy Black (American Newspaper Association); Liz Claiborne (Liz Claiborne, Inc.)

World Congress of Sales Professionals

Sponsored annually since 1991 by the Sales & Marketing Foundation, this is the governing body for setting the policies and procedures for the National Sales Certification Program. It is responsible for the professional, educational, and ethical standards to elevate sales to a recognized profession. Delegates to the annual Congress need not be members of IASP or SMF.

If you are an active sales executive, sales training director, human resource director, sales support executive, or an educator in sales at the university, continuing education, or community college level, you are welcome. For more information call (212) 683-9755.

The International Association of Sales Professionals

The International Association of Sales Professionals (formerly the Sales and Marketing Executives of Greater New York) is a not-for-profit membership association of professional men and women who represent a cross section of America's businesses. It was founded 62 years ago by a group of business executives headed by the legendary Thomas J. Watson, Sr., of IBM Corporation. Their goals were to provide a forum for the exchange of ideas and sales techniques and to increase the efficiency of the selling and distribution systems while promoting the profession of sales to capable young people. Members of IASP are board chairmen; presidents of large multinational and small fast-track companies; vice presidents of sales, marketing, advertising, and sales promotion; regional and district sales managers; and consultants. They represent all industries. IASP is the largest, most prestigious group of sales and marketing executives in the nation.

The growth of active chapters in Connecticut, Long Island, New Jersey, and Westchester, in addition to New York City, attest to the need IASP fills. Through educational seminars, workshops, and luncheon programs, it brings to members and their firms the best methods in competitive strategies and skills, presented by leading authorities. The group is headquartered at 13 East 37th Street, 8th Floor, New York, NY 10016. Telephone (212) 683-9755; fax (212) 725-3752.

Introduction

I. Martin Jacknis
Results Marketing, Inc.

A successful career in sales is an exciting journey. It has numerous rewards, not the least of which is the satisfied feeling and knowledge that you really helped someone else achieve his or her objectives. An effective, successful salesperson is a purveyor of knowledge and value.

Basic Sales Skills was developed to give new salespeople every opportunity to increase their probability of succeeding in their journey. Its chapters were written by professionals whose careers have been built on providing guidelines and practical advice to sales organizations ranging in size from Fortune 1000 corporations to regional, family-owned businesses. The markets may differ, but the strategies, tactics, execution techniques, implementation, and evaluation processes discussed can be applied to selling products and services worldwide.

Some salespeople are consistently productive pacesetters in their organization. What makes them so successful? Natural ability helps. But like a great athlete, natural ability is only part of the story. The rest is good coaching, dedication to continuous learning, and a belief in themselves and the products and services they are selling.

Another characteristic of the achiever is the ability to be honest with one's self; if they do not succeed, they typically ask themselves, "Why did I fail?" and then seek insights into the cause. If they succeeded, they would still question how they could have done it faster, or better, or at a reduced cost.

Basic Sales Skills will help you to focus on developing a conscious and systematic process to remove barriers and recognize connectivity between the sales-process steps. Figure 1, the Marketing and Sales Process, will help you to visualize the flow that begins at understanding a customer's needs and extends to growing your satisfied customer with other required products and services.

This figure graphically demonstrates how a typical sales process unfolds. Keep it handy and refer to it frequently. You will see the multitude of situations where your skills development will significantly aid you in effectively executing the process quicker, at a lower cost, and with a higher probability of success than your competition. Since this process is interconnected and interdependent, what you do or do not do at each stage usually has a dramatic impact on the outcome.

Step 1.   The first step in the process is understanding your target prospect's prioritized valid needs and wants, relative to the products and services you currently offer or plan to offer. Listening, questioning, surveying, research, and analysis skills are critical in this stage of the process.

Step 2.   Once you understand the market requirements that apply to your current or proposed offerings, you can develop your marketing program. It typically addresses policy development, positioning, packaging, pricing, and promotion. Your firm's marketing department should have sales representation and input during this developmental stage.

Step 3.   Here an overall sales strategy is developed, defining how you will attack specific markets, industries, companies, and decision influencers. Your planning will include how you will approach a given territory, encompassing its potential opportunity, demographics, and competition, to name a few key factors.

Within Step 3, you should develop an account strategy for penetrating a specific account. Determine which contact strategies to utilize, whom to approach first, second, and third. Understand what factors are the most and least important to the decision maker. Develop your strategy based on knowing your relative strengths, compared to the other available alternatives. To sell a new or modified product or service to an existing customer might mean contact-

FIGURE 1
Marketing and Sales Process

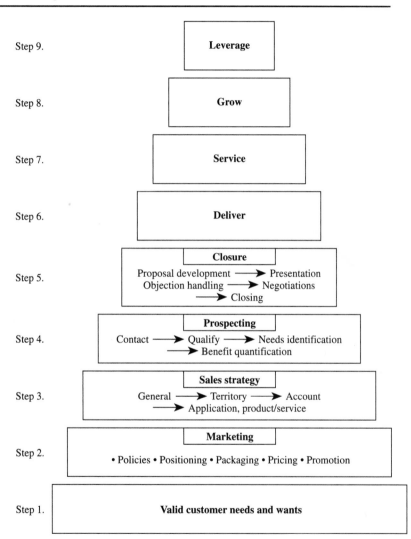

Source: I. Martin Jacknis, Results Marketing, Inc. © 1994.

ing different decision influencers and using different approaches than you utilized with your initial sale.

   Step 4. Prospecting includes: initial contact, qualifying, needs identification, and benefit quantification. Important in this is a positive attitude plus persistence; creativity; proactivity; belief in yourself, your company, your products and services; good questioning; and analysis and organization skills.

Step 5. Once you have turned a suspect into a qualified and interested prospect, develop a proposed solution and effectively present it to the key decision makers and influencers. The path to successful closure usually includes handling objections and negotiating final terms and conditions. This phase requires persuasiveness; good writing, communication, and presentation skills, including effective use of presentation tools and techniques; objection handling; and negotiation skills.
Then ask for and process your new order.

Step 6. Deliver your product or service on time, within budget, at or above the expectations you initially set with your prospect.

Step 7. Supply on-going service and support to your customer as stipulated in the contract.

Step 8. Once you have successfully completed the previous seven steps and have satisfied customers, look for more opportunities within their organizations. It is always easier to sell new products and services to existing satisfied customers than starting all over again with new prospects.

Step 9. Finally, if you delivered what you promised on time, within budget, and exceeded your client's expectations, you deserve leverage. Leverage is asking for and getting new orders, getting paid early or on time, and receiving referrals and reference letters.
Now you're on top! Keep learning and growing to stay there!

THE PATH TO SALES PRODUCTIVITY

Order taker? Sales professional? Sales consultant? Sales representatives starting out on their new journey can chart their own course.

FIGURE 2
Self-Analysis Traits

Traits	Order Taker	Sales Professional	Sales Consultant
Values:	Quantity	Quantity/quality	Quality
Approach:	Tells and sells	Sells	Listens, matches needs with solutions
Relationship:	Client tolerates you	Client accepts you	Client respects and needs you
Planning:	Hit or miss	Moderate	Have a strategy and plan
Mode of operation:	Reactive	Active	Proactive
Knowledge:	Ceased learning	Learns as needed	Always seeks and offers knowledge
Perceived as:	An intruder	A friend	An advisor and confidant
Perspective:	Short-term	Medium	Global, long-term
Goal:	Make money	Make a sale	Make a client
Selection process:	Anything	Somewhat selective	Very selective
Actions:	Unconscious, inconsistent	Somewhat conscious and consistent	Deliberate; conscious; consistent

Source: I. Martin Jacknis, Results Marketing, Inc. © 1990.

They can make their own decisions about who they want to be and how they can approach the sales process, and therefore have more control over their career path.

Figure 2, Self-Analysis Traits, is a matrix of three approaches an individual can take in selling. Sales representatives can evaluate the components of each and decide which approach best fits their markets, their image, and their objectives. It is not surprising to observe a significant difference in the quality of life and the compensation from one's efforts among members of each of the three trait groups. In most cases, it is an ascending scale from order taker, to sales professional, to sales consultant.

In following the path to productivity, salespeople should:

- Be proactive rather than reactive. Help your clients by educating them about the criteria they should use to make more informed decisions. Set attainable objectives. Determine your target markets. Then apply sales skills and strategies within the context of your particular marketing and sales process. Use the process as a compass and map to guide you through the terrain.

- Develop the skill of understanding how a customer thinks. Early in their careers, the best sales representatives became expert at putting themselves in their client's shoes. They practice the art of informed listening and know how to ask the questions that will yield the information the salesperson can then turn into benefits for the customer with the rep's product or service as a viable solution. Successful sales professionals are working to a longer-term goal: to make clients, not only sales. They build credibility and are rewarded by turning a $20,000 sale into a $200,000 client.

- Realize that age is not an issue; you will be judged on your expertise. Look to mentors in your field or your firm who have an enviable history of creative and productive selling in your field. Develop your own image at the same time you are building product knowledge. Create a comfort zone in which to work. The more knowledge you have, the better are your chances to build eye-to-eye relationships with your clients. Understand and continuously expand your comfort zone.

A ROBUST STRATEGY

1. Be thoroughly familiar with the marketing and sales process of your firm. Know the logic behind your company's five Ps—pricing, positioning, packaging, promotion, policies.

2. Gain a competitive advantage in the marketplace. Understand your prospect's prioritized decision criteria. Identify how you, your firm, its products and services meet these criteria better than all the other available alternatives. Act on news of trends, reports of technologies, findings of surveys. Set aside the time to understand the driving forces behind your industry.

3. Separate the suspects from the prospects. What are the characteristics of a qualified prospect? Prospecting combines

tenacity, psychology, and a proactive approach to *seeking, seeing, and seizing* opportunities.

4. Establish rapport and relationship. People buy from individuals they like, respect, and trust. This kind of relationship pays off, even in the toughest of times and economic climates.

5. How do you get closure? Yes or no is the culmination of days or weeks of planning, fact-finding, phone calls, meetings, building rapport, supplying information. *Basic Sales Skills* provides proven ways to close business and therefore reward your hard work.

BASIC SALES SKILLS: A BASIS FOR SUCCESS

A recent study revealed most people absorb only 15 percent of what is taught to them and apply only 15 percent of what is absorbed. *That means only $2\frac{1}{4}$ percent of what is taught is actually applied!* We believe this low level of return on your investment is almost criminal. We would like to challenge you (and ourselves) to find better ways of identifying what information is most important, how to absorb it better, and how to repeatedly apply it better. This should be our common goal.

At the end of each chapter, we would also like you to identify the top three ideas, strategies, tactics, and execution techniques that you know in your heart you are not doing or are doing but not very well. Then make a conscious, and if possible visible, commitment to try to improve these approaches for at least 30 days. Then track, measure, and analyze the outcomes. Decide if you personally want to fully embrace, modify, or reject these new ideas.

We as faculty members have committed ourselves to a process and culture of continuous analysis and improvement in our profession. We welcome you to join us in this journey to success.

Contributors

In addition to contributing their respective chapters to this volume, each contributor served on the faculty of the National Sales Certification Program, responsible for the development of this portion of the certification process.

Roni Abrams Associates Limited
2820 Avenue J
Brooklyn, New York   11210
(718) 377-6599

Roni Abrams is nationally recognized as a trainer and speaker who specializes in interpersonal communications and coaches people to listen and speak to produce results. Ms. Abrams designs Perceptual Training Programs that empower people to stretch beyond what they thought possible to develop relationships, resolve conflict, manage change, and sell effectively. Companies, business leaders, political candidates, and entrepreneurs have benefited from her counsel.

Alan Cimberg
83 Tilrose Avenue
Malverne, New York   11565
(516) 593-7099

Alan Cimberg is a much-sought-after professional sales speaker and trainer, addressing audiences from American Express to Zenith. *Sales Management* magazine has said of Mr. Cimberg, he "instructs, entertains and inspires." Mr. Cimberg is the author of the soon-to-be released book, *How to Sell in Tough Times to Difficult People.*

Sandra Lotz Fisher
Fitness by Fisher, Inc.
535 East 86th Street
New York, New York   10028
(212) 744-5900

Sandra Lotz Fisher, M.S., M.A. Energizer! Motivator! Professional speaker, seminar leader, exercise physiologist, writer and consultant on fitness, stress management, and wellness. Custom-designs programs for Fortune 500 corporate and association meetings and training programs. *Sales & Marketing Management, Success, American Health, Family Circle.* Originated "Workout While U Drive" audiotape. Ms. Fisher is an avid hiker and Outward Bound alumna who climbed Mt. Kilimanjaro.

Dr. Mel Haber
Writing Development Associates
254-39 Bates Road
Little Neck, New York   11363
(718) 279-3143

Dr. Mel Haber is the president of Writing Development Associates. For over a dozen years, Dr. Haber has taught business writing workshops for many Fortune 500 companies and government agencies. To date, he's helped many salespeople who have needed to learn to write more clearly and persuasively.

Robert B. Hartman
Rote Systems, Inc.
P.O. Box 911
Oakhurst, New Jersey   07755
(908) 530-4078

Robert B. Hartman is president of Rote Systems, Inc., a management/sales training consulting company. As a trainer/consultant for the past 18 years, he has designed and delivered scores of management/sales training programs for a variety of Fortune 500 companies.

I. Martin Jacknis
Results Marketing, Inc.
2363 Black Rock Turnpike
Fairfield, Connecticut   06430
(203) 371-0368

A nationally recognized professional speaker, innovator, expert trainer, consultant, Marty Jacknis relies on his highly successful personal experiences to create innovative thinking and positive change in firms of all sizes. Mr. Jacknis is the founder and president of Results Marketing, Inc., a marketing, sales, management consulting, and training firm that applies unique results-oriented philosophies, strategies, tactics, and execution techniques to significantly improve business generation and profitability for its clients.

Louise A. Korver
Corporate Learning & Development
1139 East Putnam Avenue
Riverside, Connecticut   06878-1411
(203) 637-6755

Louise Korver has authored hundreds of customized sales and management courses in 20 years and is a sought-after facilitator of strategic marketing meetings and process reengineering sessions. She is a graduate of the Wharton School Implementing Strategy Program and has a degree in management from the University of Bridgeport.

Richard B. Lombard, Jr.
Cal Industries, Inc.
23 East 22nd Street
4th Floor
New York, New York   10010
(212) 420-8008

Dick Lombard has developed and facilitated consultative sales and management programs for over 25 years with companies like Merrill Lynch, AT&T, Entenmanns' Bakery, Prudential Securities, Aris Isotoner, and Canon Copiers. The unique approach to developing a quantifiable "customer win" has set Dick's program apart from the competition and has uniquely qualified him to gain professional notoriety in the engineering, architectural, and accounting fields where he is currently conducting Consultative Selling Workshops.

David G. Moran
MindWorks, Inc.
25 Garthwaite Terrace
Maplewood, New Jersey   07040
(201) 763-6881

David G. Moran is president of MindWorks, Inc., a company which specializes in training companies in the areas of sales, customer service, management, presentations, leadership, and creative thinking. Mr. Moran's clients have included American Airlines, Blue Cross and Blue Shield Association, Harry & David, Inc., IBM, and Sony. Prior to forming his own company Mr. Moran held positions with Blue Cross and Blue Shield of New Jersey and Tiffany & Co.

Mark Riesenberg
Human Resources Unlimited
29 Gilbert Place
West Orange, New Jersey   07052
(201) 736-8112

Mark Riesenberg is the founder and owner of Human Resources Unlimited, which he established in 1987. His expertise is in helping management assist their salespeople to improve their prospecting, presenting, goal achievement, time management, and closing skills.

Arnold L. Schwartz
Achievement Concepts, Inc.
1963 Cynthia Lane
P.O. Box 430
Merrick, New York   11566
(516) 868-5100

Arnold L. Schwartz is founder and president of Achievement Concepts, Inc., a New York–based consulting firm which conducts customized programs in sales, sales management, and customer service. A nationally known speaker, writer, and trainer, Mr. Schwartz's client list is a who's who of corporate America.

Contents

Chapter One
PRE-CALL PLANNING   1

Prospect Sources, 3

Source Information, 4

Establishing Files, 4

Elements of Pre-call Planning, 5

    Product Knowledge, 6

    Corporate Knowledge, 8

    Industry Knowledge, 9

    Customer Awareness, 9

    Personal Appearance, 10

    Selling Skills, 11

    Setting Sales Call Objectives, 12

    Creating an Effective Sales Planner, 19

    Case Study 1: A New Decision Maker in a New Account, 22

    Case Study 2: Established Account/Seasoned Buyer, 22

    Case Study 3: Many Decision Makers but No Decision, 23

    Case Study 4: Incomplete Background, 24

    Case Study 5: Conflicting Information, 25

    Case Studies 6–10: Create Your Own, 26

Chapter Two
PROSPECTING   27

The Rationale for Prospecting, 27

Why Do Salespeople Abhor Prospecting?, 28

Developing a Prospecting Awareness, 28

Developing a Prospecting Discipline, 29

The Steps in the Prospecting System, 30

    Identifying Your Market, 30

    Finding Prospects, 32

Getting Appointments on the Telephone, 38

    Step 1: Set Prospecting Goals, 39

Step 2: Identify the Appropriate Buying Influence, 43

Step 3: Prepare a Prospecting Script, 45

Step 4: Create an Objections Handbook, 51

Step 5: Pre-call Preparation, 53

Step 6: Get through the Secretary's Screen, 54

Step 7: Set up a Record Keeping and Follow-up System, 55

Step 8: Deal with Rejection, 56

Summary, 59

Chapter Three
BUILDING RELATIONSHIPS   61

What You Will Learn, 61

The Decision Process, 61

The Sales Strategy, 62

Understanding the Problem-Solving Approach to
Marketing, 62

Becoming a Consultant, 64

Creating a Good First Impression, 66

Ego versus Empathy, 67

Ego Drive and Empathy Drive, 68

Using Empathy Skills to Establish Rapport and Build
High-Trust Relationships, 70

Intentions, 70

Acknowledging, 71

Aligning, 72

A Customer's State of Mind, 72

What Are You Ultimately Looking For?, 73

What Is the Prospect Ultimately Looking For?, 74

Summary, 75

Exercises, 76

Chapter Four
SALES PRESENTATIONS   79

Knowing the Purpose of the Presentation, 80

Knowing the Audience, 81

Selecting the Material and Audiovisual, Equipment 82
Planning the Presentation, 84
  The Introduction, 85
  The Body, 86
  The Conclusion, 86
Reading Body Language, 87
Using Eye Contact, Voice Resonance, and Gestures, 88
Summary, 89
Using Audiovisual Equipment, 90

Chapter Five
HANDLING OBJECTIONS, STALLS,
AND DELAYS   93
What You Will Learn, 93
Why It Is Important, 93
  The Prospect's Right to Object, 94
Objections Keep You on Track, 95
Forms of Resistance, 95
  Skepticism, 95
  Hostility, 96
  Concern, 96
  Dejection, 96
  Indifference, 97
Coping with Negative Feelings, 97
Responding to Objections, 99
  1. Empathize 99
  2. Probe to Clarify, 100
  3. Present and Prove, 102
  4. Close, 103
Summary, 104
  Special Note on Objection Handling, 105
  Exercise, 113
  Action Assignment 1, 114
  Action Assignment 2, 115

Chapter Six
GOAL SETTING AND TIME MANAGEMENT   117

Focus, 118

Define Your Goals, 118

Goal Setting, Goal Achieving, 123

Write Down Your Goals, 124

    S: Specific, 125

    M: Measurable, 125

    A: Attainable, 126

    R: Relevant, 127

    T: Trackable with Time Frames, 128

Profile of a Goal, 129

Take Five, 133

Getting Results, 138

    A Baker's Dozen of Time Management Tips, 140

Chapter Seven
THE ART OF LISTENING   149

A Sales Tale 149

    Example: Precision Inc., Vincent Shields, 152

    Example: Best Furniture Corporation, Helaine Gordon, 154

    Example: Medical Resource Corporation, Larry Long, 158

    Example: Alice Fields, Anthony Barnes, 161

    Example: Blue Diamond Appliance Ltd., Todd Hastings, Bernard Haas, 165

    Example: Pane & Weeks Financial Service Corp., Joyce Blake, Eric Tate, 168

Summary, 171

Chapter Eight
NEGOTIATING FOR SUCCESS   175

Preparation Is Essential to Successful Negotiations, 176

Steps for Creating Clarity, 177

Time Frame, 178

Options, 179

Positive Commitments, 181
Negotiate to Maintain Relationships, 183
Time for Listening, 184
Team Negotiating, 189
Keep Your Word, 192
Dealing with Anger, 194
Attention Getters, 196
Specific Guidelines Produce Results, 196
Steps for Making Effective Requests, 197
False Assumptions, 198
Summary, 200

Chapter Nine
WRITING FOR SALESPEOPLE   203
The "Plunging-in" Approach, 203
Planning Your Writing, 204
    Audience, 205
    Purpose, 205
    Subject, 206
    Format, 206
    Thesis Sentence, 206
The "Back-Door" Approach, 209
Seven Steps in Organizing Your Writing, 211
    Step 1, 211
    Step 2, 212
    Step 3, 212
    Step 4, 215
    Step 5, 215
    Step 6, 215
    Step 7, 221
Writing Style, 222
    Current Usage, 224
    Punctuation, 225
Summary, 231
    Suggested Readings, 231

Chapter Ten
DEVELOPING ETHICAL BOUNDARIES   233

Who Cares?, 234
What Exactly *Is* Ethics?, 235
Management Issues, 236
Testing the Legal Limits, 238
Getting Personal, 239
    Testing Your Ethical Boundaries, 240
    The Truth or Consequences Case, 240
The Ethics Debate, 246
Comparative Ethics: The Spin Doctor, 248
Powerless?, 249
    How to Spot a Pattern, 249
    Conflict Resolution Skills, 252
    Developing Ethical Boundaries, 252
    The Role of the Customer, 254
When to Speak Up, 257
Conclusion, 258
    Ranking, 259
    Case Situations, 262
    Bibliography, 264
    Mail-in Survey, 266

Chapter Eleven
STRESS MANAGEMENT   269

Why Stress Management in a Basic Selling Skills Book?, 269
    You Can't Sell if You Feel Like Hell, 270
What Is Stress?, 270
The Stress Response: What's Happening Inside
Your Body, 271
The Stress Response: What You May Experience, Feel,
and Think, 272
Handling Stress on a Sales Call, 273
    1. Breathe!, 274

2. Positive Self-Talk, 274

Your Body Speaks; Are You Listening?, 274

Can Stress Affect Your Health?, 275

How Do You Currently Manage Stress?, 277

How Much Stress Are You Under?, 278

Can You Recognize Stress in Others?, 280

Sources of Stress, 280

Stress Reduction Techniques, 282

    Coping Skills, 282

    Time Management, 284

    Assertiveness, 284

    Turn Negatives into Positives, 285

    Develop Support Systems, 285

    A Sense of Humor, 286

    SOS on Stress, 286

    Before Stress Becomes a Crisis, 287

Lifestyle Skills, 287

    Healthy Lifestyle: Choosing Wellness, 287

    Reducing Health Risks, 288

    Check Your Lifestyle, 289

    Balancing Work and Personal Life, 289

    Take Time for Yourself, 290

    Achieving Balance, 290

    Schedule Self Time!, 291

    Shape up for Success, 291

    How Fit Are You?, 293

    Planning Your Fitness Program, 294

    Simple Exercises to Do on the Job, 295

High-Energy, Nutritious Diet, 297

    Eat Healthy: The Choice Is Yours!, 297

    The Notorious Salesperson's Diet, 298

    The Unhealthy American Diet, 298

    Choosing the New American Diet—The Food Guide Pyramid, 299

How Much Is a Serving?, 299

General Guidelines for a Healthy Diet, 300

Eat for Energy: Peak-Performance versus Anti-Peak-Performance Foods, 301

Rate Your Diet, 302

Your Nutrition Profile, 303

Relaxation Skills, 304

Techniques to Aid You in Eliciting the Relaxation Response, 305

Your Personal Stress Reduction Plan, 307

Bibliography, 308

Chapter Twelve
HOW TO SELL IN TOUGH TIMES TO DIFFICULT
PEOPLE WITHOUT CUTTING YOUR PRICE   309

Achieving Balance, 310

The Positive Attitude, 311

The Sale before the Sale, 312

Selling Yourself, 312

Selling Your Company, 316

Selling Your Product/Services, 318

Selling Your Price, 319

The Benefit of Benefits, 321

Cutting Your Price, 321

Be a Pitcher, Not a Catcher, 325

Commitment, 325

Index   328

Chapter One

Pre-call Planning

Robert B. Hartman

There is no more critical activity in preparing a strategy to make a sales call than the process of *pre-call planning*. Imagine building a house from guesswork or competing in a championship final of a sporting event without a game plan. Sounds implausible? Absolutely, yet how many times do we hear of salespeople venturing on sales calls without adequate preparation? Plenty of times, unfortunately for both the salesperson and the customer. To be ill-prepared for a sales call is lunacy. As you read this chapter on pre-call planning, keep in mind that time invested *before* the actual sales call is investing in qualifying the prospect, increasing the chances of closing the sale. At the conclusion of this chapter, you should be able to separate "prospects" from "suspects," identify resources for finding prospects, and organize workable strategies to maximize the sales call.

Let's first look at the selling process, **Anatomy of a Sale** shown on page 2. As you can see, the pre-call planning process occurs in the lowest tier. Logic dictates that before you meet with a prospect, you should learn something about the person or company. Note on the stair step that compiling data and developing a strategy are both included in this process. The process of qualifying customers has been proven as an effective sales strategy for successful salespeople and will enable you to improve your close rate as well.

As you review the anatomy chart, note the arrows that encircle the entire staircase. The arrows indicate that selling is an on-going relationship-building process. The relationship you establish with your customers should be constant and never ending. Referrals for

Anatomy of a Sale

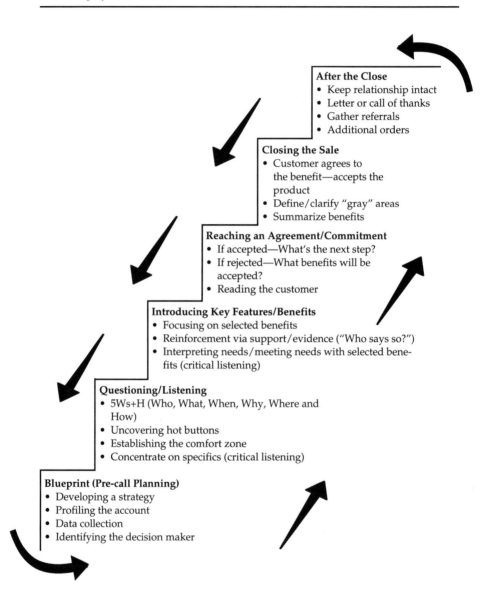

After the Close
- Keep relationship intact
- Letter or call of thanks
- Gather referrals
- Additional orders

Closing the Sale
- Customer agrees to the benefit—accepts the product
- Define/clarify "gray" areas
- Summarize benefits

Reaching an Agreement/Commitment
- If accepted—What's the next step?
- If rejected—What benefits will be accepted?
- Reading the customer

Introducing Key Features/Benefits
- Focusing on selected benefits
- Reinforcement via support/evidence ("Who says so?")
- Interpreting needs/meeting needs with selected benefits (critical listening)

Questioning/Listening
- 5Ws+H (Who, What, When, Why, Where and How)
- Uncovering hot buttons
- Establishing the comfort zone
- Concentrate on specifics (critical listening)

Blueprint (Pre-call Planning)
- Developing a strategy
- Profiling the account
- Data collection
- Identifying the decision maker

additional business and proof sources for products and services sold are the results of relationships built through your sales efforts. This chart will serve as a constant reminder that sales relationships are the key to a loyal customer base.

To begin the process of preparing for a sales call, you'll need to understand some terms that are critical in formulating strategies. The terms are *suspect, prospect,* and *qualifying criteria. Suspects* are potential customers who have *not* been qualified. *Prospects* are potential customers who *have* been qualified. *Qualifying criteria* are the critical information collected that will be used to determine if you should or should not spend time trying to sell the potential customers the product or service.

Taking time to separate those who have the ability to buy from those who are merely browsing will save you infinite amounts of time and energy that can be channeled into creating sales strategies for serious prospects. Let's identify prospect sources that can be used to separate prospects from those customers who have no intentions of buying from you or your company.

PROSPECT SOURCES

Prospecting is the process of investigating an account to determine if that person or company is a serious prospect for selling. As you begin prospecting, you'll need to identify sources of information that will lead you to the decision maker who's interested in your products or services. These sources include (but are not limited to) the following:

- Trade journals.
- Yellow Pages (includes business to business editions).
- Industrial park directories.
- Office building directories.
- Street directories.
- Direct mail lists.
- Association directories.
- Chamber of commerce membership lists.
- Financial pages of newspapers (especially Sunday editions).

Go to your local library and read such publications as:

- *The Wall Street Journal.*
- Dun & Bradstreet reports.
- Standard & Poor's.
- Local/state/federal industrial directories.

List at least five additional sources that are applicable to the products or services your company sells and the customers that buy them. If you can't find them, ask your colleagues or your boss to help identify those sources. The more resources that can be uncovered, the better the chances of identifying potential prospects.

SOURCE INFORMATION

Finding potential customers will not be your biggest challenge. *What to find out about them will be.* Note the types of information that will help you in your quest to find prospects. Consider the following: size of the company, number of employees, financial condition, competitors, position in the industry, number of locations, credit history, history with your company, key management figures, and product needs. What other types of information do you think you should include to make a determination about pursuing that company? Identify at least five bits of information that will help in separating prospects from suspects. Review this list with colleagues and your boss. Ask them for ideas in seeking information. Add their suggestions to your list.

The sources listed above should help you determine the potentiality of the account as well as the financial strength. In this age of financial instability, the *ability* to pay on time is a critical factor in separating suspects from prospects. Any record of the account with your company will help determine future business relationships. Trade magazines, periodicals, and relevant newspaper articles may shed light on buying patterns and plans for expansion or closings.

ESTABLISHING FILES

Any time you research a prospect, create a file system to compile the information. The files should consist of such basic items as: company's name, address, phone number, central headquarters, name of decision maker (if known), size of organization, past buying records (if known), competition, time of the week or month to call. Identify at least three other pieces of data and review them with colleagues and your boss. Add those ideas to your files.

How do your files appear? Do you keep them on pads or on floppy disks or are they handwritten? Whatever format you use, make sure your files are updated periodically (at least once a month) to keep them current and relevant. Make sure they're legible, too! If you have access to a computer or any other type of electronic storage equipment, find out how you can maximize its usage and store the data in it. You'll find that it will save you an incalculable amount of time.

Collecting the information is one step in the pre-call process. Interpreting it is something else. An effective file system will help you select those products or services that best suit the presumed needs of the prospect. Here's a list of suggestions that will make your file system effective:

1. Update the file with new information as required.
2. Review the file at least once a month. Changes occur. Mergers or acquisitions or a new product/service may upgrade a suspect to prospect status.
3. If possible, get on your suspect's/prospect's mailing list.
4. Keep on a schedule for suspect/prospect research each week. Review the data.
5. Make sure both suspects and prospects are on your mailing list. Keep them informed of new products or services offered by your company.
6. Allocate some time each week to do research as part of your prospecting.

ELEMENTS OF PRE-CALL PLANNING

To maximize the chances of success with prospective customers, establish a mindset of preparation. The better prepared you are before your meeting with a prospect or suspect, the better your chances of closing that sale or getting the next appointment. Face it, proper preparation takes time, and if you're a neophyte in the selling game, you'll need to manage time for each call to the best of your ability. Elements of pre-call planning that you should consider before each call include: product knowledge, knowledge of the prospect's company, industry knowledge and current events, customer awareness, your appearance, skills of selling, determining sales call objectives, sales call planner, and follow-up strategies.

Product Knowledge

Knowing which product or service to present to a prospect is almost as critical to the success of a call as establishing a strong relationship with the customer. You'll need to learn as much about your company's product line as applies to the perceived needs of the customer called. Understand the pricing structure to the best of your ability and ask yourself such questions as: What is the unit cost of the item? What prices are applicable if more than _____ are ordered? What about bulk rate orders? Are discounts or other reduced prices available to the customer? If the customer asks about future pricing, do I have the most current prices available? Other critical questions to prepare before the call are:

- What types of information should I know regarding delivery if applicable?
- What are my company's policies regarding minimal orders, short weights, short/long distances?
- What do I need to know/not know about my company's policies regarding warranties, guaranties, state or federal inspections, tariffs, specific restrictions, etc.?
- What do I know/don't know regarding follow-up service?
- Do I know the person(s) in charge at the main office if something goes wrong in the delivery process or after the product is received? What policies and procedures will be taken to satisfy the customer?
- What is the purchase order form and procedure to follow if required to complete?

Include this information in your files. If you can't find all the information, ask your co-workers or your boss to help you understand the policies and procedures regarding shipping and delivery of products to customers. Before meeting with a customer, you should also know how the product or service compares to the competition, features and benefits, common objections raised by customers, strategies for overcoming those objections, proof sources/evidence of satisfied customers, and information focusing on trends in the industry that the customer needs to know.

Product knowledge sources. The search for product information will involve numerous sources of research. Take time to organize your thoughts to create a strategy that will result in securing the types of data needed to prepare for an effective sales call. Ask yourself: What do I need to know about this customer? Whom do I need to ask to find the answers? Here are some suggestions and sources of information where you will find relevant bits of data pertaining to product knowledge:

- Product brochures.
- Marketing department of the company.
- Product manager(s) or product specialists.
- Specification sheets.
- Literature from competitors.
- Trade shows/product seminars.
- Conversations with sales colleagues.
- Local or college libraries.
- Trade magazines.
- Industry associations/clubs.

What additional sources can you identify? You may wish to ask the opinion of other reps, too.

Once you have compiled and understand the information collected, establish a "product knowledge library" for yourself. This library should be updated periodically, especially when price and other relevant changes will have an impact on the buying patterns of the customer. Make sure you are on the mailing lists of trade associations and other groups that offer additional product information. Review product information with colleagues and your boss.

Before the first meeting with prospects, review the area(s) of the product(s) to be presented to them. Think of at least five questions the prospect may ask you. Make sure you are prepared to provide accurate answers. Ask other sales reps to role-play a product presentation with you. The reps could act as the prospect and give you feedback on your product presentation. Ask for ideas from them on ways to make it more effective. Finally, you may want to record, via audio or videotape, a product presentation to hear and see how it is presented. Ask your colleagues or your boss to critique and provide constructive feedback.

Corporate Knowledge

What types of information should you have about the prospect's company? For starters, know the exact name of the company, billing address/shipping address, names of the decision makers, and the company's ability to pay. No sale is complete until the product or service is paid for. The company's credit profile is extremely important.

Other relevant pieces of company or corporate knowledge include such items as: size of the company, both dollar volume (gross annual sales) and number of employees; region in which the company operates (this is important for shipping and operational purposes); trends the company is experiencing; any relevant changes the organization has experienced over the past year or two; any critical executive changes that may affect the direction of the company. Take time to think of at least four or five additional items you think are of a "need to know" nature.

What types of information do you think you should know about *your* company? It's important to know as much about your organization as possible because prospects want to know that they can count on the company to deliver what has been promised by you. Make sure you know such things as:

- Phone number and mailing address of the company.
- Names of key personnel in accounting, shipping, operations, sales, marketing, among others.
- Company policy on product warranties/liabilities.
- Pricing policies.
- Catalog updates.
- Trade show participation for the next 6 to 12 months.

Think of at least five more pieces of information you think are of a "need to know" nature. Include this information in your company's information file.

Industry Knowledge

The third critical body of information in the pre-call planning process is data regarding your company's industry. Think in terms of the network associated with your company's products, customers, and competitors. All are sources of information to prepare you for sales calls to customers. Watch for trends and their influences on business in general and how they affect your company's business in particular. It is important to keep current with industry trends, cycles, and how each influences your customer's company. How informed should you be? The general rule is: Until experience and time have shaped your knowledge of the business, strive to become a generalist. The working knowledge of your own industry as well as that of your customer's will not only impress others but will also build your confidence in meeting your customer's needs.

Industry knowledge can be found in books, magazines, local and national newspapers, periodicals, trade journals, seminars, continuing educational courses, and in conversations with fellow sales reps among other sources. The key is to keep an open mind and to think "current." Relevant data should be included in customer files and reviewed on a regular basis.

Schedule a time during the day or evening where you can peruse newspapers and other publications to review trends or noteworthy developments. Look for information that has a direct impact on your company or industry and will influence pricing, delivery, or product availability and development. *To stay current in your industry is to anticipate potential customer concerns and buying trends.* As the marketplace becomes more competitive and global, it is critical for your success in sales to be as current and savvy as possible. The more informed you become, the better your chance of gaining the edge over your competitors.

Customer Awareness

Thus far, pre-call planning has focused on your ability to know the product, the company, the industry, and current events and trends. Another key element is your ability to *know* your customer. This includes some objective and subjective criteria.

The first course of action includes learning as much about your cus-tomers as time allows. This means you try to find out as much as you can about the buying patterns of customers and any information that has a direct effect on why they buy. How will you gather this type of critical customer information?

To answer this question, think in terms of the prospect's position, history of the account, previous buying patterns, contact with col-leagues, or prior history with other companies. Read sales reports and check company files on previous purchase records (if applic-able). You also may want to consider the type of personality the prospect has displayed in phone conversations or any other type of interaction (if applicable). Try to establish a profile of him or her. Use this information to help in preparing for the sale.

Other customer-focused areas are:

- Researching the customer's job responsibilities or promotions.
- Identifying the competition and the amount of business cur-rently generated.
- Determining the customer's needs by placing yourself in the role of the customer.
- Understanding the type of behavior demonstrated by the cus-tomer so you can adapt your presentation to fit the customer's "comfort level."
- Determining how similar or dissimilar the customer is to your own temperament.

Believe it or not, chemistry is a key element in the customer's mind. The success or failure of a sales call may rest on likes or dis-likes. Try to anticipate the type of personality that you'll deal with during the sales call. Understanding customer behavior is the sub-ject of several sales training programs. You may want to research programs or seminars that focus on these themes and become knowledgeable to upgrade your skills in dealing with divergent behaviors.

Personal Appearance

When you do make that first sales call, the first impression you make with the prospect can make or break your entire presentation. Your appearance can be as important as dealing with the customer's personality. Customers have an idea or image of how a successful salesperson should appear. *Dress for success in your industry.* Find out what is considered appropriate garb and what is considered inappropriate. When in doubt, dress conservatively. Think about the types of jewelry you wear; the perfumes or colognes you use; your hairstyle, shoes, briefcase; visual aids and brochures given to prospects; and your *attitude.*

Selling Skills

Preparation for the sales call includes an introspective look at your selling skills. Assess your skills level and objectively evaluate the areas you need to fine-tune before the call is made. Have a solid understanding of the basic elements of the selling process. Know the difference between the elements and be prepared to use them throughout the sales call. Selling skills include knowing when to speak and when to listen. You'll need to know when silence is the best strategy, too. Selling skills involve the use of brochures, visual aids, and specification sheets. Review your visual aids before using them. A word may be misspelled or omitted and can embarrass you and the customer. Check all audiovisual equipment before using it.

It is recommended that plenty of *practice* occurs before the sales call so you become comfortable with product information, the customer, and action to be taken as a result of the sales call. Take time to record calls into a tape recorder or in front of a video camera and play the tape back. Identify those areas that went well or poorly. You may want to ask colleagues or your boss to critique the tape and provide meaningful feedback before the sales call. Selling is like any other skill—*you need to practice to get better.*

If you believe you have difficulty in any selling skill area, investigate various sales training vendors available to help fine-tune your approach. Confidence in selling is everything. Lack of confidence is correctable. Ask your co-workers or boss to recommend a seminar or in-house workshop to help you overcome your area of weakness. After each sales call, review things that you thought went well and the areas that still need improvement. Be candid with your performance. If you make a team call with a fellow sales rep, ask for an appraisal of your sales performance. *Keep an open mind when receiving the feedback.*

Any number of effective how-to books on the subject of selling may help you. Check them out at your local bookstore or library.

Setting Sales Call Objectives

As you prepare to make a sales call ask yourself the following questions: (1) Do I know enough information about the needs of my customer? (2) Can I meet his or her needs with the products/services of my company? (3) Can I adjust my personality/behavior to the comfort levels of this customer? If the answer to these three questions is yes, then your primary goal is to make the sale. If the answer is no, more information is needed before you can close the sale with the customer. Do not begin a sales call by assuming the customer's needs. It is your responsibility to uncover those needs or to redefine those needs with the customer.

The following questions are designed to help you make the proper decision about what type of call objectives you should set. Keep these questions in sight before each call to remind yourself to gather these meaningful bits of information to close the sale. Find answers to these questions:

- Who are my customers?
- Why should they deal with me?
- What are their needs?
- When is the best time for them to make the purchase?
- How should they purchase my products or services?

To help you gather these critical pieces of information, you should use an *account blueprint*. It will serve as a sales call planner and will help you organize your thoughts and create a direction for the sales presentation. The blueprint identifies such items as: current status of the account, profile of the customer, sales objective(s), strategies, and action steps. A sample of the blueprint appears on pages 14–15. Study the sample carefully, and begin to think of information that you'll collect for your customers.

Account blueprint. Throughout this chapter, the discussion has focused on a multitude of considerations for collecting data. We've discussed the files that need to be established to store

the data as well. Let's study a sample form (account blueprint) that not only captures the information already mentioned but also creates workable strategies to use before the next sales call. Keep in mind that a plan such as the one that appears on pages 14 and 15 does not include *everything* that should be known about the customer, yet it provides a detailed analysis you'll be able to use effectively.

Account Blueprint Analysis. The first page of the blueprint identifies general account information—the customer's name, address, current volume, and so on. This information can be collected from the sales department's records (if applicable). If the account is new, some of this information will be missing. At this stage in your development, it is more important to think in terms of items to *include*. The list of facts that appear on the blueprint should trigger the types of data to be included in your account research.

The next area of discussion in the blueprint is competitive information. Any information that can help you further your understanding of the competition should be considered. Note the types of data listed in this segment. What importance would you place on each piece of information seen in this segment? You would be able to determine that Acme has been doing business with XYZ company and the product sells for $300 per kit and current inventory is 50 kits. At this point, you at least know the account is active, and you know the competition and what product is sold to the customer today.

What does the next section, history of the account, tell you about the prospect? This is a new account. A new account indicates that more information is needed. You will have to spend time gathering enough data to determine whether the account is worth the time and effort to pursue.

The next area of attention on the blueprint form is the sales objective. The sales objective merely states the purpose of the sales call for that day. It provides you with a goal to achieve and helps you to focus on the reason for the call.

The "assumed customer need" provides you with another layer of information that gives you a direction for selling. If you actually know the need(s) of the customer, more power to you! In most

Account Blueprint

Account Blueprint

Rep's Name: Mary Smith   Date: Today's Date

Financial Profile/General Information | **Competitive Information**

Company Name:	Acme, Inc.	Currently using:	XYZ Co.
Address/Phone:	Anywhere, USA (555) 555-1212	Rep's Name:	Peter Forrey
Key Contact:	Harry Smith, V.P. Sales/Marketing	Relationship to	
Day/Time to Call:	Tuesday - 10:00 a.m.	Decision Maker:	?
Current $ Potential:	$50,000 (Annually)	Inventory of Products:	50 Sales kits
Y.T.D. Gross Sales:	$15,000,000	Pricing Structure:	$300 per kit
No. of RoTe Products used:	None	Other:	Considering purchase of
Name/Key Players:	Dawn Welk (Secretary)		"Delegating" product

---

History of Account

New   ____√____ New Account
Have been in business for 25 years   _____ Est. Account
AAA credit rating   _____ House Account
Bought 1st program 5 years ago   _____ Inherited from previous Representative

---

Sales Objective

To meet decision maker and arrange 1 hour overview of our "Strategic Selling Skills" program.

Assumed/Customer Need

To upgrade existing selling skills of internal/external sales force.
Based upon pre-call research, customer is interested in "hands-on-learning" training program.

Product(s) to Discuss

Strategic Selling Skills

Features	**Benefits/General**	**Benefits/Specific**
• Interaction	• Group + individual practice skills	• Each rep practices
• Detailed, individual role plays	• Individual opportunity to practice sales skills	• Acme reps will be able to sell more products

Account Blueprint (concluded)

Sales Strategies

Fact Finding Questions:

How many reps in-house/field do you have?

What do you want the training program to accomplish?

What skill(s) need to be developed?

Focus Questions

What do you like/dislike about your current program?

Ideally, what skills would you like your people to develop?

Behavior Profile (perceived)

____ Submissive   √ Responder   ____ Investigator   ____ Dominator

---

Decision Maker's "Hot Button" Area

Likes to discuss his years as a Sales Representative. Loves selling and talks openly about it.

Action Steps

Date/Time: 4/16 at 1:00 p.m. will meet with Mr. Smith on my follow-up call. I will focus on what he currently uses and why he selected that product. My goal is to set-up an actual overview of the program.

Target Date: 1 week from today. I'm trying to find out if Mr. Smith has total decision making powers.

cases, especially with new accounts, the need(s) will have to be uncovered through research and probing. Experience will help you gain insight into the general needs of most customers. Remember, as a new sales rep, assuming will hurt *not* help you.

Under the section product(s) to discuss, the need for product knowledge is never more evident. You'll need to know not only the products your company has to offer but also the salient features and benefits of them. Product brochures and product training should shed light on the product needs of your prospect. *Make sure you have the most current product information available to you before you create a final strategy for presenting to the customer.*

The next category in the blueprint, sales strategies, focuses on the questions you should formulate before the sales call. The sales strategy is no more than asking yourself, "What's my game plan for this sales call?" Combine the strategies with the next segment, focus questions, to direct your efforts toward yourself with the customer. These focus questions are designed to ask how they feel about their current situation and to allow them to reveal their concerns and needs. The direction of the sales call and the future of the sales relationship between the customer and you may rest on the answers to these questions. Take time to formulate them before the next call.

The next category, behavior profile, is based on the perception you or others have formulated about the customer through direct or indirect conversations and face-to-face meetings. This information deals with the chemistry factor discussed earlier.

The behavior and personality of the customer should indicate how you'll approach the customer based on your own personality. You may have to adopt a style of presenting that is more or less dominant, faster paced or slower, higher energy or lower. The need for you to be flexible is very critical. When you have determined the perceived type of behavior of the customer, try to determine what the hot buttons may be. A hot button increases the interest levels of the customer. An example is price. Perhaps when you mention that the price of your product or service is $5 *less than* the competition, that turns on the customer. Another example is quality. The customer is interested in the "five extra steps" taken in the preparation of the product. Whatever the area of interest is, note it in the blueprint.

The next area to note in the blueprint is action steps. This is the section in the form where you identify the action to be taken based on the information found in the form. In other words, the data collected will now be used to take such action as selecting a product or service for presentation, presenting spec sheet data, setting sales appointments, and setting a time or date for product demonstration. The listing of action steps to take is the final strategy before the call is made. The action that follows, the call itself, will be analyzed and reviewed in the first step in the form titled "Revised Blueprint."

The revised blueprint is the one-page form found on page 18. Immediately after the sales call, take time to review. Record the action by completing the section marked, "Objective Achieved/ Results of Previous Call," which serves as a summary of the completed sales call. What *did* occur in the meeting? List the action. Next, identify the decisions reached (if any) and record that information in the box marked "Decision(s) Reached." The next two boxes ask for information related to new needs and new information. This information can be known if you probe for facts by asking the customer the right types of questions. The new information will be beneficial to you for the next sales call to the customer and help you to set new call objectives.

The next segment in the revised blueprint deals with identifying the decision-making team. What new players (if any) have been identified during the sales call? Who'll be the chief decision makers in future negotiations? Equally as important as the identification of these individuals is the recognition of the behavior profile of each person. As mentioned in the original blueprint, understanding the personality of the decision makers is crucial to the success of the sales relationship between yourself and the customer(s). After you've met with the customer ask yourself: What behavior did the customer demonstrate to me during this sales call? Was the customer different from the perception before this call? What did I perceive to be the same or different this time? Did I adjust my behavior to meet the comfort levels of the customer? How did he or she react when I asked specific questions that resulted in emotional/ nonemotional responses?

As you determine the type of behavior displayed, what new hot buttons, if any, were evidenced? Note them on the revised form as well. You may wish to include the hot buttons of all those who

Revised Blueprint

Revised Blueprint

Rep's Name: _____   Date: _____

Objective Achieved/Results of Previous Call (Summary)

Decision(s) Reached

New Needs	New Information

Decision Making Team (Additional Players)

Names/Titles: _____   _____

                 _____   _____

                 _____   _____

Behavior Profile

___ Submissive   ___ Responder   ___ Investigator   ___ Dominator

Hot Button Areas: _____
_____
_____

Time Frame for Next Action	Cross-Sell Opportunities

Next Step

I will: _____
_____

Customer will: _____
_____

Comments: _____
_____

are influencers and decision makers as you prepare follow-up calls to them.

Identify a time frame for action to provide a window for follow-up action to occur. As you set the time frame for action, think in terms of the opportunities for cross-selling additional products or services. If you probe successfully during the sales call, you'll find that the needs of the customer become more multidimensional. Think of the possibilities that exist for additional business through cross-selling ventures.

The final segment in the revised blueprint is called the "Next Step." As the name implies, this is the action you wish to take to close the sale or take the call to the next step. It identifies the actions of you and the customer and should summarize steps to be taken for the future of the account. Review the copy that appears on the revised blueprint. Note the blank account blueprint and revised blueprint forms on the next pages. You'll have an opportunity to practice completing blueprints in the case studies that follow.

Creating an Effective Sales Planner

You've had an opportunity to study a sample sales planner as shown in the account blueprint, and you've seen the revised blueprint. Both of these plans are designed to provide you with a format to collect as much information as possible about the prospect before making the initial face-to-face sales meeting. Now, you'll have several opportunities to practice completing blueprints for prospects who appear in this text. Please read carefully the following case studies. Develop a sales planner (account blueprint) for each case. When you believe you've included all the pertinent data required, review the information with an experienced colleague or your boss to evaluate its effectiveness. When you feel comfortable with the blueprint, begin to set up your own customer files using the same format or adopt a format that you think is equally effective.

Pre-call planning includes a written plan. Success depends on preparation and execution of the written plan. Before you read the cases, consider these thoughts: more than one goal can be identified in the planner, streamline your information-gathering techniques to save time, make sure you set objectives per call, analyze your strengths and weaknesses in meeting the objective and recognize them before the action is taken. Work your plan!

Account Blueprint

Account Blueprint

Rep's Name: Date:

Financial Profile/General Information

Company Name:
Address/Phone:
Key Contact:
Day/Time to Call:
Current $ Potential:
Y.T.D. Gross Sales:
No. of RoTe Products used:
Name/Key Players:

Competitive Information

Currently using:
Rep's Name:
Relationship to
Decision Maker:
Inventory of Products:
Pricing Structure:
Other:

History of Account

How long ago _____   _____ New Account

Reason for discontinued business _____   _____ Est. Account

$ amount generated previously _____   _____ House Account

Name of previous contact _____   _____ Inherited from previous Rep

---

Sales Objective

Assumed/Customer Need

Product(s) to Discuss

Features	Benefits/General	Benefits/Specific
•	•	•
•	•	•
•	•	•
•	•	•

Account Blueprint (concluded)

Sales Strategies

      1. _____

      2. _____

      3. _____

Focus Questions

      1. _____

      2. _____

      3. _____

Behavior Profile (perceived)

_____ Submissive   _____ Responder   _____ Investigator   _____ Dominator

---

Decision Maker's "Hot Button" Area

Action Steps

Date/Time: _____

_____

_____

_____

For next call: _____

_____

_____

_____

Case Study 1: A New Decision Maker in a New Account

Frank Nosal has recently been hired by Acme Brands as its new purchasing agent. You've received little information about this account, but several facts are available. This prospect has been in business for over 20 years and manufactures a variety of food products. It ships its products all over the country and to several foreign countries as well. Frank oversees the purchasing of a variety of vendors, most notably, packaging materials for shipment. With over five years of experience in purchasing, Frank is eager to prove himself in this $50 million company. He has a staff of two clerks and a junior associate.

Your company, Pafko Packing, is a major packaging company in the state. The company manufactures and sells packaging for a variety of industries, including food products. As a rookie sales rep, you've conducted research on both new and established accounts in your territory. Your boss has given you a lead card. Before you make your first call to Acme and its purchasing agent, you need to gather as many facts as you can. Where do you start your research?

Case study assignment: Complete an account blueprint for Acme. On a scratch pad, fill in the information that composes the account blueprint. Complete as much information as you can about the account that exists from the information available. Identify the information that is lacking. Where will you go to find the missing pieces? When you believe you have completed as much of the form as possible, review it with your co-workers or boss. Ask them for their opinions in completing the blueprint. As you review the data with your colleagues, make sure you can identify the following: sales objective, assumed customer need, sales strategies, and sample focus questions.

Case Study 2: Established Account/Seasoned Buyer

Don Paseo of Franklin Communications is the vice president of information systems (data processing department) and the chief decision maker in acquiring new or upgraded computer systems. As the senior officer in the department with over 15 years at

Franklin, he's quite familiar with the vendors that service his needs. Don is a seasoned veteran in the computer field. He has well over 25 years' experience either testing various systems or installing them for the dozen or so companies that compose the Franklin Communications family of subsidiaries.

This account was transferred to you just a week ago from a rep who has since left the company. Your company, EQIX Systems, is small computer hardware company that is an innovator in the design of PCs. EQIX has sold Franklin several prototypes for evaluation as recently as 15 months ago. The company has selected Franklin for testing of its latest PC, the T2500.

The T2500 has been written up in a variety of trade publications over the past three months and received mostly favorable reviews. As a rep for EQIX, you have been assigned the task of introducing the T2500 to Franklin. More important, your boss has insisted you develop a working relationship with Paseo, who remains somewhat skeptical about this latest "innovation" from the "gods of EQIX" (his term for the R&D department at EQIX). You've spoken to Paseo for just a few minutes a couple of days ago. He seemed all business and somewhat aloof.

Case study assignment: Develop an account blueprint for a sales meeting with Don Paseo of Franklin Communications. Remember to identify your sales call objective, ID the customer need(s), develop sales strategies, create focus questions, ID his behavioral profile (perception of his behavior/personality), and plan strategies that involve the presentation of the T2500 involvement with product specialists. Ask yourself: What additional information do I need to make an effective presentation to this customer? What sources should I include in my research of this account? What product information will I need to present to the customer?

Case Study 3: Many Decision Makers but No Decision

Early this morning, you received information from your boss about an account that used to be serviced by your company, Morton Consulting Services, a management consulting company. The prospect, Tomalson Brothers, is a chain of 20 electronic parts stores. About two years ago, Morton Consulting was contracted by Tomalson to conduct a comprehensive study of the stores' management teams to determine skills proficiency. The project came to an abrupt end, however, due to a severe case of "decision by committee." Too many senior executives were involved in too many decisions that resulted in missed deadlines.

Tomalson could generate staggering business for your company. The obstacle to the account, however, is finding the chief decision maker. At this stage, there are several players you can contact. They are: Dave Tomalson, vice president of store operations; Bill Wellington, general manager of stores; Peter Tomalson, senior vice president of sales; and Marianne Conklin, vice president of human resources and training. Two years ago, all these officers were involved in one degree or another. According to the notes you've received about this company, Dave Tomalson is a "big picture" person. Wellington is a hands-on manager who sometimes overlooks the obvious. Peter Tomalson is concerned with sales generated and concentrates his efforts on maximizing margins on profits. Conklin is aware of the skills that need to be developed but feels overwhelmed by the other personalities. The chain generates almost $25 million in annual sales. Your company's chief competitor is Burton & Crable Associates, a consulting firm that specializes in retail chains.

Case study assignment: Prepare an account blueprint that will be a workable strategy as you try to secure this account. Capturing this account will be a real coup for both you and Morton Consulting. You'll need to identify the chief decision maker as well as: a sales call objective, customer need, personality profile of each, questions, and some hot buttons that could establish your credibility with Tomalson. When completed with this case study, ask your colleagues or boss to comment on the blueprint. Explain your reasons for the strategy and discuss other bits of information that may help you prepare for the sales call.

Case Study 4: Incomplete Background

As a sales rep for a cleaning chemicals company, ALLKLEEN, you're always in search of new prospects. Recently, while reading the local newspaper, you discover that a commercial leasing company called Gorham Realty Inc. has taken management control over several commercial buildings in town. The takeover involves control of the maintenance of more than 100 small and medium-size companies. Potentially, the Gorham account can be a gold mine if you can determine its cleaning needs and whom to contact. At this point, all you know is what you have read in the newspaper: Gorham is about to take over the RealShores commercial complex in the commercial part of town.

Case study assignment: Develop an account blueprint for Gorham Realty. Since you have limited information available, what resources will you use to gain additional data about this account? What will your call objective be? Where will you find competitive information about this account? When you've completed the blueprint, ask your boss or co-workers to review the information with you. Ask yourself: Do I have enough information to make a sales call to this prospect? What additional data do I need? Where should I go to find it?

Case Study 5: Conflicting Information

You are a sales rep for Huff Stationery Products, a company that sells office supplies to the business community. You've been a rep for six months and have both established accounts and new ones acquired over the past few months. Recently, you've researched a number of prospects in old files and discovered a company called McGuire Kalman & Company, a paralegal firm. A few years ago, a rep from your company, Dawn Marshall, called on this account and conducted some business with it. The records of the purchases, contacts at McGuire, and status of the relationship with Huff are incomplete.

The few facts you do have are: The account generated $25,000 in revenues for at least one year, at least three departments at McGuire bought a variety of paper products and computer-related products, and the office manager's name is Sandy Welch. According to Dawn's notes in the file, McGuire Kalman always paid its bills at least 30 days later than other accounts that spent the same or near the same amount. You want to reopen the account but need more facts to formulate a sound sales strategy.

Case study assignment: Develop an account blueprint for McGuire Kalman & Company. What facts do you have? What facts do you need to find out? As you develop the blueprint, remember to set a call objective, identify the contact, establish the need, and identify the action to take. When completed, discuss the plan with your boss or co-workers for input.

Case Studies 6–10: Create Your Own

To reinforce the skills of pre-call planning that have been discussed here, select five prospects or customers that you currently have. Some of these customers should be new accounts, some established accounts. Complete blueprints for each account. Review call objectives. When you have completed a blueprint for each, review them with your boss or co-workers and ask for comments on the plan for each. Since these are *real* prospects or established customers, the additional information you develop for each becomes much more meaningful and should help you in generating additional business with each account.

Remember to identify sales objectives for each call as well as the other elements that appear on the blueprint form. Take time to methodically plot your strategy and gather enough data to complete the form for each of the five accounts. When you've completed the blueprint and after the sales call has been made, the next step is to complete the revised blueprint.

Chapter Two

Prospecting

Arnold L. Schwartz

THE RATIONALE FOR PROSPECTING

Selling would be a piece of cake if you could wake up each morning knowing you had a full day's schedule of qualified appointments set up for you. These would be interested, prospective buyers eagerly awaiting your arrival.

If this fantasy were true, recruiters' waiting rooms would be crammed with sales applicants because it would remove one of the real drudgeries of selling, one that results in a high rejection rate and a test to any salesperson's ego: *prospecting*.

Every company needs to add new customers and to sell existing customers additional products or services. Prospecting is the lifeblood of an organization if it is to grow and compensate for the normal attrition every organization experiences. The loss of just a few key accounts can cause a company to fail if they are not replaced.

In the challenging economy of the 1990s, prospecting takes on even more importance. Markets are shrinking, competition is keen, and prospective customers are guarding every dollar. They are no longer raising their hands in a gesture of interest. They must be ferreted out by industrious salespeople.

This chapter deals with the mental as well as the skill aspects of prospecting. In short, you will have a blueprint for becoming a better prospector and feel more comfortable and confident doing it.

WHY DO SALESPEOPLE ABHOR PROSPECTING?

The answer is obvious. You are setting yourself up for rejection.

1. Often the prospects have never heard of you or your firm.
2. The timing is wrong.
3. They are not in a receptive mood.
4. They have been bombarded by phone calls.
5. Secretaries screen their bosses' calls and are often curt and impolite.

Prospecting can be an unsettling experience.

DEVELOPING A PROSPECTING AWARENESS

How do we overcome these negatives and make prospecting a satisfying and productive experience?

To start with, you must accept prospecting as a necessary part of selling, as basic as being well-groomed or having product knowledge. Successful salespeople develop a prospecting awareness. This means they "see the world" in terms of prospective customers for what they are selling.

They see prospects *everywhere,* in restaurants, planes, social situations, and family gatherings. While I am not advocating that you should be talking and thinking business all the time, dedicated and enthusiastic salespeople are constantly aware of people's needs and wants as they relate to what they sell.

Psychologists refer to this awareness as "selective perception," the act of seeing your world in terms of the dominating thoughts that occupy your mind. If you do not believe there are prospects out there with the money, authority, and need for what you are selling, you will not pursue them diligently.

Perhaps you are thinking, "That all sounds fine, but I don't like cold calling. Talking to strangers is not my forte. The company should provide leads. They should do more advertising. My time should be spent in selling, not talking to a lot of deadbeats." (The "shoulds" can be translated into "if onlys," which can be translated into wishful thinking.)

You may not appreciate the following response, but this is the way it is.

You don't have to like prospecting—you just have to do it! Many people out there need what you are selling but do not respond to advertising, direct mail, or computerized telemarketing. They may, however, respond to a warm, enthusiastic, knowledgeable person who can help them make a decision that is good for them.

Prospecting is often a case of finding the person that is looking for you. When you find each other, it's love at first presentation. However, in the process, you have to wade through a lot of disinterested suspects and a lot of negative reaction. If you are fortunate enough to have leads provided, you still need to qualify them. Even if you have others making appointments for you, my strong recommendation is that you also do some prospecting on your own. No one can tell *your* story as well as you.

There is an additional benefit to prospecting. When you initiate a deal, you can skew it to your strengths, build a strong relationship with the buyers, and "spec" the deal to effectively stymie competition. You can avoid the price rat race by setting standards not easily matched by others.

Conversely, when prospects call you, generally they have also called your competitors. You then find yourself in a price war where often the only winner is the customer.

Prospecting tests a salesperson's ego, discipline, and motivation. It is far easier to make presentations to existing customers who you know will accept you or to prospects who have already declared their interest. But whether you are new in the territory or have a solid following, you must develop new business.

Prospecting will hone your selling skills, keep you on top of what's happening in the marketplace, and put money in the bank. And surprisingly, you will get good at it and even learn to enjoy the challenge.

DEVELOPING A PROSPECTING DISCIPLINE

Paul Meyer, president of SMI International states, "I would rather be a master prospector than a wizard of speech with no one to tell my story to."

Prospecting requires discipline. **Prospecting is not a hit-or-miss activity, something you do when you have some time.** It is a planned activity that must be scheduled into your selling day or week. Let's face it, who likes to prospect? As Bill Good writes in his book, *Prospecting Your Way to Sales Success* (New York: Charles Scribner's Sons, 1986), most salespeople "would rather stand in a cold shower ripping up one hundred dollar bills then make cold prospecting calls."

Like depositing part of your paycheck in your savings account, if you wait for what's left after meeting all your expenses, your bank account is likely to be zero. But if you take it off the top and deposit it immediately, you will probably find a way to manage with what is left and have a growing savings account as well.

Prospecting is like that. Do it first and you will never want for a pipeline of prospective buyers. Schedule your prospecting time into your calendar as if it is an appointment with your best prospect or customer. It's inviolate—it can't be broken.

This is a commitment you make to yourself. Winners do the things that losers don't like to do. Winners don't like to do them either, but they do them anyway.

You'll leave 98 percent of your competition in the dust solely by sticking to your prospecting commitment.

THE STEPS IN THE PROSPECTING SYSTEM

Identifying Your Market

Who should you call on, who are the best prospects for your product or service? Pareto's principle, the well-known 80/20 rule that states 20 percent of effort yields 80 percent of the results, suggests 80 percent of the business comes from 20 percent of the prospects.

Let's start by asking who are your best present customers, the ones that give you the biggest payoff for your time invested? What particular need are you satisfying? Do they have a unique problem that your product or service solves better than the competition? What characteristics do they have in common?

If you are selling to only one or two vertical markets (lines of business), identifying prospects is relatively easy. But even in this case, it is important to focus on the high-potential users.

When your product has a broad market potential, you have to zero in on a few specific markets and specialize. Salespeople who sell pension plans can sell everyone, but the successful ones select a specific market such as doctors or accountants and work that market. They become familiar with the jargon, problems, and proven solutions unique to that line of business. They become *experts* rather than generalists.

Too many potential prospects can lead to no prospects. You find yourself wandering all over the place with no real plan of action. **Decide on the industry classifications you want to penetrate and concentrate in those areas.**

Here are some criteria you can use to categorize your best customers:

1. Line of business (SIC codes).
2. Revenue (i.e., more than $10 million or less than $5 million).
3. Number of locations, plants, branches.
4. Number of employees.
5. Type of distribution (i.e., sells through distributors, dealers, or direct to end user).
6. Geographic location.
7. International business.
8. Net worth, credit rating, etc. (and in these times, do they pay their bills?).
9. Life of present equipment or contracts.
10. Obsolescence factors.
11. Company's policy and culture affecting purchasing.
12. Past experience with your company or product.

Creating an ideal prospect profile.   Narrow the key factors that describe your "ideal" prospect to a manageable number such as five. Then list them in declining order of importance. In addition to quantitative criteria, you may want to include cultural characteristics such as the company's traditions, values, attitudes, or philosophy. Your ideal prospect company might have a strong people orientation or pride themselves on their reputation for creativity and innovation.

You now have a model that you can use to evaluate potential prospects. Figure 2–1 is a sample profile sheet that will help you analyze your present customers.

FIGURE 2–1
Ideal Customer Profile

Name of customer/client _____

Type of business _____

SIC codes _____

No. of employees _____ Sales volume_____

Divisions or subsidiaries_____

Other information _____

Decision makers _____

Associations customer belongs to _____

Customer special characteristics as they relate to my business _____

Special needs my product/service fills for client _____

Customer's competitors _____

Names of other companies, people, or organizations that have similar needs

Finding Prospects

Now that you have identified the prospects, what is the best way to get to them?

In the following pages, we've listed more than 20 ways to find prospects. We will cover telephone prospecting in a separate section. Not every method listed may apply to your product or service, but I urge you to keep an open mind before passing judgment. Perhaps a slight variation on the theme might be the appropriate approach for you.

1. Referrals. Getting referrals is one of the best ways of prospecting, yet many salespeople do not take advantage of it.

When was the last time you got a referral? Perhaps a better question is: When was the last time you *asked* for a referral?

Don't be passive about asking for referrals. If you have done a good job for the client or customer, they will generally be glad to recommend you. But you need to help them help you by giving them the criteria for the people you want to meet. Here's an example of a referral presentation.

> Jim, I need to meet forward-looking, open-minded people like yourself (stroke, stroke) who could benefit from our service. Could you give me the names of five financial officers of firms that deal with companies in the $5 to $10 million range?

Asking for a specific number is helpful. Of course, be careful not to give the impression that you will be helping your client's competitors.

You may further help your customer come up with some names by directing his thinking in this way: "Are there some people in your association that fit that criteria?"

Once you have a satisfied customer, here are a number of ways they can help you generate additional prospects. In effect, you transform your customer into a "center of influence."

- Referrals.
- Testimonial letters.
- Invitation to speak to their association.
- Permission to have other prospects call.
- Use as a "demo" site.
- Article in industry magazine.
- Word-of-mouth advertising.
- Use in your company advertising.
- Appear in your company audio and/or video as satisfied user.
- Keep you posted on competitive activity.
- Keep you informed on what's happening in his company and industry.

2. Prospect by line of business. This is called vertical or even niche marketing. You develop an expertise in a particular industry and are able to offer a value-added service because of your knowledge of your customer's operation. This enables you to become more than just a salesperson—you become a consultant. Prospective customers like to think you know their problems and have successfully addressed them before.

Think of some of the business classifications you'd like to become expert in. Then work those classifications.

3. Existing customers.   One of the best sources of new business is your existing customers. Many salespeople take for granted that their customers know them, remember them, and will call when they have a need. Not so! It is best to assume that "out of sight is out of mind," and make sure you constantly update your customers on your latest product enhancements, literature, and services.

See that they get periodic mailings, seminar invitations, and other promotions that show them you are pursuing their business just as diligently as when you were trying to convert them from prospects to customers. Taking existing clients for granted permits competition to invade your accounts. Many smug salespeople sitting on their laurels have been surprised to learn the accounts they thought were "locked up" were "stolen" by persistent, hungry competitors who let the customer know they wanted the firm's business and were willing to work for it. **Remember, your customer is someone else's prospect.**

Do not limit yourself to one department, operation, or buying influence. There may be other opportunities within the customer organization that you are unaware of. "Penetrate" and "proliferate" are two activities to work at.

4. Associations. Joining the associations where your prospects are members will enable you to meet them in a different environment and get to know them on another level. This is a form of networking.

Making presentations at association meetings is an excellent way to attract prospects. Seek out opportunities to give presentations on how your industry, company, or product impacts the audience's concerns. Keep it nonsales oriented.

The way to maximize the benefit of being a member of an association is to get active; serve on a committee or head it. You will get to meet the movers and the shakers and have visibility with the total membership. This an investment and you are not likely to see short-term results. Be patient.

5. Directories.   A good business library has many kinds of directories. Some of the well-known ones are:

Standard & Poor's Registers of Corporations, Directors & Executives.

Million Dollar Directory (published by Dun's Marketing Services).

Coles publications (street or "reverse" directories).

Polk's city directories.

Gale's Encyclopedia of Associations and *Directory of Directories.*

Standard Directory of Advertisers.

Yellow Pages. The Yellow Pages of your phone book are very good prospecting tools because the listings are by line of business and the addresses and phone numbers are up to date.

Other directories. Many associations publish directories as do special issues of magazines and newspapers. The local chamber of commerce is another source.

6. Seminars and trade shows. Conducting seminars, staging open houses, and exhibiting at trade shows are excellent ways to find prospects. You maximize your time by attracting many potential prospects to a single location. Another way to use trade shows is to attend as a visitor and contact the exhibitors who are prospects for your product or service.

7. Newspapers and magazines. These sources provide current information on executive promotions, transfers, and company activities. The classified section indicates which companies are hiring and possibly expanding. Check the Sunday display section of your local paper.

Here are a few sources of personnel changes:

The Wall Street Journal: "Who's News."

The New York Times: "Company News" and "Executives On The Move."

Crain's New York Business: "Profiles/Executive Moves."

8. Networking. Networking is a burgeoning method to make new contacts in a quasi-social environment to enable people to increase their spheres of influence. Networking groups are springing up all over the country.

There are several important things to remember when networking:

• You must help others if you want to be helped. It's not a one-way street.

- Find out what people are looking for in the way of prospects and help them get it.
- Be proactive. Don't wait for people to come to you.
- Don't dismiss individuals because they are not prospects for you. They may know someone who is.
- View networking as a process. Don't expect immediate results in terms of business.

9. Direct mail/advertising. Send personal letters to prospects and follow them up with phone calls. Follow up company mailings with phone calls. Advertise in appropriate publications that cover your territory or reach your prospect base.

10. Newsletters. Develop a newsletter to keep your name in front of your prospects and customers. It does not have to be fancy; a one-page version will do as long as it contains something of value to the reader. A newsletter is an excellent way to reach hard-to-contact prospects.

11. Former customers. Another source of prospects is people who used to buy from you but stopped. Perhaps the reason is no longer valid. Maybe there is a new decision maker who would be open to your suggestions. Examine old records. Look through past invoices to get the names of those accounts and contact them. You may find that the perceived barriers are nonexistent.

12. Former prospects. Check old prospect cards and files. Review past proposals. Companies' needs change. Get back to the former prospects—there may be some nuggets in "them thar hills."

13. Public relations. Write articles, give talks, or do community work where you and your company will be recognized.

Getting involved in charitable organizations such as Muscular Dystrophy, United Way, The Ronald McDonald House, and so on, will not only give you a feeling of personal satisfaction and pride but will also enable you to meet some of the most important and wealthiest individuals in your community.

14. Cold calls. This means physically calling on a company or individual without an appointment. Make cold calls when you are already in an area and have limited free time before your next appointment. The chief value of this method is usually information gathering. However, certain products lend themselves to cold calling.

15. Videos. Sending videos unsolicited can be effective if you have a clearly targeted audience and know their specific needs. Of course, your video should be highly professional and not overly long.

16. Audiocassettes. As in the above, a professionally narrated cassette can be an effective way of getting your message across.

17. Free samples. Most of us have received personalized pens, diaries, and similar items in the mail. A free seminar or service is another way of introducing your offering to potential prospects. Make it easy for them to buy.

18. Free trials. Let prospects try your product for a period of time. Sometimes called the "puppy dog" technique, if the users have a successful experience and get used to the offering, they will purchase it.

19. Forming strategic alliances. Develop relationships with salespeople whose product lines complement your own, who can provide "intelligence" and even enable you to provide a total solution combining your products or services.

20. Postcard mailer decks. This is a relatively inexpensive way to reach a large number of targeted prospects. The prospect receives a deck of 20 to 50 cards advertising a variety of products.

21. Broadcast fax. Utilizing a computerized fax service, you can send a fax message to a large number of people simultaneously and automatically.

22. Surveys. This involves sending questionnaires to a targeted list to gather information about buying habits and preferences. A crisp, new one dollar bill often accompanies the survey to encourage the recipient to respond.

23. Company service or repair department. Nonsalespeople with customer contact can be very effective in developing prospects. Their recommendations are often received as being objective and accepted as having the prospect's interest in mind.

24. Teach adult courses. The students who attend could become prospects for your services since they regard you as the expert.
What can you add to this list? It is limited only by your imagination and creativity.

GETTING APPOINTMENTS ON THE TELEPHONE

Whatever means you use to prospect for new business, referrals, networking, and so on, you will probably end up phoning the person for an appointment.
For many salespeople, cold calling by telephone is the *primary* method of getting appointments.
This section is devoted to helping you become more effective on the phone, with an emphasis on cold calling, that is, calling people you have never met or called before, but whom you have identified as potential users of your product or service.
The steps in getting appointments on the phone are:

Step 1: Set prospecting goals.
Step 2: Identify the appropriate buying influence.
Step 3: Prepare a prospecting script.
Step 4: Create an objections handbook.
Step 5: Pre-call preparation.
Step 6: Get through the secretary's screen.
Step 7: Set up a record keeping and follow-up system.
Step 8: Deal with rejection.

Step 1: Set Prospecting Goals

How much time should you devote to prospecting? When is the best time to prospect? How do you set up a prospecting schedule?

It all begins with a goal. The goal could be what you want to earn, the amount of sales revenue you want to generate, the number of product units or new accounts you want to sell through your prospecting efforts. Let's take a hypothetical case.

Bill Barnes sells widgets. His widgets range in price from $3,000 to $10,000 and his commission ranges from 7½ percent to 12½ percent, depending on the model. His annual salary is $20,000, and he is paid commissions in addition to his salary.

Bill Barnes's earnings goal for the year is $50,000. Thirty thousand dollars will be in commissions. At an average commission rate of 10 percent, Bill will have to sell $300,000 worth of widgets annually.

The average sale is $5,000, so Bill will need to make 60 sales to reach his goal. This means he will need to produce $25,000 in monthly revenues, or five sales per month.

Bill estimates he needs eight prospects to close one sale. This means he will have to call on 40 new prospects a month (five sales × eight prospects) or approximately two per day.

Bill's previous experience with getting appointments indicates he usually closes one of four phone contacts for an appointment. A phone contact is defined as talking to a qualified decision maker or influencer. He will need to make 160 phone contacts per months to get his 40 appointments (40 appointments × 4 contacts).

Because Bill does not make contact with everyone he calls, it requires about three dials to make one contact. Therefore, it requires 480 dials to make 160 contacts. The monthly totals look like this:

Dials: 480
Contacts: 60
Appointments: 40
Sales: 5
Revenues: $25,000
Commissions: $2,500

Based on these numbers, Bill earns approximately $5.21 in commissions each time he dials a phone number ($2,500 divided by 480). It certainly is motivating to know you're making money every time you dial a prospect, isn't it?

Based on 20 dials per hour, it will require approximately 24 hours per month or 6 hours per week of phone prospecting time for Bill to reach his goal. Figure 2–2 contains an illustration of Bill's plan.

Set up a prospecting schedule. When is the best time to prospect? It depends on a number of factors: when your prospects are generally in, when you are in your office, and when you are at your telephone best.

The important thing is to schedule the same time each week and be thoroughly prepared with your cards, script, records, and anything else you need to work on the phone.

Have a goal for each session and do not stop calling until you have reached your goal. Then, reward yourself in some way.

To relate what you have just read to your own situation, complete the information in Figure 2–3.

You now have your productivity goals for prospecting. Keep a record of each prospecting session to fine-tune the numbers. If it takes you fewer calls to get the desired number of appointments, you can either spend less time on the phone or spend the same amount of time and make more appointments.

Once you have determined the inputs required to achieve your goals, that is, the dials, contacts, and appointments, concentrate on performing those activities. Remember, the input that you have the most control over is the dials, so concentrate on making the required number.

No one can stop you from dialing the phone. No one can stop you from asking for the right person. If you will perform the inputs, the outputs will take care of themselves.

If you have been in your territory for a long time and work mainly with existing customers and referrals, set a goal to make 5 to 10 prospecting calls a day to keep yourself sharp and in selling shape.

If you are not getting the sales results you are looking for, it is probably because you are not making enough calls! Refer back to the bottom of Figure 2–3, "Telephone Batting Average," for a simple way to keep track of your productivity.

FIGURE 2–2
Bill Barnes's Prospecting Plan

Salary: $20,000
Commission goals: $30,000
Total revenue required to reach goal: $300,000
Average sale amount: $5,000
Commission rate: 10%

Prospecting Productivity Planner

1. My (Bill Barnes) earnings goal for the year/period is $50,000.
2. I need to generate $300,000 in sales for the year/period; $25,000 in sales each month.
3. I need to make 5 sales to achieve $25,000 in sales each month.
4. I need to make 40 presentations to get 5 sales (assumption: 8 presentations to make 1 sale).
5. I need to make 160 phone contacts* to get 40 presentations (assumption: 4 phone contacts to get 1 appointment).
6. I need to make 480 dials to get 160 phone contacts (assumption: 3 dials to make 1 contact).

I will achieve the following productivity goals each week. Making 120 dials, I will:
1. Reach 40 people (contacts): 1 contact every 3 dials.
2. Get 10 appointments (presentations): 1 appointment every 4 contacts. Resulting in 1.25 sales: 1 sale every 8 appointments. Generating $6,000 in weekly revenue @ $5,000 revenue per sale. I will earn $600 in weekly commissions: 10 percent of $6,000.
3. Designate the following days and hours for phone prospecting each week (assumption: 20 dials per hour).

Monday and Friday 9:00 AM to 12:00 PM (6 hours to make 120 calls)

Day(s)	Hours	Dials

(Telephone Batting Average)

Dial	Contacts
1 2 3 4 5	1 2 3 4 5
6 7 8 9 10	6 7 8 9 10
11 12 13 14 15	11 12 13 14 15
16 17 18 19 20	
21 22 23 24 25	
26 27 28 29 30	
31 32 33 34 35	*Appointments*
36 37 38 39 40	
41 42 43 44 45	1 2 3 4 5
46 47 48 49 50	6 7 8 9 10

---

*Contact = reaching the desired individual on the phone.

FIGURE 2–3
Sample Prospecting Plan

Prospecting Productivity Planner

1. My earnings goal for the year/period is $_____.
2. I need to generate $_____ in sales for the year/period; $_____ in sales each month.
3. I need to make _____ (number of) sales to achieve $_____ in sales each month.
4. I need to make _____ presentations to get _____ sales.
5. I need to make _____ phone contacts* to get _____ presentations.
6. I need to make _____ dials to get _____ phone contacts.

I will achieve the following productivity goals each week. Making _____ dials, I will:

1. Reach _____ people (contacts).
2. Get _____ appointments (presentations).
   Resulting in _____ sales.
   Generating $_____ in weekly revenue.
   Earning $_____ in weekly commissions.
3. Designate the following days and hours for phone prospecting each week (based on 30 dials per hour).

Day(s)	Hours
(Telephone Batting Average)	

Dials	Contacts
1 2 3 4 5	1 2 3 4 5
6 7 8 9 10	6 7 8 9 10
11 12 13 14 15	11 12 13 14 15
16 17 18 19 20	
21 22 23 24 25	
26 27 28 29 30	
31 32 33 34 35	*Appointments*
36 37 38 39 40	
41 42 43 44 45	1 2 3 4 5
46 47 48 49 50	6 7 8 9 10

*Contact = reaching the desired individual on the phone.

For many salespeople, their performance chart looks like a series of peaks and valleys. That's because they stop prospecting when business is good. The best time to prospect is when you're "hot," when you need it the least. A confident, expectant attitude has an uncanny positive effect on prospects. The less you seem to need them, the more they want you.

When business is slow and you need new prospects, that slight eagerness is picked up by the prospects and they tend to draw back.

Make prospecting an activity for all seasons and you will straighten out your performance chart on the high side.

I was approached recently by a young woman who had attended our sales training course and was making an auspicious beginning as a salesperson. She eagerly told me about the number of appointments she had obtained and the sales she was closing.

I asked her how her prospecting techniques were working. An embarrassed look crossed her face and she replied guiltily, "Arnie, I'm so involved with servicing the accounts I've sold and handling the details, I have no time for anything else. I can't even think of prospecting."

I advised her to set aside one hour each day, preferably the first hour, to do nothing but prospect for new business. "Keep calling until you get at least one good prospect," I said, "and don't take any calls during this time. In this way, you'll keep the pipeline filled while you're taking care of existing business."

Step 2: Identify the Appropriate Buying Influence

It is important to reach the individual who can make the decision to buy what you are selling. However, this individual may be difficult to reach, and to complicate matters, others may also be involved in the decision-making process.

To simplify your job of identifying buying influences, we've broken them down into four categories or roles.

Decision maker
Decision influencer
Decision implementer
Center of influence

People may play several roles, sometimes all four, and roles may change depending on economic conditions, the dollars involved, experience with the product or vendor, and who will be using the product or service. Let's examine the typical characteristics of the four buying influences.

Decision maker. This is the individual who has final authority to buy or not to buy. He or she can release the funds. In short, the decision maker can say yea or nay to your proposal at any time. For large purchases, it usually is a senior executive of the firm. Generally, this individual is measuring the impact of the purchase on the entire organization—taking a "big picture" perspective.

Decision influencer. This individual has significant input into the decision-making process but needs final approval. A lot of the frustration in selling is because salespeople cannot get past this individual to the decision maker. The decision influencer is often a department head or manager of an operation such as sales or customer service and evaluates your product or service on its ability to improve results.

Decision implementer. This is an individual who has firsthand contact with your product or service. An example would be a PC operator if you were selling personal computers. While decision implementers cannot make final decisions, they can significantly influence them if they feel strongly one way or another and their input is valued by management.

Center of influence. This is an individual either inside or outside the organization who has credibility with all the buying influences and who favors you and your offering. He or she can offer you advice and guidance in your selling efforts. They can be consultants, CPAs, attorneys, or anyone whose judgment is valued by the prospect.

Any of the other three buying influences can also act as a center of influence. It is important to develop a center of influence in accounts if you want to do on-going business.

FIGURE 2–4
Identifying Buying Influences

Decision Makers

Have authority to authorize or deny request for purchase.
Can initiate purchase process or terminate it at any time.

Decision Influencers

Can recommend purchase but cannot make final decision.
However, can often make a no decision.
If strong, recommendation may be tantamount to purchase.
Performance or productivity usually directly affected by the performance of product or service.

Decision Implementers

Potential users of the product or service being presented.
"Hands-on" relationship with vendor, product, or service.

Centers of Influence

Guide salespeople through the purchasing process; has
personal and/or position power with all parties to the decision.

Figure 2–4 illustrates the buying influences we have discussed.

In larger organizations and where the purchase amount is large, all the buying influences can be involved in the decision. It's important that you contact each individual who has a stake in the purchase and show them how they benefit.

Committees. It is not uncommon for buying committees to make decisions. However, there is usually a "first" among equals who is, in effect, the decision maker. Try to identify this individual. Keep in mind that the committee may be composed of decision influencers and even decision implementers. Don't ignore any buying influence.

Step 3: Prepare a Prospecting Script

"A script? That's terrible. It's canned. I'll sound stilted and unnatural. It's boring. I'll never get any appointments."

The word *script* evokes images of rote learning and recitals—monotonous incantations of facts and figures. That's not what I have in mind. The purpose of phoning for an appointment is just that: to get the appointment.

Prospects are inundated with phone calls. It's tough to even get through to the person you're calling. So when you do, you need to say what you want to say, exactly the way you want to say it— every time—and with maximum impact!

You will have ample opportunity to be spontaneous and creative. Remember, the prospect plays his role as he sees fit. By knowing what you are going to say and having a track to run on, you will be able to concentrate on what your prospect is saying and how he says it. **You will be able to listen better.** With practice, you will deliver a presentation that sounds fresh and spontaneous. Program a few "ah," "you know," and pauses if you have to.

When was the last long-running stage play you saw? Didn't it seem to you and the audience that the performance was given just for you? Yet the actors were speaking the same words in the exact same way, performance after performance. Using a script will prevent you from getting emotional and saying the wrong things, especially when the prospect is rude or putting pressure on you.

Think of your telephone presentation as a stage play. You are the author, director, and star performer. Unfortunately, the other performer is ad-libbing his role, so you have to anticipate his responses as much as possible.

Scripts will vary based on your product and the type of buying influence you're calling. Some scripts will be very short and to the point to quickly capture the prospect's attention and interest.

Writing a script is evolutionary. You start with what you think is an effective script and make changes as you go along. What will ultimately develop will be a script that gets you the best results in terms of appointments.

Basic steps in a telephone presentation. The following is an example of the type of script you will use. It begins when the person you have asked to speak with answers the phone.

Identify your prospect, yourself, and your company.
Prospect:
(answering phone) "Hello."
Salesperson:
"Mr. Prospect?"

Prospect:

"Yes."

Salesperson:

"Mr. Robert Prospect?"

Prospect:

(coming to life) "Yes, who's this?"

(The repetition of the prospect's name using first and last name is used as a preoccupation breaker. It ensures that you have your prospect's complete attention.)

Salesperson:

"Mr. Prospect, this is John Q. Salesperson with the ABC Courier Company. Does that name ring a bell?"

Prospect:

"I'm not sure it does. What is this about?"

Salesperson:

"Mr. Prospect, ABC is an international courier that offers overnight delivery around the world for your time-sensitive documents."

Make a rapport-building statement.

Salesperson:

"I've heard a great deal about your firm's international activities and have been looking forward to speaking with you."

or

"We've helped other companies in your industry and perhaps we can be of service to you."

or

"Your company (use name) enjoys a fine reputation, and I've been looking forward to meeting with you to see if we can be of service."

(You are attempting to establish a common bond with the prospect at this point. If you have some information about his firm or if you are aware of an event affecting his company, use it.)

Prospect:

"What can I do for you?"

Qualify your prospect.

Salesperson:

"Mr. Prospect, do you make the decision as to which courier to use for your international work?"

Prospect:
"Yes."

Salesperson:
"Is there anyone else involved in the decision?"

(If the person you are talking to is not the decision maker, find out the name of the person who is.)

Prospect:
"Yes, Bill King, our shipping department supervisor is also involved."

(The salesperson takes note of this information.)

Find out the facts. Ask the questions necessary to determine whether the prospect has a need or application for your services.

Salesperson:
"Mr. Prospect, to what countries do you presently ship? (Wait for answer.) "What is the frequency? What kind of documents do you ship?" (Wait for answer.) "How critical is overnight delivery?" (Wait for answer.)

The prospect's responses will dictate the kinds of questions you will ask. In this step you are qualifying for need. Once you have ascertained that there is a possible need for your product or service, you move to the next step.

Deliver your sales message.

Salesperson:
"Mr. Prospect, ABC Courier is small enough to treat every client individually—with a personal touch. You are assured of flexible service to meet your most unusual requirements—and at the right price."

Your selling message should answer the questions in each prospect's mind: "Why should I see you?" "What's in it for me?" (WIIFM). Your sales message needs to be persuasive and interesting. It should promise benefits that whet the prospect's appetite to hear more. Don't clutter your sales message with features.

Request an appointment.

Salesperson:
"I'd like to show you how we can handle your shipments to your com-

plete satisfaction. Let's get together. How does your calendar look for Monday at 10 AM or is Tuesday at 3 PM a better time?"

(This is the alternate choice close, giving the prospect a choice of two positive alternatives. Other examples are: "Are mornings or afternoons better for you?" or "What's more convenient, earlier in the week or later?")

Prospect:
"Well, I'm kind of busy right now. Can you send me something in the mail?"

Handle the objection.
Salesperson:
"I appreciate the value of your time, Mr. Prospect. But literature sometimes raises more questions than it answers. It will take just 18 minutes for me to show you how our service can benefit you. Is Monday morning a good time for you or is Tuesday afternoon better?"

(The salesperson was prepared for the prospect's "Send it in the mail" response. We'll cover handling objections later in this chapter.)

Prospect:
"Monday is OK; I can't give you much more than 18 minutes though."

Confirm the appointment.
Salesperson:
"That's fine. Perhaps Bill King would want to be present, also. I'll see you Monday, September 15, at 10 AM. I've marked my calendar. Thank you, Mr. Prospect. Have a good day."

You may want to leave your phone number so the prospect can reach you.

Review the basic steps in a telephone presentation and some key points shown on next page.

Don't say too much on the phone. The goal is to get the appointment, not to regurgitate everything you know about your product or service. If you want the appointment more than the prospect does not want to grant it, you will get a lot of appointments.

Developing a Phone Presentation	*Key Points*
Identify your prospect, yourself, and your company.	Be enthusiastic, friendly, and confident.
	Be clear and concise.
	Don't keep your prospect guessing as to what your call is about.
	If you have a difficult name to pronounce, repeat it. Say "sounds like" or use your first name only.
	If you are not sure of the prospect's name, ask him or her to please spell it.
Make a rapport-building statement.	Referral (the best).
	Favorable comment.
	Related event.
	Industry knowledge.
Qualify your prospect.	Identify the decision maker.
	More than one?
Find out the facts.	Criteria to sell.
	Learn more about the company.
Deliver your sales message.	Short and persuasive.
	Stress benefits.
Request an appointment.	State reason.
	Use alternate choice.
	Assume acceptance.
Handle the objection.	ARC: Acknowledge. Respond. Close.
Confirm the appointment.	Restate time, date, your name, and company name.
	You may want to leave your phone number in case the prospect needs to reach you.

Remember that the goal of the phone call is to get an appointment. If you say too much on the phone, there may be no need for the prospect to see you in person. *Do your real selling face-to-face.*

Features and Benefits. Before we leave scripting, here are a few key points to remember about features and benefits.

- People don't buy features. They buy the benefits that result from the features.
- A feature is a prominent part or characteristic of your product or service. It is a *fact*.
- A benefit describes what the feature does for the person using it.
- We don't buy air conditioners. We buy comfortable, cool homes and offices and a good night's rest.
- We don't buy airbags and ABS brakes. We buy safety and security for ourselves and our loved ones.
- Remember, only people can realize benefits.

Translate your product or service features into meaningful buyer benefits—that's what adds persuasiveness and impact to your presentations.

Voice mail. Voice mail can be a roadblock or opportunity. I prefer to view it as an opportunity to deliver an enthusiastic, friendly, well-scripted, benefit-oriented sales presentation of about 20 to 30 seconds. State your name, company, and telephone number slowly and distinctly, and repeat it.

Invite the prospect to return your call or request information. End the call with the benefit to your prospect.

If prospects who return your call reach an answering machine or voice mail, have a friendly, enthusiastic message that shows your appreciation and desire to render prompt service.

Step 4: Create an Objections Handbook

Objections are a fact of life. You are going to get them, so be prepared. They are knee-jerk reactions to your solicitation, a predisposition to say no. Most phone objections are stalls, put-offs, excuses to get you off the phone. They are invalid objections. They are more emotional than logical and have to be treated as such.

As mentioned, the three-step process for meeting objections is the **ARC** method.

1. Acknowledge or agree
2. Respond
3. Close

This has to be done quickly and positively, and it has to be followed by a request for an appointment.

We hear certain typical objections on the phone. They are listed below along with the suggested responses. Make a list of the objections you get on the phone and then write the best answers. If you can do this in conjunction with other salespeople in your company, you will get the benefit of choosing from a variety of responses.

When you have finalized your responses to objections, test them in actual phone presentations. Fine-tune them until you get them exactly as you want them.

Then set up an "objections handbook." Go to a photo store that sells albums with plastic holders for 4-by-6-inch pictures in a flip-up or shingled (overlapping) arrangement. Type each objection on the bottom of a 4-by-6-inch sheet so it will project out from the one above. Then type the actual answer above each objection.

Keep your objections handbook next to your script when making calls. When you hear an objection, flip to the appropriate place, and presto, there is the answer, exactly as you would like to present it. After a while, you will memorize the responses and will no longer need to refer to your book. By that time, you will have become a fine prospector and be on your way to success in phone prospecting.

Typical Telephone Objections and Responses

"I don't think I'm interested."

"I can understand that, Mr./Mrs. _____. It would be presumptuous of me to expect you to be interested until I can show you how you might increase productivity, reduce costs, and save money with our system. We've been able to accomplish this for other companies such as yours. (Mention names if applicable.)

   "May I take just 22 minutes to explain how we can accomplish this. What's better for you, morning or afternoons?"

"I think you're wasting your time."

"Mr. _____, thank you for being so considerate. I appreciate the value of your time, as well as my own, that's why I phoned ahead. What I have to say may be worth thousands of dollars to you and your company. I believe I can prove it if you can spare 22 minutes. Might you have some time on Tuesday morning or perhaps Thursday afternoon?"

"I really don't have the time right now."

"Mr. _____, I appreciate that you are working on a tight schedule. It's important that you hear this information, and I'd be glad to arrange an appointment at your convenience. Perhaps before 9 AM or after 5 PM, if that's better? I promise we won't go beyond 18 minutes. How about 8:45 AM tomorrow, and I'll bring the coffee. How do you take yours?" (A little feisty, perhaps. Use your judgment.)

"Would you drop the information in the mail?"

"Ms. _____, I really feel that sending you a brochure would do an injustice to both of us. It may raise more questions than it answers. I could give you a much more meaningful picture of how you may benefit from this system in just 18 minutes in person. What's better for you, Monday at 10 AM or Tuesday at 11 AM?"

"We're satisfied with our present supplier/equipment/system/service, etc."

"Ms. _____, I respect your loyalty. All I want to do is to keep you current on the most up-to-date information on _____. You're entitled to this service and there is no obligation. It's my job. At the very least, you'll keep your current supplier on his toes."

or

"It's good business to have an alternate source. It keeps everyone on their toes, and you get the benefit of the best service. Would early next week be a good time to see you, say Monday or Tuesday?"

Step 5: Pre-call Preparation

Prepare yourself emotionally, physically, and logically for this critical selling event. Have a goal for dials, contacts, and appointments. Have your score sheet handy.

Emotionally: Check your attitude. Are you ready to call? Are you ready to win? Use affirmations and visualization to mentally experience the results you will achieve.

Physically: Using a mirror on your desk will ensure that your facial gestures and posture are reflecting the enthusiasm and confidence you want to project. Dress for business, even if you are calling from home.

Logically: Have all your materials ready. This should include your prospect cards, headset, customer list, notepaper, account records, pens and pencils, script, "objections handbook," calendar, score sheet, map, and anything else necessary for phone prospecting. Clear your desk of anything not pertaining to the job at hand.

- Do not schedule anything else during times of the week you will be prospecting.
- Make an unbreakable date with yourself. Get into the habit of making your prospecting calls at the same time each week.
- Do not accept incoming calls while prospecting unless they are urgent.
- Concentrate on the job at hand.

It's money-making time!

Step 6: Get through the Secretary's Screen

Secretaries, assistants, or whoever screens the call can be difficult to get through, but that is because they have been instructed to carefully guard their boss's time. Using gimmicks or tricks or trying to power your way into the inner sanctum will work against you more often than not. Annoying a secretary may have a similar effect on the boss.

First, find out what the screener's actual title is. It may be administrative assistant and the person may take umbrage at being addressed as a secretary.

The best approach is to build rapport with assistants or secretaries and to sell them on the benefits their bosses will gain by speaking with you. This may take time, effort, and patience. Show the secretaries that you understand their boss's problems and have a possible solution. After all, secretaries have their boss's interests at heart. Have a good reason for wanting the appointment.

Humility is a powerful tool. "I've got a problem. I need your help," softens up a lot of hard-boiled people. When you openly acknowledge that someone has the power and position to help you or thwart you, that person is more likely to use that power in a helping way. Most people find it a lot easier to refuse an arrogant demand for action than to deny a humble request for assistance.

It will take multiple calls to get through to a busy decision maker. It may be an "A" priority to you, but it's only a "C" or "D" to him or her. Don't let your ego get in the way. Don't take it personally. He or she is reacting to your role as a salesperson. Visualize the end result and keep trying. Some of my best clients are people that were extremely difficult to reach initially. **Persistence is a must in prospecting.**

Make the call productive by getting qualifying information from the secretary.

> "Ms. Jones, we're looking for companies with a profile of 50 employees or more. Does your firm fit that profile?"
>
> "Do you sell direct or through distributors?"

Plan the questions you need to ask so when you do talk to the decision makers, you're more knowledgeable about their operation. Some salespeople prefer to make an information-getting call before calling for the appointment. This works well when working from a small list.

If you cannot get anywhere with the secretary, call early in the morning, after hours, during lunch, or even on weekends, times when the secretary is not likely to be there. You can write and say you will be calling for an appointment, send a mailgram, or try a person-to-person long-distance call. Sending pertinent bits of information to your prospect periodically may serve as a door opener. If at first you don't succeed, well, you know the rest.

Step 7: Set up a Record Keeping and Follow-up System

First, remember the *KISS rule: Keep it short and simple.* The following system is designed as a prospecting system and requires these materials:

- 3-by-5-inch cards.
- 3-by-5-inch card file box, your prospect box.
- January to December dividers.
- Two sets of 1 to 31 dividers (one set behind the current month and the next month).
- A to Z dividers (these go in the back of the prospect box).
- Business card file (to keep customer business cards in alphabetical order).
- A monthly calendar with space to enter in appointments each day of the month.

Transfer your prospect information to the 3-by-5 cards. If you have a large territory, you may use a different color for each geographic area so they are easily identifiable. The information on the front of the card should include:

- Company name, address, and ZIP code.
- Telephone number.
- Person(s) to contact and title.
- Secretary's name.
- Any other personal information.

The back of the card is used to record the date and result of your last call.

The system I am describing here is a simple one using 3-by-5 cards. There are many automated systems available with calendaring and letter-writing features that will not be covered in this chapter. It is suggested that you become familiar with a manual system and define your needs before automating.

As you make each call, note the date and result on the back of the card and place it behind the month and date of the next call. You simply keep moving the cards in the file as you make appointments or schedule the next call. Make sure to jot down pertinent information so you can use it to build trust and rapport on your next contact.

Follow-up.   If you send literature as a result of the call, follow up in five to seven days. If you don't get through the first time, make your next call in about a week unless you have uncovered information that indicates a decision is to be made.

Spread out the time frame between each elapsed call, but usually no longer than a month. It may take four or five dials or even more before you get through to your contact.

Leave your number even though the vast majority of prospects will not return your call. Some will, and the ones that do may have an interest in what you're selling.

Step 8: Deal with Rejection

Telephone prospecting has a high rejection rate. It is not a reflection on your ability, personality, or product. No one likes to be turned down, but if you are oversensitive to the negative reactions you get, you'll never be a successful prospector.

Selling is a numbers game. The more calls you make, the more appointments you will get; the more appointments, the more presentations; the more presentations, the more sales; the more sales, the more income, recognition, title, and prestige. It all begins with prospecting.

Focus on the end result, not the process. If your average is one appointment for every 10 calls, view the nine misses as stepping-stones to the one hit! Visualize your new condo, tooling around with that spiffy sports car, the latest digital audio ensemble in your den, not the fact that nine people missed the opportunity of talking to you.

No one cares how many you lose. It's the ones you win that count. If it takes you more calls to get an appointment than someone else, then make more calls. There are few "natural" salespeople. Most of us have to use our persistence and determination to earn our keep.

Listed below are some of the all-time strikeout leaders in professional baseball. Do you recognize any of these "failures"? (The asterisk indicates a Baseball Hall of Fame member.)

1. Reggie Jackson*
2. Willie Stargell
6. Mickey Mantle*
13. Frank Robinson
14. Willie Mays*
22. Hank Aaron*
24. Babe Ruth*

In 50th place on this dubious list is the all-time hit leader, Pete Rose.

The message is clear: You need to lose some to win some. There are several things you can do to minimize the effect of rejection.

1. Focus on the "inputs." Set a goal for the number of dials you'll make in the session. Starting with that number, 20 for example, write all the numbers in descending order (20, 19, 18. . .) down to 1. As you make each call, simply cross out the highest number until all 20 calls are made. Concentrate on making the calls, not whether you get appointments. Let the law of averages work for you.

Caution. Don't give up after a few calls and say, "It's not my day." You can never tell when you'll hit a hot prospect; it might be on your last call.

My view of prospecting is that it is the process of "finding someone who's looking for you." As mentioned previously, there are people out there who don't respond to direct mail or other forms of solicitation but who will respond to a warm, friendly, concerned voice on the phone. There is no substitute for persistence.

2. Make phone prospecting an "assembly line" operation. Have all your cards ready with telephone numbers already on them. As soon as one call is completed, begin the next. Use a headset—it will free your hands for making notes. Don't physically hang up the phone. In this way, you won't have time to commiserate with yourself over an unsuccessful call.

Adopt an attitude of positive expectancy. Here is what a successful salesperson said about getting through the secretary screen:

> I always find it helpful before I make a call to visualize Mr. Johnson, whatever his position, as a friend of mine, as someone I know personally, who always talks to me and who will welcome hearing from me. It's easy then to imagine that it would be silly for me to telephone this friend of mine and expect his assistant or secretary to keep me from talking to him. Because I know she wouldn't. Now how do you suppose Johnson's friends would ask for him when they talk to his secretary?
>
> As I said before, I'd say, "Mr. Johnson please, this is Joe Salesperson," and 9 times of 10 he will pick up the phone a second later.

We might disagree with the success rate, but the principle is valid.

No sales technique works all the time. To be worthwhile for you, it need only work 1 more time out of 10 than your present approach. For example, if what you are presently doing is getting you two appointments out of 10 contacts and you get three appointments using what we have suggested, you have realized a 50 percent increase in productivity.

When you get through to the decision maker, make sure your phone presentation is benefit oriented. It should answer his unspoken question, "Why should I see you?" Present a realistic benefit early in the interview, preferably in your opening statement.

Be prepared for resistance. No prospect is sitting by the phone hoping you'll call because he needs your product or service.

Don't be tempted to stray from your prepared script. If it has proved to be successful, stick with it. You may be getting a bit bored with it, but the prospect who is hearing it for the first time is not. Visualize your little production as a successful, long-running show on Broadway. The financial backers would not permit you to tinker with the dialogue as long as the theater was packed.

Practice, practice, practice. Listen to yourself on tape, or watch and listen on videotape. Check your pronunciation, enunciation, pacing, and expression. Put a smile into your voice. Smile while you dial. Enjoy yourself. Create a desire for your prospect to want to see you.

Remember, nothing worthwhile comes easy. Selling is not a profession for dabblers. It requires courage, commitment, and perseverance. Stick with it. Keep calling. Will you begin Monday at 10 AM or Tuesday at 11 AM?

SUMMARY

- Prospecting is the lifeblood of your business. Accept the fact that it has to be done. The more prospects you have, the greater your sales productivity. As a rule of thumb, have three times your monthly sales target in prospective business.
- Prospecting must be done regularly. Set a schedule and stick to it.
- Profile the best prospects for what you sell. Find the directories they are listed in, the organizations they belong to, and the publications they read.
- Your present customers are your best prospects. They are also excellent sources for referrals.
- Set up a simple prospecting system using 3-by-5 cards.
- Set prospecting goals. Determine how many dials, contacts, and appointments you need to achieve your goals and perform these "inputs."
- Remember, if you are not getting the results you want, it's probably because you are not making enough calls.
- Prospecting requires commitment, discipline, and persistence.

Winners do the things that losers don't like to do. Winners don't like to do them either, but they do them anyway.
BE A WINNER!!

Chapter Three

Building Relationships

Richard Lombard

WHAT YOU WILL LEARN

In this chapter you will learn:

- The problem-solving approach to marketing.
- How to create a positive first impression.
- How to use empathy skills to establish rapport and build high-trust relationships.
- How to use specific empathy skills: intentions, acknowledging, listening, and aligning.
- How to move a prospect into the proper frame of mind for making a sale.
- How to define the comfort zone for your sales relationships.
- How to look at the business relationship according to the prospect's needs.

THE DECISION PROCESS

Before you can begin to build a sales relationship with a prospect, you must first understand purchasing. The purchasing decision process is actually a series of minor decisions that move the discussion step by step toward the final decision. Typically, it follows a pattern similar to this (read from bottom up):

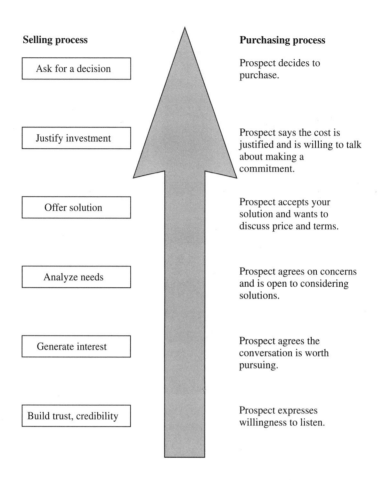

Selling process	Purchasing process
Ask for a decision	Prospect decides to purchase.
Justify investment	Prospect says the cost is justified and is willing to talk about making a commitment.
Offer solution	Prospect accepts your solution and wants to discuss price and terms.
Analyze needs	Prospect agrees on concerns and is open to considering solutions.
Generate interest	Prospect agrees the conversation is worth pursuing.
Build trust, credibility	Prospect expresses willingness to listen.

THE SALES STRATEGY

The sales strategy is a step-by-step process that parallels the decision process. Salespeople who follow the strategy and earn the right to advance from step to step will succeed in selling their products and increasing their prospects' profits. (Read from bottom up.)

UNDERSTANDING THE PROBLEM-SOLVING APPROACH TO MARKETING

Successful selling is solving people's problems. We can picture a successful sale as having four key elements:

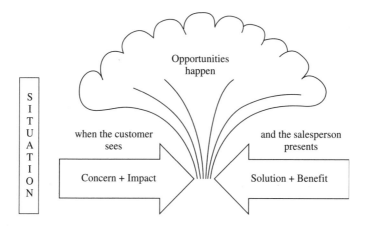

No prospect will purchase from you unless these four elements are in place: (1) a real *concern* that the prospect is facing or is having, (2) a noticeable *impact*—organizationally, financially, or personally; (3) a *solution* from your company that will produce; (4) a genuine *benefit* for the customer.

For example:

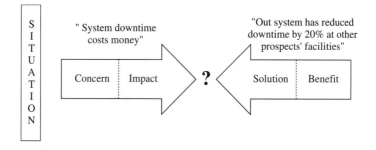

Will this make the sale? Maybe. And then again, maybe not. Just because you know downtime should be a real concern for your customer and your company has the sales solution does not mean you will get a commitment for the service. If that's all there were to it, we could sell our services by dropping a postcard in the mail.

The key is the customer. The salesperson must help the customer *see* the problem, *feel* the impact, *suffer* the consequences—the urgency of finding a solution. When a solution is offered, the customer will not purchase until it is possible to *see* and *touch* the solution, *understand* the simplicity, *experience* the results, and anticipate the *excitement, relief, pride, and sense of accomplishment* the solution will bring.

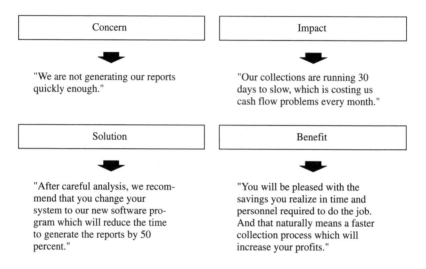

That is the problem-solving or consultative approach to marketing. And that is why your "sales" role is crucial to the success of your company. It is the salesperson who, using vivid word pictures and sales tools, creates the total realization that results in profitable applications of our products and services.

BECOMING A CONSULTANT

Unfortunately, you can't expect to simply walk into someone's office and become his or her sales consultant. Many customers are suspicious of those they consider salespeople. They may have had bad experiences with incompetent or unscrupulous vendors. Many of the people you will be calling on have a built-in resistance to you and a low tolerance for anything they perceive as a sales pitch. Yet, to be successful in today's marketplace, you must be assertive. For that reason, successful salespeople must play many roles: consultant, counselor, educator, negotiator, sometimes friend. Most of all, they're flexible. They adjust to each situation and to each person they meet. They don't sell by a fixed approach. They understand

The Consultative Sales Approach to Selling

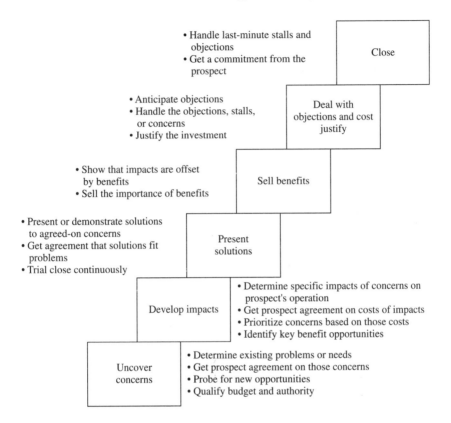

- Handle last-minute stalls and
  objections
- Get a commitment from the
  prospect

Close

- Anticipate objections
- Handle the objections, stalls,
  or concerns
- Justify the investment

Deal with objections and cost justify

- Show that impacts are offset
  by benefits
- Sell the importance of benefits

Sell benefits

- Present or demonstrate solutions
  to agreed-on concerns
- Get agreement that solutions fit
  problems
- Trial close continuously

Present solutions

Develop impacts

- Determine specific impacts of concerns on
  prospect's operation
- Get prospect agreement on costs of impacts
- Prioritize concerns based on those costs
- Identify key benefit opportunities

Uncover concerns

- Determine existing problems or needs
- Get prospect agreement on those concerns
- Probe for new opportunities
- Qualify budget and authority

that building good relationships is just as important as making sales. They see as their key role to:

- Help prospects solve problems and satisfy needs, rather than just push services.
- Build a strong relationship with the purchaser based on trust, integrity, and openness.
- Convey a genuine interest in helping them.
- Show respect for the prospect's point of view and right to decide.
- Listen intently, rather than to guess or presume what the prospect will say next.
- Ask prospects for commitments and decisions without pressuring them.

- Adjust the pace of the discussion and vary the sales approach to match the prospect's level of understanding, acceptance, and interests, rather than to conduct a one-way, nonstop monologue.

By approaching the marketing process in this manner, the salesperson will begin to establish a high level of credibility with the customer. Some of the techniques and attitudes that will hold you in good stead include:

Enthusiasm.	Customer focused.
Knowledge of:	Develop custom win.
Systems.	Success stories.
Products.	Probing and listening skills.
Markets.	Analyzing capabilities.
Services.	Relating skills.
Flexibility.	Presentation skills.
Persistence.	Empathy.

CREATING A GOOD FIRST IMPRESSION

The first three minutes of an initial face-to-face meeting with someone often determine whether or not you build a successful relationship. Because of the importance of these crucial moments, you will want to make sure you:

1. *Dress appropriately.* Dressing appropriately won't get you a commitment but not doing so may prevent you from getting it.

2. *Observe office or area etiquette.* People work very hard at their jobs to earn respect, so it is prudent on a first visit to be polite and respectful of the person's position without being overly solicitous. That means you should:
   - Enter an office or work area only with an invitation or permission.
   - Smoke only when offered.
   - Sit only when and where the customer indicates.
   - Touch nothing without the customer's permission.

3. *Demonstrate a positive attitude.* Your body language—the way you walk, your expressions, your tone of voice, your posture

and movements—tell a great deal about you. Make sure you:
- Smile.
- Shake hands firmly but not excessively.
- Maintain good eye contact.
- Use a friendly, relaxed tone of voice.

Remember, the impression you create in the first three minutes is the one that may stay in the mind forever. Be sure to put your best foot forward . . . and not in your mouth!

The First Three Minutes

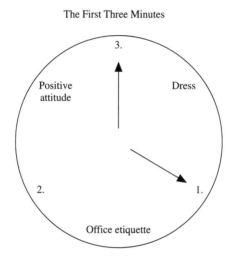

EGO VERSUS EMPATHY

All people have two strong drives that affect how we sell and how we are perceived by the purchaser. Ego is the drive that compels us to get the order, to win, to succeed, to excel, to achieve. Empathy

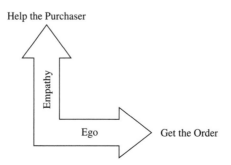

encourages us to help customers, to be sensitive to their feelings, to be interested in them.

Marketing requires a balance of both—ego (to push for a decision) and empathy (to continue building trust and rapport).

EGO DRIVE AND EMPATHY DRIVE

When our ego drive is much stronger than our empathy drive, the customer often perceives us as aggressive, pushy, self-interested, dominating, competitive, intimidating, and high pressure.

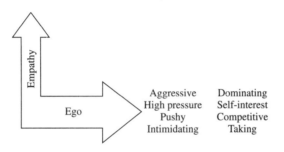

When our empathy drive is stronger than our ego drive, we are often perceived by others as sensitive, interested, helpful, accommodating, and giving.

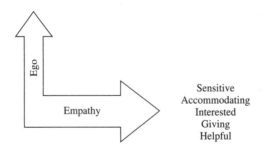

When we display strong but equal amounts of ego and empathy, we are perceived as assertive, firm but fair, give and take, cooperative, and leading.

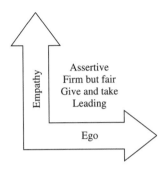

The accompanying chart summarizes how you will be perceived by a prospect, depending on your mix of ego and empathy:

	Understanding Accommodating Giving Interested Sensitive Patient Accepting Tolerant Easygoing	Assertive Firm but fair Give and take Empathic Listens Cooperative Leads Problem solver Not intimidated Leading
		Directive Intolerant Dominating Intimidating Taking High pressure Competitive
	Withdrawn Intimidated Passive	Pushy Aggressive Impatient

(Vertical axis: Empathy; Horizontal axis: Ego)

You use ego skills to inform customers—to present enough information for them to make decisions. You use empathy skills to build instant rapport. Both happen simultaneously. The best salespeople use them without conscious thought or effort—they become second nature. But never fear, they can be learned by anyone.

USING EMPATHY SKILLS TO ESTABLISH RAPPORT AND BUILD HIGH-TRUST RELATIONSHIPS

Empathizing means identifying with what the customer is saying. When customers believe you are really listening, rapport is strengthened and they are more likely to open up and honestly express their needs and concerns. You can help yourself build high-trust relationships by recognizing these four important elements:

1. Intentions: convey to the prospect intentions that encourage trust and relaxation.
2. Listening: actively tune into the customer's thoughts and feelings.
3. Acknowledging: show and convey to someone that you are interested, pay attention, understand, and respect the prospect's point of view.
4. Aligning: talk at the same level as the other person to maximize rapport, understanding, and communication.

Your ongoing relationships with prospects are an integral part of your success as a salesperson. Relationships built on your ability to exercise these empathy skills will bring payoffs throughout the years ahead. Let's examine each of these elements in more detail.

Intentions

People's willingness to listen to you and accept your recommendations depend to a large extent on how much they trust your intentions. You improve your chances of being heard, understood, and accepted if you convey these helpful attitudes throughout the sales process:

Ego (Sell)	*Empathy (Relate)*
"Let's solve this problem"	"I'm here to help."
"My recommendation is . . . "	"I'm here to learn."
"Will that work for you?"	"I'm here to listen."
"How soon do you expect to make your final decision?"	"I'm here to discuss."
"It's the right decision for you."	"I'm working for you."
"Let's do it."	"I care about my customers."
	"I respect your opinion."

When you demonstrate these balanced intentions, you build credibility, earn trust, win acceptance for your ideas, accomplish your objectives by finding out what customers want and need, continue to hold the customer's attention, avoid collisions of feelings, and move the discussion purposefully toward a decision—all of which improve your chances of getting a commitment and future opportunities.

High trust earns you the right to be more persistent and assertive without turning the prospect off.

Acknowledging

Anything you say or do that conveys to the other person that you are attentive, listening, and interested and that you understand and accept their point of view will enhance your relationship. Acknowledgments can be implied:

- Nodding.
- Taking notes on key points.
- Steady eye contact.
- Giving full attention.

Acknowledging can also be expressed by:

"That makes sense."	"I recognize . . . "
"I share the same opinion."	"I see."
"Seems fair to me."	"I agree."
"I appreciate your position."	"I hear you."

Acknowledgments facilitate conversation. They open channels of communication. They relax customers and encourage trust. By your acknowledgment of their feelings, they are encouraged to listen and be more receptive to your ideas. Your acknowledgments create a favorable climate for discussion and for decisions.

Aligning

You communicate best with people when you talk at their level. When you enter a conversation, you pick up cues from the other person that alert you to adjust your pace, your loudness, your tone, or your intensity. If you are talking to nontechnical people, you make allowances and adjustments. That's aligning—getting on the other person's wavelength, so he or she can hear you better.

Aligning can be done in several ways:

Language: Change your choice of words, using simpler, non-technical language.

Tone: Regulate the volume, pace, and tone of your voice to be closer in tune to your listener's needs.

Emotions: Talk at the same emotional level.

Social style: Become more or less formal to suit the occasion.

When you empathize and align with people, a remarkable thing happens—they become more receptive to you.

A CUSTOMER'S STATE OF MIND

When you talk to anyone about anything, the person can be identified as being in one of three states of mind about the subject: They are positive, neutral, or negative.

```
+ Positive
0 ———————————————— Neutral
− Negative
```

For the sake of discussion, let's picture neutral as a horizontal line. Positive is the area above the line and negative is the area below. You can't have a productive conversation unless both you and the prospect are at neutral or above. Another way to think of it is that two people can't have a productive conversation unless they're both "above the line."

A prospect relationship that stays above the line is one that moves toward solutions to problems and gives everyone involved a good feeling, a feeling that the best that can be done in this particular situation is being done, a feeling of cooperation, of being on the same team. Naturally, it would be great if all your prospect relationships stayed above the line. However, life isn't always that easy, is it?

The difficulty lies when you start with someone below the line. It's often very difficult to get someone from negative to neutral and positive. People tend to hold on to their viewpoints, especially if they feel pushed. Leading people up to positive is a two-step process:

1. Empathize to get them to neutral, then
2. Offer an alternative idea or benefit to get them to positive.

When the customer shows . . .	You should . . .
+ Positive	Close for acceptance
0 —————— Neutral	Present ideas
− Negative	Empathize

When you shift gears in a car, you use the clutch to go through neutral first—otherwise you get a grinding of gears. Marketing is like that, too. If you attempt to shift someone's point of view from low to high without first going through neutral, you may get a grinding of wills. That's what happens when you try to overcome the customer's strong negative feeling with your strong positive one. First, you have to shift the negative to neutral. Then you can approach with a positive.

WHAT ARE YOU ULTIMATELY LOOKING FOR?

If you have the opportunity to work with a customer year after year, you are obviously doing some things right. You have established some kind of rapport and high level of comfort with that customer that keeps him or her asking for your products or, more likely, your services. We like to say you and your customer are living in the "Comfort Zone." In this zone are all those attitudes and personal skills that encourage a solid salesperson/customer relationship. There is only mutual trust and confidence. There is high credibility for both parties. The relationship is interactive and well-aligned with enthusiastic problem-solving capabilities, and so on. In the Comfort Zone, the sales interaction is always "above the line."

Outside the Comfort Zone are all those attitudes and barriers that inhibit good customer relationships. There is hostility and distrust on one or both sides. There are time restraints that get in the way of effective communication. Interruptions cause mistakes and misunderstandings. Preoccupied minds fail to focus on the necessary concerns that must be identified and solved. Outside the Comfort Zone, the sales/prospect interaction is always "below the line."

Therefore, it's your job to find a way to identify and to stay in the Comfort Zone—for each of your prospects and customers. And remember, every situation is unique. What works in one relationship may not work in another. It's up to you to remain flexible and attentive to the needs of each particular situation.

WHAT IS THE PROSPECT ULTIMATELY LOOKING FOR?

We've spent a lot of pages talking about why you want to build good customer relations and what you must do to get them built. Well, let's step back for a moment and remind ourselves that it's **what the prospect wants that is most important**—that is, the essential factors in establishing a good relationship must be measured from your prospects' points of view. Those factors are:

1. To be taken seriously as a person.
2. To have their problems or concerns taken seriously.
3. To be able to effectively communicate their problems or concerns to you.
4. To feel that you are on their side.

This may seem overly basic and simplistic. However, just think how many times you've personally encountered a salesperson who has not fulfilled one or more of these factors. **When in doubt, put**

yourself in the prospect's shoes and think how you'd like to be treated. Then get your own shoes back on and do it!

SUMMARY

We have covered the following key concepts and ideas:

- Successful salespeople practice a problem-solving approach to marketing, adapting their style to each situation and prospect.
- Successful salespeople don't sell by rote, but understand that the key to marketing in all highly competitive industries is to build strong relationships based on trust. This trust will help them earn the right to be assertive with their customers.
- The first three minutes of an initial meeting can determine success or failure. That is why it is crucial to develop trust quickly.
- Successful salespeople dress professionally, observe proper etiquette, and project a positive attitude.
- The intentions you project have a great influence on the marketing process. Projecting a helpful attitude will build credibility with the prospect.
- The empathy skills of a positive, helpful attitude, acknowledging a prospect's ideas and feelings, and aligning your style and tone to suit your listener are key ingredients to creating rapport and building high-trust relationships.
- A prospect's state of mind can generally be described as negative, neutral, or positive to any suggestion or recommendation.
- The only way that positive agreements are made are when the customer and salesperson are dealing "above the line"—that is, both in the neutral or positive mind-sets.
- Trying to get an agreement with one party above the line and one party below the line is like trying to change gears in a standard transmission without using the clutch . . . you get nothing but loud grinding sounds.
- The ultimate aim of the salesperson should be to get all customer relationships into a Comfort Zone.
- The ultimate aim of prospects is to be respected personally and professionally, to have someone with whom they can communicate, and to feel that someone is on their side.

Exercises

1. In your own words, define the problem-solving approach to marketing.

   _____

   _____

   _____

2. Explain how people typically make purchasing decisions and list some questions they consider as they move toward a final decision.

   _____

   _____

   _____

3. To what extent do you believe people make decisions logically and emotionally?

   _____

   _____

   _____

4. What is empathy? How does it influence your ability to sell?

   _____

   _____

   _____

5. What is ego? How does it influence your ability to sell?

   _____

   _____

   _____

6. Is there an ideal mixture of ego and empathy that works best?

   _____

   _____

   _____

7. What are a prospect's three potential mind-sets in relation to a suggestion or recommendation? How would you attempt to move a prospect from one level to another?

_____

_____

_____

8. Describe the "Comfort Zone" in your own words. What would you describe as the hardest part about existing in such a zone with all your prospects and customers?

_____

_____

_____

Chapter Four

Sales Presentations

David G. Moran

Many salespeople still fear making a presentation. This fear can be reduced, if not eliminated, by knowing the mechanics of a presentation and practicing those mechanics, or skills. When you have finished reading this chapter, you will have gained knowledge about the following seven topics:

1. *Knowing the purpose of the presentation.* This is not always as easy as it may sound. Learn how to uncover the most important purpose, and how to prove it!

2. *Determining the results you want from the presentation.* Learn how to identify the results you want to achieve from the presentation.

3. *Knowing the audience.* Eliminate surprises. Find out in advance what the audience's hot buttons are.

4. *Selecting the materials and audiovisual equipment.* Learn the ins and outs of the effective methods and equipment techniques. See the addendum, "Using Audiovisual Equipment."

5. *Planning the presentation.* Organizing the talk into an introduction, body, and conclusion will help present information that meets the audience's needs.

6. *Reading body language.* Sometimes what is seen speaks volumes about what is happening with the audience.

7. *Using eye contact, voice resonance, and gestures.* Become knowledgeable and proficient using verbal and nonverbal skills.

KNOWING THE PURPOSE
OF THE PRESENTATION

Three factors will help you determine the purpose of your presentation.

1. Is the purpose related to one of three general issues? These are: increasing something (sales), decreasing something (costs), or explaining something (total quality management).
2. Your company contact wants you to be successful and is an excellent source for explaining the company and participant issues.
3. If you already know the audience, include the information the audience members need to arrive at the decision or action you want them to make.

In addition, the answers to these five questions will assist in establishing priorities and direction.

1. What should the audience members be able to do after my presentation?
2. What decisions are within their authority to make?
3. What information do they need to make valid decisions?
4. Why should they agree with me?
5. What do they already know about me, my company, my product or service?

Having more than one priority is common with more intricate presentations. When this occurs, simply look at each of the priorities and rank them from the strongest to the weakest. Next, determine the logical order to present this information. This serves as a second check to assure a logical flow in the presentation. Some presenters like to save the strongest point for last, so they start with the weakest information first. These presenters also believe that what is said last is remembered most. Unfortunately, in today's fast-paced environment if you start off slowly, you may not be around for the finish. If the audience members are bored from the beginning, will they be enthusiastic listeners at the end?

Try the opposite strategy. Start with the strongest, most compelling point first. This approach grabs the attention of the audience immediately. This also assures that anyone who leaves the presentation early has at least heard the most important information.

Have available enough information to prove every point you make in the presentation. Proof information can come from statistics, books, articles, historical data, and so on. Of course, be aware of the audience's acceptance of the sources of information.

Determining the priorities and organizing the points and proofs are the first steps in preparing for a successful presentation.

KNOWING THE AUDIENCE

Make it a goal to find out about everyone who will be attending the presentation. The best source for this information is your contact. Remember, the contact wants your presentation to succeed and will usually be glad to supply any supportive information needed.

If you do not know the composition of the audience, you run the risk of not achieving the desired results from the presentation. A potentially embarrassing situation for your contact can result. Imagine presenting to five people and the one you never found out about is the comptroller of the company. Had you known the comptroller would be present, you could have included specific information and prepared yourself for possible questions. Lack of information about the audience may set up one big nasty surprise! Take the time to investigate!

In general, you should be familiar with the major corporate functions and their general responsibilities within a company. This information can offer an idea of what someone from one of those areas might be concerned about and provides another means to identify and understand the needs of your audience. Listed below are seven major disciplines and their typical roles of responsibility.

Finance:	Budgets, profit, use of assets, investments, and investment guidelines such as return on investment (ROI).
Marketing:	Advertising, promotion, printed materials, sales aids.
Human resources:	Hiring, retention, policies, procedures, labor relations, compensation, benefits.
Sales:	Increasing sales, increasing market share, selling particular products/services, meeting established quotas and budgets.

Production:	Machine and person performance, operating profit, teamwork, effective and efficient use of assets.
Systems:	Communication, reporting, networks, support.
Customer service:	Supporting sales, handling orders and/or complaints, promoting the business.

In addition to this functional information, Figure 4–1 presents another way to think about and capture information about the audience. The figure asks three questions. Do they know the topic to be presented? What are their backgrounds? What are their possible attitudes? Answers to these questions can provide you with powerful information to tailor the presentation to address this audience.

SELECTING THE MATERIALS AND AUDIOVISUAL EQUIPMENT

It is advantageous to know how to support the presentation with handouts and a professional use of audiovisual equipment. Let's first address handouts. The age-old question has been whether or not to place the handouts on participant tables in advance, or distribute them when needed, or distribute them at the conclusion of the presentation. All are both correct and incorrect. Thinking through what needs to be accomplished with the audience will point to the right choice.

If the audience needs the handouts to refer to for more than 50 percent of the presentation, then distribute them in the beginning. If they never need to refer to the handouts, then distribute them at the end. If they will need to refer to them later in the presentation, then distribute them appropriately. The handouts become invisible support.

Be certain all the handouts are related to the material you are presenting. If you have prepared your own handouts, be sure all words are spelled correctly and there are no grammatical errors. Provide a binder; it will help organize the information for the audience.

Despite the tremendous advances in technology, there are still just three very common presentation media. Knowing how to use

FIGURE 4–1
Audience Information

Issue	Concern	What to Do
How much do they know about my topic?		
What backgrounds do they have?		
What attitudes will they have?		

them is important. The three most common are flip charts, overhead projectors, and slides.

Flip charts

- Use double sheets of paper for better control and to prevent see-through from a preprinted chart. This also protects against the marker ink from bleeding through.
- Stand and write from the side of the chart, and don't talk while writing.
- Keep your attention on the audience. When you have finished writing, return your attention to the audience.
- Prepare yourself for the next chart. Write a light pencil note on the top corner of the chart. This will help keep the correct place.
- Practice using transitions or bridging statements between charts.
- Practice printing ahead of time.
- Use blue markers for narrative, red and green for highlights.

Overhead projectors

- Make sure the bulb works and know where the spare is kept and how to replace it.

- Determine whether you will use preprinted overheads or will create as you present.
- Get estimates to produce color overheads before you decide to use them.
- Practice using the machine and overheads in advance. Practice writing and staying in touch with the audience. Practice talking about an overhead without looking at it. Practice turning the machine on and off between overhead transparencies.
- If you plan to use a pointer, practice!

Slides

- As with the overhead, check the bulb and know where the spare is kept and how to change it.
- Practice setting up the projector and focusing the image.
- Make sure all the slides are in the right order and facing forward. Then secure the slide tray with a locking ring.
- Know what to do if a slide jams.
- Practice using a remote control and talking to the audience without looking at the screen.

One new presentation medium is the LCD (liquid crystal display) panel. An LCD panel is a glass panel that is placed on top of an overhead projector. The panel is wired to a computer. Information on the computer monitor is sent to the panel where the overhead projector shows the image on the large screen. In many companies, LCD panels are replacing overheads and slides. The panel displays live and/or preprogrammed computer data. Check prices and the budget before making a suggestion to purchase one.

PLANNING THE PRESENTATION

A convenient way to organize your presentation is to think of the presentation as three interconnected parts, each supporting the other.

The first part, the introduction, is designed to establish rapport with the audience. Let them know:

a. Who you are.

b. That you are someone to listen to.

c. What is going to be presented.

d. What they will be able to decide after the presentation.

During the middle part, the body, you present all the points of information with supporting documentation (the proof). For example, the product or service may reduce costs, but before the audience will believe it, you must demonstrate proof. It is during the presentation of the body that the majority of audience questions are asked.

The last part, the conclusion, is a brief summation of the presentation and a request for action from the audience.

The Introduction

Establishing rapport is very helpful to you and the audience. It sets up an initial friendly tone. Ways to establish rapport include:

- A personal, short, and entertaining account of some event.
- A joke that relates to why you are there.
- An entertaining comment about the weather, the room, etc.

Next, introduce yourself, if your contact has not already done so. Briefly explain your topic and why the audience should listen to you. This explanation answers very typical audience questions well before they are asked.

Telling the audience why they should listen helps them to understand how and why you know the topic. Explain your knowledge of the topic from job experience, interviews with people from the prospect's company, education, or previous experience with this and other companies. A truthful, briefly stated reason for knowing the topic will usually satisfy audience curiosity. This brief explanation in the introduction usually prevents this topic from becoming an issue later in the body or conclusion.

Briefly tell the audience the major points or important topics to be raised in the presentation and what they will be able to decide at the conclusion of the presentation. For instance: "My presentation today will cover three main points of concern. These are increasing sales in a sluggish economy, reducing support costs, and sharply reducing customer complaints. At the end of my presentation, I would like to know if I can return to demonstrate how this will work. Any questions about me, the topic, or what my expectations are from you?"

The more that is known about you, the topic, how the information will be presented, and what the audience is to do with the information, the better they will listen to the body of the presentation. They are ready to *hear* the presentation!

The Body

The body of the presentation contains all the important points along with all the supporting proof. The points were determined by working with your contact and include your own ideas. Remember to start with the most important point and prove it with the most compelling proof. Typical proof sources are:

Experience: yours, your company, the audience, the product, the industry.

Experts: you, leading authorities, print sources, subject/issue authors, or researchers.

Examples: case studies where the same or similar actions have been taken and the results.

Have more supporting proofs for each of the points than you think are needed. This can become a helpful resource when answering customer questions.

Depending on the length of the presentation and the number of points being raised, you may want to encourage questions during or after each point or at the conclusion of the presentation. Keep in mind that questions should be prompted during the presentation when audience agreement is needed to proceed. For instance, audience agreement may be needed on the first idea to improve sales results, before audience members can agree to the next idea regarding reducing costs.

The Conclusion

When you are finished discussing the last point, briefly recap all the points that were made, along with any key proof that emerged. This signals to the audience that the presentation is ending. It also reminds them of the other points of the presentation, particularly if there were lots of questions.

If questions were asked and answered during the body of the presentation, it can be safely assumed it would be redundant and counterproductive to ask for more questions at this time. Instead, this is the time to ask for what you said you would ask for in the introduction. For example, "Given the evidence for improved sales, reduced costs, and reduced complaints, can we secure your agreement for a demonstration next Thursday at 10 AM?" As with most questions, after you ask it, keep silent and give the audience the chance to think. If they have a question, answer it.

Remember your presentation priorities; this is the time to fulfill them. Don't be shy!

It is common for a sales professional to feel comfortable in one-to-one presentations and uncomfortable when presenting to a group. There is no need to get psychological about it. The biggest difference between the two is that with a group, you are most likely standing, doing most of the talking, and do not know everyone. It is not fear you are dealing with, it is just the feeling of awkwardness.

The best way to get over feeling awkward is to practice. Practice the presentation standing up, looking into the mirror, or talking to imaginary or real people. Do this several times or until you feel comfortable with the topic and the flow of the introduction, body, and conclusion. Remember, *don't practice in front of a customer.*

The probability of success is greatly improved if you take the time to practice, practice, practice.

READING BODY LANGUAGE

After practicing the presentation and feeling more comfortable, you can focus less on yourself and more on the audience body language during the presentation.

If the audience is looking at you; nodding heads in agreement; smiling; sitting in relaxed, slightly leaning forward positions, the group is attentive and listening.

The other situation is characterized by very few or no people looking at you. Many are checking their watches, yawning, holding their heads in their hands, frowning, or leaning back away from you. You can pretty much guess that the mark was missed.

Quite frankly, most body language between these two extremes is a best guess. That is because it's usually neutral. It can also be referred to as "enrollment" body language. This means they are neither for nor against, just waiting to be persuaded. They are giving the presentation a fair shot. When the points and proofs are on target, the enrollables are sold.

USING EYE CONTACT, VOICE RESONANCE, AND GESTURES

Eye contact, voice resonance, and gestures are natural expressions of how you communicate. When talking with friends, you look them in the eye or they think you are hiding something from them. In these conversations, you also raise and lower the volume and expression of your voice, as well as using numerous gestures to make your point. You can do this with friends because you are comfortable and acting naturally. The idea is to be as comfortable as possible or manage any discomfort so formal presentations can be made with the same inherent ease. In formal presentations, make eye contact with audience members. Practice with peers and maintain eye contact for three seconds with each person.

Speaking in a monotone will drive an audience up the wall. Practice raising and lowering your voice at various times in the presentation.

Get comfortable with your hands. Mindless flailing of hands is a big distraction to the audience. Generally, hands held loosely waist high look comfortable. One hand in one pocket and the other held waist high close to the body is also a relaxed look. Don't play with jewelry, coins, and so on.

Eye contact and gestures fall into the category of nonverbal communication. Other nonverbal areas include:

- Physical appearance, mode of dress.
- Facial expressions.
- Posture.
- Total body movement.

- Partial body movement.
- Interaction with objects.

If a demonstration of any object is required, practice beforehand.

SUMMARY

Take the time up front to determine the priorities and objectives and the information that is required to convince the audience of the truth and value of the information you will be presenting. It will help you improve the probability of a successful presentation.

Organize the material into the introduction, body, and conclusion. Support your verbal presentation with well-thought-out audiovisual presentations, and ride the high road to success. Now practice the whole presentation until you feel comfortable. Your homework is done. Make it work and the sale is yours. Just ask for it!

Using Audiovisual Equipment

1. Flip chart

Pros:

- Easy to set up, captures information quickly, mostly inexpensive.
- Standard flip chart pads, lined, unlined, and grid, are readily available and can be prepared in advance and also used spontaneously.
- Professionally designed appearance can be created with equipment such as a PosterPrinter.

Cons:

- Depending on the size of the audience and the room, visibility could be a problem.
- Hand-drawn information may lose impact with the audience.
- Not good for complex graphics or many lines of text.
- Without practice it can be clumsy to use.

2. Slide projector

Pros:

- Use of color creates a very dramatic presentation.
- Audience focus is on the slide since lights are normally out.
- Can present a very formal look.
- Cost to produce slides is lower than just two years ago.
- Can be linked to a recorder for voice-overs and to other projectors for more dramatic presentations.
- Slides are very easy to carry.

Cons:

- Projectors can be expensive and bulky to carry around.
- Presenter loses eye contact with the audience when the lights are dimmed or turned off.
- Presenter must know how to change lightbulbs and remove jammed slides.
- Slide trays can be clumsy, and must have a retaining ring to keep slides from falling out.

- While prices to produce slides dropped, they can still be expensive.
- Slide may have a onetime use.

3. Overhead projector

Pros:

- Can have the impact of slide projection with fewer potential equipment problems.
- Less expensive than slide projectors.
- Overheads can be produced from computers and printed in color.
- Easy to operate, and lights dimmed slightly.
- Can write on transparencies.

Cons:

- Because of its size limitations, the overhead is not good for very detailed or complex images.
- Must know how to change the bulb.
- Not easily moved.
- Changing transparencies is an art unto itself, so practice is important.

4. Liquid crystal display

Pros:

- Any image on the computer monitor can be projected onto the screen.
- Changing information is easy.
- Can be programmed to present at timed intervals.
- Looks exactly like slides.
- "Live" nature of display enhances attention from the audience.
- Easy to carry attaché case.

Cons:

- Most expensive of the four; active matrix color LCD is in the $4,000 range.

- Requires an overhead projector that can illuminate by 4000 lumens or better.
- Requires several electrical connections.
- Much more technical than the other three.
- Presenter must not just practice, but learn the equipment's technology as well.

Chapter Five

Handling Objections, Stalls, and Delays

Richard Lombard

WHAT YOU WILL LEARN

Objections can crop up throughout the sales cycle, from the moment you contact a prospect to your final close. In this unit, you will learn about:

- The prospect's right to object.
- Types of sales resistance.
- Coping with negative feelings.
- Common objections.
- An objection-handling process.

WHY IT IS IMPORTANT

Being able to handle objections, whenever and for whatever reason they are raised, is essential to any type of selling. It is especially true in the ever-changing sales world of today. If you cannot resolve a prospect's objections quickly—and satisfactorily—you may not get a commitment to utilize your company's products or services.

In any selling situation, there is bound to be some skepticism, confusion, uncertainty, and disagreement. If a prospect has a valid question (or even an invalid question), you must acknowledge it respectfully to maintain rapport, provide solid reasons to overcome the objection, and eventually gain agreement that it has been handled.

The Prospect's Right to Object

Selling is most effective when you and the prospect or client can look at the issues together. Overcoming an objection implies a strategy of defeating the objection and—by implication—the prospect. This viewpoint envisions selling as a contest between buyer and seller, as a contest to see if you have better answers than the prospect has questions. But selling is not a battle of wits. Instead of dueling with prospects, or "matching wits," work with them to help solve their problems.

The greatest opportunities lie in providing a prospect with that which best meets his or her needs. Confrontations may prove who's tougher or smarter, but seldom contribute to a favorable outcome. That is why handling objections works best when:

1. You respect the prospect's right to disagree, have concerns, or just plain have questions.
2. You listen and acknowledge the prospect's objections, rather than react immediately and challenge them.
3. You recognize that objections are often a necessary part of the prospect's decision-making process to test his or her own convictions and assumptions.
4. You anticipate objections and prepare yourself for them.
5. You think of objections as opportunities to move the sale forward to a decision.

By welcoming objections, you no longer fear them but treat them as opportunities to clear up misunderstandings, dispel doubts, and help the client or prospect resolve conflicts.

An unresolved objection simmering below the surface can postpone or even stop an agreement. It's better to bring it out, deal with it, and get a yes or no decision. A *maybe* is like a telephone call on hold—you can't hang up and you can't finish the conversation. Therefore, it's better to raise issues and resolve them to the point where you can move on with the sale. Often, you will have to set the objections aside in terms of a final resolution, but it is now on the table and has been dealt with.

OBJECTIONS KEEP YOU ON TRACK

You may have heard the expression, "Selling begins when the prospect says no!" An objection is often a prospect's way of asking for more information. It may mean: "I'm interested, but I can't make my final decision just yet." Viewed this way, an objection is not threatening; it's an opportunity to move the prospect toward a decision.

Objections also help you pace the conversation. They reveal how interested the prospect is, and how far you are from the close. Use objections as signposts pointing you in the right direction to a decision.

The entire process of handling objections can be viewed as helping people change perspectives. When an objection occurs, the prospect is focusing on his or her perspective, and you are focusing on yours. It's your job to reorient the client's point of view. You do that by first creating an environment in which the prospect can say things like:

"I never looked at it from that point of view."

"That's an interesting way to approach the problem."

FORMS OF RESISTANCE

All points of view have an emotional element in them. To respond accurately and empathetically may require clarifying exactly what someone is thinking and feeling. Resistance can be expressed in several ways:

Skepticism

One type of resistance is skepticism. You'll hear it expressed as:

"Sure, but . . . "

"Every service says that."

"Show me."

"Prove it."

"Can you substantiate that?"

"That's a little hard to believe."

"That's what you say . . . "

And this often results in a *challenging* situation.

Hostility

One of the most difficult kinds of resistance to handle is hostility or anger, especially when it's focused on you.

"Look, I've told you several times . . . "

"Stop! I heard you the first time."

"You're not listening to me."

"No, I don't want to think about it now."

And this requires *control*.

Concern

The third type is concern. Concern is generally based on uncertainty, insecurity, hesitation, worry, and fear.

"I'm concerned about . . . "

"My worry is . . . "

"How do I know that'll work?"

"Without some assurance, I might wind up . . . "

And this requires *control*.

Dejection

Another type is dejection. The client feels the situation is hopeless, too difficult, too much hassle. The salesperson sounds defeated.

"We've tried that before."

"Forget it. They'll never buy the concept . . . "

"You're wasting your time."

"If you're wrong, it could cost me my job."

And the salesperson becomes *defeated*.

Indifference

Indifference is not really raising an objection; it's total disengagement, disinterest, lack of involvement. It's actually further away from acceptance than resistance is. At least someone with an objection is involved. Indifference sounds like this:

"Not interested."

"Not now."

"Maybe later."

"It's not for us."

"Too busy."

The result is your prospects *ignore* you.

COPING WITH NEGATIVE FEELINGS

Overcoming a negative with a positive is simply not possible. As you can imagine, the prospect can feel pressured and overwhelmed by your enthusiasm. Trying to jump a client or prospect directly from resistance to acceptance with overabounding enthusiasm seldom works. Just as a child falls down when it misses a stair step, an agreement will fall through if steps are missed. In fact, even if both parties are talking civilly, problems can occur if you try to move the client too quickly from neutral to acceptance. It always works better if you go step by step, discharging the negative feeling to neutral, then move up to positive steps to acceptance.

Once a prospect's negativity has receded to receptivity, you are then in a position to present your ideas to someone who is listening, not resistant. It is usually necessary for you to leave your positive stance, and utilizing your empathy skills, join your prospect in the neutral zone. Then together you can hope to move to the positive areas of receptivity and acceptance (see diagram on p. 98).

That is why it is important to avoid colliding with or overwhelming the prospect's feelings. Instead, you should show understanding and respect for the person's position. Your prospects are then more willing to open-mindedly consider your alternatives, thus enabling you to lead them up to acceptance—and ultimately to a decision. For example:

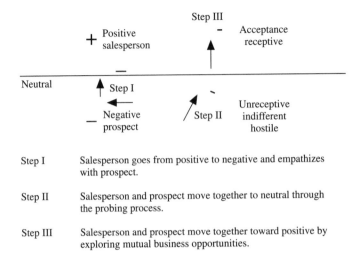

Step I   Salesperson goes from positive to negative and empathizes with prospect.

Step II   Salesperson and prospect move together to neutral through the probing process.

Step III Salesperson and prospect move together toward positive by exploring mutual business opportunities.

Prospect:
"I don't know, we've been doing business with the HRC Group a long time." (concern)

Salesperson:
"No problem! We'll do just as well . . . and you'll thank me for it in a few months. Trust me. I've seen it happen before." (enthusiasm)

Prospect:
"Let me think about it. If we decide to go with another firm, I'll let you know." (avoidance)

Salesperson:
"What's to think about? Our services are perfect for your operation. It's a good decision." (more enthusiasm)

Prospect:
"If you don't mind, I'd like to make my own decisions." (hostility)

Without *empathy* and *probing* most objections will provide the basis for not doing business, and in this vignette *presenting* was the only skill utilized by the salesperson. The results: confrontation.

There is a better way for salespeople to deal with resistance. First and foremost, it is to view objections as an opportunity for more dialogue—with the focus on probing to better understand the resistance and prepare a platform from which you can present valid reasons to overcome the resistance.

RESPONDING TO OBJECTIONS

Whenever a prospect expresses or conveys a negative thought or feeling, you can respond to it using the following four-step method.

1. Empathize—Acknowledge, show understanding, and be receptive to their feelings. Let them know you recognize their right to object.
2. Probe—Use the objection opportunity to ask questions to establish a platform from which you can present.
3. Present and prove—When the prospect shows some receptivity, present an alternative idea or benefit for the client to consider. Prove it if necessary with a success story.
4. Close—Ask if the prospect accepts your ideas.

This skill model will work, regardless of the prospect's attitude. You can use it to help lead his or her attitude up the ladder to acceptance. In addition, it may not be necessary to use all four steps every time. Let's look at the model in more detail.

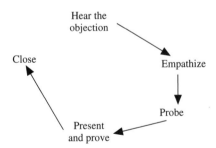

1. Empathize

Empathy is the ability to convey to someone that you understand and accept how they feel—even if you do not agree. It is essential not only to empathize with the prospect's concerns but also to express that empathy.

Empathy can be expressed in three basic ways:

Acknowledgment:	Expressed As:	Message Conveyed:
1. Attention	"Uh huh." "I see."	"You are worthwhile."
2. Understanding	"I see what you mean."	"You make sense."
3. Acceptance	"That's fair."	"You're OK to be feeling that way."

Any time you convey in words or actions that you are attentive, or that you understand or accept the other person's viewpoint, you strengthen your relationship. Most important, it gives you increased power with this person—not power over them, but influence with them. Acknowledgments are not manipulative. You use them to fortify relationships, not to deceive someone or gain advantage. The very instant that another person senses your intentions are manipulative, all trust and communication are destroyed.

When you hear resistance of any kind, don't fight it. Go with it for a while until it loses much of its potency. You might say:

"You've raised a good point."
"I can understand why you'd be concerned about that."
"That throws a different light on it."
"That certainly seems fair."
"I can appreciate your views on that."

Any statement that conveys to the other person . . .

"I'm listening." "I appreciate your point of view."
"I'm receptive." "I'm not rigid or dogmatic."
"I understand." "I accept your right to hold that view."

. . . sends a powerful message to the other person that encourages mutual trust and rapport. They listen to you. They become receptive to your suggestions. This is the art of persuasion.

2. Probe to Clarify

At the beginning, it is important to make sure you understand the objection before trying to answer it. Ask questions to:

- Make sure you understand the facts and the feelings.
- Find out how important, how serious, how deeply felt the objection is.
- Find out if the prospect has a valid concern or has misunderstood something.
- Give the prospect an opportunity to talk through the objection. (Sometimes people will reason away their own objections!)
- Give yourself time to formulate a response so you can respond accurately and nondefensively.

Sometimes you may have to probe a bit first just to gather enough information to be able to make an empathetic response. For example:

Prospect:

"I don't know. We're doing everything possible to lower our accounting costs."

Salesperson:

"What do you mean by lowering the costs?" (Probe)

Prospect:

"Well, you do know there are a number of ways to minimize accounting fees."

Salesperson:

"Well, I can understand your concern over costs, but let's see if we are talking apples to apples . . . " (Empathize)

You might also ask questions like:

"Could you be a little more specific?"

"What, exactly, are you being offered?"

"What are your primary goals in reviewing alternative recommendations?"

"What do you think might be the result?"

"How do you feel about that?"

Without answers to these questions, it is difficult to respond accurately. And just to make sure you got it right, summarize the objection and check the accuracy of your understanding with the client.

"So you've been able to reduce your current accounting costs by 20 percent, but you're still not satisfied with your retirement

plan and your lines of credit aren't going to be adequate for
your future business plans?"

3. Present and Prove

By probing to clarify, you have accomplished two objectives:

1. You have led the client to receptivity by treating the objection with empathy and respect.
2. You have gathered the information you need to effectively respond.

You can now match your response very precisely to the stated
worries and concerns. You might begin by saying:

"I have an idea that might work."

"There may be a way to resolve those issues for you."

If the other person expresses receptivity, it's a clear signal to offer
a solution.

"You'll be happy to know that . . . " (clear up misunderstanding).

"My idea is to . . . " (offer alternative)

"I don't think that will be a problem because . . . " (offer fea-
ture/benefit and prove it)

Every objection has a different answer and may require different
proof. A successful salesperson will know the "answers" to the
most common objections. But be careful! Those answers work best
when you use them in the context of this four-step method for handling objections.

Proving is usually best accomplished by utilizing a success-story
reference—and as we stated earlier, references are probably the
most powerful selling tool you possess.

What is important about using a reference to prove your point is:

• You know the success story.

  What the situation/problem was before you and your firm
  entered the picture (with an emphasis on the quantitative size
  of the problem).

  The solution your firm offered.

The results (what that has meant to the client).

- The success story fits with the point you are trying to prove. (It works when it's a similar company, in a vertical market, or a similar situation.)
- You are comfortable with having your prospect contact the reference if appropriate.

Example:

Salesperson:

"So with an expanding outside sales force you will need to expand your lines of credit and need financial statements that will support the request for expanded credit."

Prospect:

"Sure will, but what does that have to do with your business? Besides, we really can't afford to spend too much money preparing those financial reports."

Salesperson:

"Well, Cal Industries, you know, the office equipment company just down the street, had a similar situation. They were doubling their sales force and hoping to add over a million dollars in new sales. When we discovered that their $100,000 line of credit was inadequate to support the sales increase, we created a new banking relationship for them with a revised method of financial reporting and forecasting. The new result for Cal was a dramatic increase in sales and profitability and a banking arrangement that proved in the long run to be more cost-effective than their previous relationship."

Prospect:

"Interesting—let's review just how you developed that approach."

4. Close

The final step is to test for acceptance. After you've answered the objection and proved it, make sure the issue is resolved before moving on.

"Does that take care of it?"

"Will that work for you?"

"Do you have any other problems in that area?"

"Does that help you?"

Once the close has been obtained, you may proceed with the sales process. However, if the prospect replies with a *no* you must start again with empathy and clarification. For example, you may have to say, "I guess I misunderstood; perhaps you could elaborate a little further on that point." From there you will probe until you feel you have a solid reason to present your solution.

Finally, a good technique at the end of objections is to ask a general question: "Are there any other concerns we have yet to talk about?" In this way you will hopefully be able to put all "open items" on the table so you do not leave the prospect with unshared or unresolved concerns.

Some unique objection-handling tips for salespeople:

- Hang time. When the prospect states an objection or a concern, you often do well to pause a few seconds. Give clients time to continue on and clarify what they really mean or are really thinking. This is often referred to as "the power of the pause."
- Positive, immediate feedback. "I'm glad you brought that up because it's an important consideration."
- Use a work-with approach. "You know, that's a good point, and if we can't come up with an appropriate solution together there'd be little reason to switch."
- Finally, view the objections as a communications opportunity to move the sale forward and respond with positive body language, which might include:

  Nodding to show understanding.

  Smiling to reflect it's OK.

  Changing position a little to communicate, "that's good because we're moving forward."

  Pausing to think out the response even though you may have it on the tip of your tongue.

SUMMARY

- Objections play a positive role in the sales process. Not only do prospects have a right to object, but also objections allow you to clarify issues and resolve them.

- Prospects can rarely be taken *directly* from a negative to a positive position. Attempting to do so only creates more resistance. It is better to first lead the prospect to neutrality by discharging their negative feelings.
- Objections are often combinations of feelings and/or a need for clarification or better understanding, and therefore generally require a process for objection handling.
- A simple, four-step process provides a reliable model for handling virtually any objection: empathize, probe, present and prove, close.
- If the prospect still objects, you can "recycle" the four-step process.

Special Note on Objection Handling

There are numerous considerations in handling objections including:

- How is the prospect feeling—confused, angered, indifferent?
- How does the prospect voice his or her objection—an open question, a challenge, a positive or negative statement?
- How legitimate is the objection?
- Where are you in the sales process when the objection arises?

Depending on the situation, you will utilize the four steps of objection handling to varying degrees.

CLOSING: WHAT YOU WILL LEARN

Closing doesn't happen just at the end of a sale—it happens throughout the sale. Selling is a process of trial closing—getting step-by-step commitments that advance the sale from initial contact to final commitment. You determine how far along you are in the decision cycle by the commitments a prospect is willing and able to make.

You will find the words *close* and *trial close* throughout this program. It is important that you understand their significance at every stage of the sales process. If the process is conducted properly, the final close, that is, asking for the commitment, becomes a fairly easy task.

Therefore, we will:

- Close on getting appointments.
- Close on agendas for the first meeting and subsequent meetings.
- Trial close on concerns, impacts, and business opportunities.
- Close on solutions and benefits.
- Close on final commitments, next steps, referrals, etc.

These commitments, or trial closes, are milestones that help you:

- Know where you are and what to do next.
- Stay aligned with the prospect's decision-making process.
- Time your final close.
- Forecast more accurately.
- Shorten the sales cycle.
- Improve your close ratio.

In this chapter, you will learn how to prevent stalls and ask for the order (the final close). To do that effectively you will need to review several skills:

- Know when to ask for the order.
- Know how to ask for the order.
- Know how to be persistent without turning people off.
- Know several types of closes that you can use in the various situations you find yourself.

WHY IT IS IMPORTANT

When is a sale "closed"? Is the sale closed when the prospect:

- Says yes to a company's recommendation?
- Gives you approval to move ahead?
- Gives you referrals?
- Adds on an additional service?
- Allows you to become his or her sales consultant?

A sale is never completely closed. We are always selling and reselling ourselves and our company to our clients and prospects.

When you take clients and prospects for granted, you can lose them as quickly as you got them, and as you know, your business is all about closing new prospects and retaining existing customers.

KEY CONCEPTS AND IDEAS

- Throughout the sale you ask for commitments and decisions that move the discussion to a final decision.
- You ask for the order when there are no remaining unresolved issues and the prospect has shown high interest.
- Closing techniques based on trick questions, setups, or slam-dunk tactics usually turn people off and backfire on you.
- People will respond favorably to assertive, persistent closing provided you have built high trust and rapport and have made recommendations that make good business sense.
- One of the best times to ask for the order is after a big issue or objection has been resolved.
- Prospects indicate their readiness to make a final decision in a variety of ways: making positive statements, asking questions that imply that they are satisfied with your solutions, saying they'd like to buy but can't for some reason, bargaining for concessions, and showing other similar buying signals.
- Trial closes enable you to test the water before closing to prevent a "no" or mistiming your close.
- People who fear rejection are afraid to close. A "no" is not a rejection, it's just a business decision. Sometimes you have to accept a "no" and move on, if that's the right decision for this prospect at this time.
- There are dozens of ways to ask for the order—the best one is simply to summarize and assume the answer is "yes."

WHAT IS CLOSING?

Every time you ask for agreement, a commitment, or a decision, you are closing. Every prospect commitment is a step toward the final decision.

- "Do you have time on Thursday to see me?"
- "Could I have a look at your MIS department?"

- "Do you agree that would help?"
- "Would you like us to survey your space now or next week?"
- "How soon could we talk to the president?"
- "Are there other firms you work with who could use the service?"

FOUR IMPORTANT QUESTIONS

The four questions most often asked about closing are: "When do I close?" "How do I close?" "How hard do I close?" "Why don't people buy?"

1. When to Close

You can ask for a minor decision at any time. There is no right or wrong time. You ask for minor decisions throughout the sale.

- "So are we in agreement that you currently have 20 outside salespeople who are using the office on an average of three times a week?"

It is important you get into a closing mode early on so that the prospect begins agreeing on committing to the concerns and impacts that will in turn set up the sale. It creates a climate for listening and deciding. It sets a precedent for asking for decisions early and often. You can set up any close you want early in the process. Obviously one of the early closes will be agreement on the agenda you've prepared for that meeting. A second close will be on agreeing to supply you with some information on their company, and a third close will be on "next steps" as you conclude the initial meeting.

Buying signals. But when is the right time to ask for the order? Knowing when to close isn't a matter of guesswork. You ask for the order when:

- The prospect has agreed there is a definite need for one of your company's products or services.
- The prospect feels definite concerns and understands their impacts on his business.
- The prospect has expressed interest in your solutions.

- The prospect has agreed that your products and services will solve a problem.
- There are no remaining unresolved issues, questions, or objections.
- The prospect is comfortable with the decision.
- The prospect gives you a strong buying signal.

How do you know all this? You ask. If you don't ask, you won't know. Prospects don't always give you obvious buying signals. When they're impressed, most people will show definite buying signals. Some buying signals to look for:

- Positive statements that indicate high interest.
  "I like it."

  "That workstation sounds like it could be helpful in our new MIS department."

  "It sure would be nice not to have to worry about coordinating the timing of the various furniture deliveries."

  "It looks like a good way to get a better handle on our internal cost controls."

  "At least we could look for improvement in the use of our conference room for sales presentations."
- Questions that sound like they've bought.
  "Is the coordination going to create confusion?"

  "What sort of lead time is required?"

  "Who else in this area is using your company?"
- Asking about a contract, or returning to a specific area of discussion.
  "If we decide to use your company, do we need to sign a contract?"

  "Let's go over the delivery coordination process again."
- Saying they want to buy without giving reasons why they can't.
  "I agree, but I'm not sure I can get it approved."

  "It'll be a tough sale with the owner, whose a pretty strong supporter of one of your competitors."
- Requests for details on service, reliability, and competence.
  "How long will it take you to get us a revised proposal?"

"Do you have a checklist on the ways we might best ensure a smooth, coordinated move?"

2. How Do I Close?

There are a number of accepted ways of closing for an order—you only need to know a few. If you want more, there are a dozen books in print on additional closes. A word of caution: many traditional closing tactics rely on manipulative, high-pressure gimmicks that can trigger prospect resistance. Before trying out any method of closing on a prospect, try it on yourself. Would you be offended, put off, or threatened by that close? If so, don't use it.

Here are some proven ways to ask for the order.

Minor point trial close.   Instead of asking for the final decision, ask for a minor decision that tests the water.

- "Would you be able to give me your latest office survey for a review?"
- "Will you be looking at all your MIS departments?"
- "Do you want me to include the report analysis after one month?"

Summary of benefits close.   Many sales reps feel the best close is to (1) briefly recap the key reasons why the prospect should buy (only points you've gotten agreement on), (2) make your recommendation, and (3) ask for the decision.

- "Let me see if I can recap the situation. What you said you need is . . . " (summarize benefits)
- "Based on that, I recommend . . . " (summarize recommendations and benefits)

Statement close.   A closing statement, rather than a question, is a stronger close. Some examples:

- "Mr. Jones, all I need is your signature, and we'll get the program underway next week."
- "Fine . . . let's try to schedule the first deliveries for the week of . . . "
- "I just need you to sign the authorization and we'll schedule the meeting to inform your senior management team."

Assumptive close.   When a prospect gives you a clear buying signal, assume it's a decision and recommend a course of action.

Prospect: So you recommend the desk, chair, and cabinet ensemble for our clerical people. (buying signal)

Sales Rep: Yes. So let's get the paperwork in right away so we can program the right deliveries for your company.

Similar situation.   Cautious people often need reassurance that they're making a good decision. Use referrals. When you sense that a prospect is hesitant to give you approval on something, relate a story about somebody else who had a similar need and made the decision to go with one of your manufacturers. In this situation, local testimonials are useful.

- "Mr. Jones, have you ever heard of Summit Tech over in Redding? They had about the same size MIS department that you have . . . and we were able to save them a few hundred dollars per workstation by utilizing the Executive Office Concepts program in place of individual desks, chairs, and cabinets. Why don't you call Bob Shea. He'll be happy to talk to you."

Relate the story matter-of-factly. Don't oversell or embroider; it'll sound phony. Let the facts sell the decision. If the hesitant prospect senses he is being pushed, it may heighten his resistance.

Calendar of events close.   The last step in any decision cycle is start-up. Many successful salespeople like to transition into the final close by reviewing the schedule. You can usually judge by the prospect's response if he has given his final consent.

- "Okay, let's review what happens during the delivery. The first step is . . . "
- "Now all you need to proceed is . . . "

Alternatives close.   You may close by presenting the prospect with alternatives as to level of service or timing.

- "Do you prefer we start the file case delivery on the 3rd, or next week on the 10th?"
- "Do you want the complete delivery to start on the 1st, or hold back on the MIS workstations until we've delivered the sales office furniture?"

OVERCOMING FEAR OF CLOSING

There are three basic fears in closing:

1. Fear of getting a "no." Asking for the order won't alienate the prospect or ruin your chances of getting the order if you've given the prospect enough good reasons to buy and gotten agreements on each point throughout the sale. You're asking them to make a good decision.

2. Fear of rejection. What about rejection? Forget it. A "no" is not a personal rejection of you, it's a decision not to buy today. Tomorrow they may say "yes." How many Arcadia customers become Knoll or Herman Miller customers in three to four months and vice versa? There is no room in this business for fear of rejection.

3. Fear of applying pressure. How hard can you close? If you believe that what you are recommending will really help them, close with confidence and conviction. Your conviction communicates an urgency and a sincerity that this is a good decision. You won't be perceived as high-pressure. You may close by presenting the prospect with alternatives as to level of service or timing.

SOME FINAL THOUGHTS ON CLOSING

Any close will work if your intent is genuine and helpful and you have total conviction that it's a good decision for the prospect. If your timing is good, you have successfully identified business concerns and opportunities and agreement on the business impacts, and your prospect is at a high level of interest, you can be persistent and assertive in asking for the order. At that point you are truly consulting on ways for your prospect to improve on some aspect of his or her business.

Keep closing throughout the decision process, from the initial appointment to after the sale. But as a sales rep, your job has just begun. Remember: the sale is never over. Existing customers must be retained, services added on as appropriate, and references gained wherever possible.

Exercise

1. What are the different forms of resistance you may encounter?

   _____

   _____

   _____

2. Describe the basic four-step model for handling objections.

   _____

   _____

   _____

3. Why is it important to empathize during the objection-handling process?

   _____

   _____

   _____

4. Provide three examples of closes you may use after the "present and prove" phase of objection handling.

   _____

   _____

   _____

5. What is meant by "the prospect's right to object"?

   _____

   _____

   _____

6. Describe the process of moving a prospect from resistance to acceptance.

   _____

   _____

   _____

7. What are the three most important things you need to know about a reference when *proving* a point to a prospect?

   _____

   _____

   _____

Action Assignment 1

Complete five copies of this form and submit them to your manager. You may use objections you have encountered either over the telephone or in person.

Objection Report

Prospect: _____ Date: _____

Objection: _____

_____

_____

_____

_____

_____

Type: (Skepticism, Hostility, Worry, Dejection) _____

_____

_____

_____

_____

Response to Objection: _____

_____

_____

_____

_____

Result: _____

_____

_____

_____

_____

Action Assignment 2

List your five best references (see if you can provide a reference for as many industries and sizes of companies and applications as possible).

Company and Person	Prior Situation	Your Company's Solution	Results
1. _____	_____	_____	_____
_____	_____	_____	_____
2. _____	_____	_____	_____
_____	_____	_____	_____
3. _____	_____	_____	_____
_____	_____	_____	_____
4. _____	_____	_____	_____
_____	_____	_____	_____
5. _____	_____	_____	_____
_____	_____	_____	_____

Chapter Six

Goal Setting and Time Management

Mark Riesenberg

The focus is on *you! How can I best help you?*

I believe that learning how to set, achieve, and exceed goals is the most powerful skill I can teach you. Personally and professionally, goal setting is the most important thing you can do to rapidly move you toward the use of your full potential.

The strategies and techniques you will learn in this chapter are skills you can start applying immediately and for the rest of your life. Obviously, goal setting is something I am very passionate about. Because of its far-reaching impact into many different areas of your life, we will be exploring the who, what, why, how, when, and where of goal setting.

The *who* we already know; it's *you*. The *what* is goal setting. Remember the classic scene from *On the Waterfront* when Marlon Brando uttered those memorable words, "I could have been a contender?" He expressed so clearly what unfortunately so many of us experience: the pain of regret. There are two pains in life—*the pain of discipline* and *the pain of regret*. Which one will you choose? *The pain of regret* is more centered around what we did not do than around what we did. Lack of focus causes us to waste so much of our precious time/life.

FOCUS

Goal setting means focus. Focused individuals know where they are and where they're going, know how to get there, and discipline themselves to do it, to take action. Focus creates mission, vision, goal achievement, and balance in one's life.

That's what goal setting accomplishes for you. It creates a focus for your life. We're all familiar with KISS: "Keep It Simple, Stupid." Well, I'm going to take a little poetic license and change it to, "Keep It Short and Simple." I promise you I will supply you with a short and simple yet a highly effective goal-setting system that has the potential to create wonderful things for your life if you will simply discipline yourself and apply what you learn in these pages.

Goal setting remains, even in our highly sophisticated world, one of those simple skills that can get you results that far outdistance the effort you put in. The system I propose will take you 15 to 20 minutes once a month to implement and continue.

Goal 1: START! Begin the process, the journey.

Goal 2: CONTINUE!

I will supply you with all the necessary tools to get started.

Whenever I ask my audiences why we set goals they always come up with a great many of the right answers. You set goals because:

- It gives you a target to shoot at.
- It gives direction to your life.
- It gives you something to measure against to let you know how you're doing.
- It leads to happiness, contentment, fulfillment.

Yes, to all of the above. Any one of these would be reason enough to get yourself quickly into a regular program of goal setting.

If I were able to ask every adult on this planet, "By a show of hands, how many of you believe that setting goals is important?" 100 percent of the people would raise their hands.

DEFINE YOUR GOALS

In 1953, Harvard University approached Yale University about doing a 20-year study on motivation and the role goals play in motivating people. Harvard received permission from Yale to interview

Focus!

Goals: Written and visible

Priorities

Organization

Execution

Accountability: Coaching and fine tuning

Breakthrough results: Exceeding goals and quotas

Increased sales, income, and job satisfaction

the graduating seniors. Harvard asked these seniors 20 questions, 3 of which specifically had to do with goals: (1) Do you have goals? (2) Do you write them down? and (3) Do you have written action plans for their accomplishment?

What percent do you think were able to say yes to all three? Only 3 percent of these graduating seniors answered yes to all three questions. The study further revealed another 12 percent had goals but did not write them down. I meet people like this all the time. They tell me they have goals but they simply carry them around in their heads. (More in a moment about the difference between goal achievement when you write down your goals and when you don't.)

The other 85 percent came up with a resounding "duh" when it came to having goals. And whatever goals these 85 percent did have were universal in nature such as, "I want to be happy," "I want to be healthy," and of course that all-time favorite "I want to be rich!"

These are not goals; these are common to the wishes and dreams of all of us.

The power of this study does not lie merely in pointing out how a few people set goals. The power is in the *results*. The researchers followed these seniors over the next 20 years through questionnaires mailed on a regular basis, ending in 1973. Again the Harvard researchers asked these people 20 questions. Many of the questions were subjective about the quality of their lives, the quality of their relationships, how much they enjoyed work.

But one of the questions was extremely measurable and objective. The respondents were asked, "What is your financial net worth?" The 3 percent who had written goals from 1953 and later had a greater net worth than the other 97 percent *combined!* These high financial achievers had literally written down what they planned to earn in 1953 and within 2, 3, 5, 10, and 20 years! When the researchers looked deeper into the profile of these goal setters, they found a wide range of grades achieved, IQ levels, and family backgrounds. Some had high grades and some were average students. Some had high IQs while others were average. Some came from well-connected families while others came from blue-collar backgrounds. *The single determining factor of their financial success was that they had written goals with action plans.* The best news was that these people had also scored well when answering the more subjective questions about career and family relationships.

Another study by the Gallup organization further supports the finding of the Harvard–Yale study. Gallup randomly chose 1,500 people from *Who's Who in America*. These are people who are nominated by their peers and perceived to be successful. These 1,500 people were asked the same three goal-setting questions from the Harvard study: Do you have goals? Do you write them down? Do you have action plans for their accomplishment?

A resounding 66 percent answered yes to all three questions, further supporting the role of setting goals in achieving personal and professional success. The other one-third probably fell into the category of people who definitely do have goals but do not write them down.

I hope that at this point it is clear why goals are important. Some of my favorite motivational quotes on goal setting are:

"The best way to predict the future is to create it."

Peter Drucker

"Success is not a matter of chance, it is a matter of choice; it is not a thing to be waited for, it is a thing of vision to be embraced and achieved with direction and passion."

Helen Keller

"If you don't know where you're going, you'll probably end up there . . . no where."

Cheshire Cat

"There are two pains in life, the pain of discipline and the pain of regret."

Anon.

Now on to the tougher question. We all know why it's important to set goals. Now let me ask, "Why don't people set goals?" We have close to 100 percent of the adult world population in agreement that goals are important, but study after study shows that only 1 to 5 percent of the world's population consistently sets and achieves goals. So why do so few people actually write down their goals?

There is no one set of absolutely correct answers, but the following are an excellent representation of what holds people back from really going for it.

1. *They don't fully realize the importance of setting goals.* They really don't understand deep in their heart and mind that goals are truly all that important.

One interesting study on the role of goals in motivating people said the determining factor of whether a child picks up on the importance of goals or not is something as simple as the conversation around the dinner table. The children who really "get it" when it comes to goal setting invariably pick it up from their parents. If your parents weren't goal setters, you probably won't be either.

2. *A lot of people just do not know how to set goals.* How many of you received some formal classroom training on how to set and achieve goals? In my 12 years of school and then into college, I never once received any instruction on how to set goals. Schools are finally starting to realize this gross oversight, and many schools now offer courses on goal setting. It's about time! By the end of this chapter I promise you will know how to set goals. And it's easy.

3. *People have a fear of rejection.* Not many of us look forward to and enjoy being criticized. When we are young and enthusiastic about something, we often hear words like this from our friends: "Oh, who do you think you are? You can't do that!" We feel the pain of rejection and being put down, and we unfortunately fall into the trap of listening to our friends and dropping our dreams. One of the most important things to us when we are young is fitting in. So we listen to our friends and conform.

And it doesn't end just with friends. As we get older, we may hear similar messages from family and peers.

When I started my business, I heard it from several family members and colleagues. They thought I must be crazy to be thinking of leaving a great job. I almost took their advice to stay because of the pressure that was put on me. I'm glad I didn't.

I recommend that you keep your goals and dreams confidential, for the most part. There seem to be a lot of "well-meaning" people out there who would be more than happy to rip apart your pursuits and tell you all the reasons you shouldn't do what you know is right for you. Share them only with other goal setters and with people who are going to support you.

4. *People have a fear of failure.* This last reason why people do not set goals is probably the biggest killer of goals and success. Our greatest enemy—fear—teams up with the thing we seem to fear the most—failure.

To successfully combat this enemy we need to understand the role of failure in achieving our goals and success in life. If you fear failure enough, you'll fail. That's the double-edged sword of failure. *Failure is indispensable to success.* People who understand this won't be afraid to start a project, an endeavor that has no guarantees. People who do not understand the role of failure in bringing about success will never start; at best, they will give up soon after they start, never really giving the goal a fair chance for success.

One of the greatest failures of his time lived for 37 years in my hometown of West Orange, New Jersey. Thomas Edison. A failure? Yes, this man failed more than anyone else in history. But obviously he also succeeded more than just about anyone else in history. From visiting his labs in West Orange, I found out that Edison attempted over 4,000 experiments until he got the electric lightbulb to work and worked over 10 years on the electric storage battery.

Legend has it that a young reporter once asked Mr. Edison why he kept going (referring to the light experiments) when he had failed so many times. Edison looked the reporter right in the eye and without missing a beat said, "I haven't failed 2,000 times; I have successfully identified over 2,000 ways it won't work." Edison knew the role of "failure" in bringing about success. He understood that the attitude of someone who succeeds in life is "I cannot fail; I can only learn and grow." Edison knew how to "fail forward." He knew the secret of learning from his mistakes, of failing forward. That is why failure is indispensable to success, because success is a process, a learning process. *And as long as you are learning from your mistakes, you are moving forward, moving closer and closer toward your destined success.*

Your philosophy in life has a very profound effect on your achievements. Having the attitude that the world is basically a good, supportive place will positively affect your thoughts, your actions, and your results.

GOAL SETTING, GOAL ACHIEVING

Let's start looking at a goal-setting and goal-achieving system, a pattern to take your goals through that assures greater goal accomplishments. The starting point of all goal achievement is desire—how badly do you want it. It is the burning desire, the fire in the belly, the passion that you throw into the pursuit of your dreams and goals.

While reading about successful people who had overcome great obstacles and odds, I found a common thread. Their success boiled down to two things: (1) They all knew exactly what they wanted and (2) they were willing to make the necessary sacrifices of hard work and study. And that was because the desire was powerful. They not only wanted their goal to be reached, but they also *needed* the goal to be reached. There was no question of ever turning back. They were fully absorbed and committed to their mission. They had no choice. It was this and nothing else.

Following are three examples from popular movies that depict what I mean by desire and how it can dramatically propel you forward.

- *Dead Poets Society.* The characters talked about the importance of *carpe diem,* Latin for "seize the day." Know and treat each day as the precious gift that it is. Be filled with a sense of purpose that your dreams can give you. Few people that I meet have a clear sense of purpose. And for those who do, you can see it in their eyes and feel it in their movement through life.
- *Stand and Deliver. Ganas* is Spanish for "desire." A teacher had the vision and desire to help a group of poor students achieve exceptionally high scores on the National Advanced Calculus Aptitude Test. He helped them to attain the high level of *ganas* that was necessary for them to achieve the goal, which they did. But it all started with *ganas;* if it wasn't there they would never have achieved such heights.
- *Rocky 3.* Clubber Lang, as portrayed by Mr. T., had that burning desire. He knew exactly what he wanted. He wanted to fight and beat Rocky Balboa. "I want Balboa. I want Balboa."

The starting point for you too is how badly you want and need your goals to become reality.

The intimate cousin of desire is belief. Just as important as having a burning desire, you must also have total belief in yourself, in your ability to make your desire(s) come true. *Your belief and faith in yourself is the potion that gives action to your thoughts.*

If you do not believe you can make something happen, you'll probably never take those all-important first steps and will not persist when the going gets tough or when you come up against obstacles. The depth of your conviction will spur you constantly forward. Successful people have the attitude that they are unstoppable, that whatever they put their mind and heart into and want badly enough they can make happen. They possess an inner optimism that whatever they pay attention to and focus on strongly enough will come to be. The combination of an unwavering desire with an unstoppable attitude and belief is your most powerful tool in setting, achieving, and exceeding goals. As political leader Lech Walesa said, "Faith can move mountains."

WRITE DOWN YOUR GOALS

The challenge of success is the challenge of balance. Now that we have attained these spiritual heights through desire and belief, it is important to keep our heads in the clouds while our feet are firmly planted on the ground.

It is now time to *write down your goals!* Don't just think your goals, ink them! Study after study reveals that people who write down their goals get more results. So stop fooling yourself into believing you don't have to write them down. Sure you can get results without putting them down on paper, but my job is to help you maximize your results and your chances for great achievements. *The best way that I know to assure your success is to simply write down your goals.* This simple act may be the one thing that you need to do to make the difference between winning and losing. Losing is not moving toward the use of your full potential.

We need to make sure you know *how* to write down your goals. There is not just one right way to write goals, but what I am going to teach you now is one of the simplest ways. We are going to discuss how to write goals in two parts. Part one is from Ken Blanchard. Many of you know him as the author of the best seller, *The One-Minute Manager.* Ken is the master of KISS—"Keep It Short and Simple." Ken also taught me goals need to be SMART, each letter standing for the following:

S: Specific

A goal must be specific. It shouldn't be something so generic and universal as "I increase sales." "I'm better at doing my work." It needs to start with a specific category.

M: Measurable

Goals also have to be measurable. "I make three new prospect calls every weekday." "I have 10 appointments this week." "I lose 7 pounds this month." The first challenge of goal setting is to get your goals to be more and more specific and thus measurable. This first challenge can also prove to be the most formidable. Most goal-setting pursuits are smashed because the goals are not specific or measurable enough.

This whole goal-setting system will boil down to a simple, once-a-month 15- to 20-minute exercise, which I will explain toward the end of our discussion on goal setting. When you start this month-to-month process, one of the first things you may notice is that your goals may not be very measurable because they were set with too wide an angle. Over time, and usually in a very short time, your goals tighten up and become more specific and more measurable.

Practice, practice, practice. Constant practice will lead to perfect execution of writing and exceeding goals.

"M" also stands for motivational. Your goals must turn you on. They must excite and inspire you. Goals must come from within.

Quotas are a management process. They are what management is saying is needed to keep the company financially healthy. Your personal professional goals may be lower than the company's short-term quotas, the same, or higher than what the company is saying it expects from you. Many times this can be the problem with a company's top performers.

They have been lulled into a rut by always accepting the company's quotas as the final target. They may win all the contests and remain at the top, but did they stretch themselves? If they had set their own goals well above the company's demands, would they have been able to double their results? Would they have truly reached for and achieved their personal potential? I see this at some companies where the top performers are operating far below their potential, an injustice to the company as well as to the individual. Goals must be something you set, not what someone else tells you they are. They may be the same as the company's, but they are what *you* feel are your best shots.

A: Attainable

People are always asking me, "Mark, should I set my goals high or should I set them low?" My response is, "Yes." Yes, get started. At first we may not have a solid handle on what is high or what constitutes low goals, so in some cases the answer is just to start. As you continue with your month-to-month commitments, you will recognize more clearly obtainable, realistic goals for yourself.

The rule of thumb in goal setting is to set challenging and flexible goals. I recommend establishing goals that are a stretch for you but are not so high that you are setting yourself up for failure. Some people fall into the trap of setting high goals, goals they could never realistically achieve. When they inevitably fall far short, they get down on themselves and the goal-setting process and convince themselves it doesn't work anyway and so they stop setting goals.

That is why I advocate lowering unrealistically high goals so they remain a stretch but you believe they can be achieved. Remember, belief plays a very important role in the accomplishment of your goals. *If goals are set too high, they can demotivate you from the beginning.*

A United Way study from 1987–88 showed the effect of setting goals too high. One group of 20 managers was given realistic fund-raising goals and achieved a very healthy 17 percent increase. Another group of 20 managers was given outrageously high fund-raising goals and fell far short of its targets. Setting the goals too high caused the second group of managers to think there was no way they could ever hit those goals. Essentially, they were demotivated right from the start, and this had a very negative effect on their performance output.

R: Relevant

We get truly involved in activities only when they are relevant to us and will have a high impact. We need to set goals that are meaningful. In my discussions with managers and employees about goals for a job, it often sounds as though they are talking about two different jobs. The employees are not clear about what the manager expects, and the manager has a whole different perspective on where the employees need to put their attention. Each has a different understanding of what the top priorities should be. *It is paramount that both the manager and the employee are in full agreement on what is going to most positively impact sales.*

Top priorities, high impact. Too many people are involved in the trivial many and not the vital few. The vital few are those high-impact, doing-what-counts activities. A simple exercise can get everybody pointed in the right direction.

At the top of a piece of paper write three column headings, "Where I need to put my attention." "How I plan to increase sales." "What are my high-impact, top-priority activities?" List these to the best of your ability without consulting your manager and make it account specific whenever possible.

Some activities you might list are:

- Prospecting.
- Setting up appointments.
- Getting appointments.

- Making sales with specific accounts.
- Organizational issues.

There are no right or wrong answers at this point. Just write down everything that will lead to a positive result on sales.

Then sit down with your manager and share your list. At this point, you will be adding, deleting, and fine-tuning. The end result will be a mutual agreement between you and your manager about where you should put your attention and where you have to set and achieve some goals. *It will be an action plan with your input and buy-in.*

Now set some specific and measurable goals around these categories for the next month. Although it is a simple exercise, it is probably the one area where I have been able to help my clients the most. After doing this exercise, everybody should be in agreement about what will maximize results.

This exercise minimizes the "chicken syndrome." I meet a lot of very busy people. They are busy all day long, and at the end of the day they go home with a tight knot in their stomach, thinking, "I have been busy all day, but what have I accomplished?" Our goal is for no more chickens. Yes, you will continue to be busy *but now you are busy with those activities that will get you the most return on your energy.* You will be busy *and* productive.

T: Trackable with Time Frames

Goals must be trackable. If you have set six-month goals, know where you are after two weeks, after three months, and the general progress toward your goal. This trackable information holds true for *any goal of any length.* You have to know how you're doing so you can make any necessary adjustments.

"T" also stands for *time frames.* A goal without a time frame merely remains a wish. By putting a time frame to your goal, you will create a sense of urgency, a deadline. Without the deadline, you will run the risk of adopting too lax an attitude about the goal and may not take the necessary action steps to make the goal come true.

I like to think of a deadline as a lifeline. Time frames put purpose into your day. This sense of purpose gives meaning to your life. Examples would be some of the following: "I call XYZ Corporation by 3 PM, September 22." "I get an appointment with Mrs. Jones by the end of this week." "I get a go-ahead decision from Mr. Doe in the month of September."

PROFILE OF A GOAL

The first part of writing goals is knowing that goals are specific, measurable, motivational, attainable, relevant, and trackable with time frames. Part two will show you how to keep your goals simple and to the point, a series of one-liners. Before we get into part two, we will do a few easy exercises to get you started. Massage that brain of yours to facilitate the writing of meaningful goals.

First, I want you to think about what you value in life. What is important to you?

A *value* simply means: What are your core beliefs? What are you willing to live for? Your values should fit you like a hand in a glove. *The clearer you are on what is important to you the clearer, more specific, and meaningful your goals will be.*

Ideally, you want your goals congruent with your values. For instance, if family harmony and spending a lot of time with your family is a core value and your goals continually take you away from your family, then your goals will be creating a life that you may eventually regret. If creating tremendous wealth is your number one priority, then your goals must reflect action steps that will move you in that direction. *Balance as a core value will force you to set goals that will harmonize seemingly contradictory goals.* You will put together plans that satisfy both family values and economic security.

Let me make two suggestions that can help you better understand your values and how to get them to be consistent with your aspirations in life. I recommend that you read *The 7 Habits of Highly Effective People* by Stephen Covey (New York: Simon & Schuster, 1989). A bestseller for several years, Dr. Covey does an excellent job of covering the role of values, integrity, and honesty with yourself in setting and achieving worthwhile goals. I also recommend attending a seminar, "Managing Personal Goals," by the Blessing-White Company of Princeton, New Jersey. The seminar includes a wonderful two-hour value clarification exercise.

The next exercise will give you momentum in inventorying your goals. It is a very easy and fun area in which to set goals because it involves products. Pretend you have just won one minute in a free shopping spree. In this one minute, everything you write down, regardless of the price, you can keep. Get a blank piece of paper, set a timer for one minute, and begin to write down *everything* you would want if money were no object. When I say *things,* I mean cars, boats, houses, clothes, anything you want to have. There are no limitations. Let your imagination run wild.

Now begin to write; you have one minute.

The purpose of this exercise is to get you to think big. Put an estimated dollar amount next to each item and come up with a grand total. How much were you able to spend in one minute? Did you want a lot of things? If you came up with only a few things, it means either you have most of the things you need or you do not really know what you want. Now that you have had some practice in writing down goals and have gained some momentum, you are clearer on your values and have some ideas about what you want. Let's really inventory your dreams, your goals.

Get 12 blank pieces of paper. Put one of these 12 headings at the top of each sheet:

Family goals
Health and fitness goals
Personal development goals
Travel goals
Community goals
Material goals
Financial goals
Productivity goals
Career goals
Emotional goals
Social goals
Spiritual goals

Family goals. Family does not mean just the immediate family. It includes the extended family—cousins, aunts, uncles, grandparents, brothers, sisters, parents. Goals might include spending more or less time with these people and developing stronger bonds, stronger relationships.

Health and fitness goals. This includes exercise goals, weight, nutrition, or learning relaxation techniques.

Personal development goals. Activities such as reading, attending seminars, listening to audiocassettes or watching video learning cassettes are in this category.

Travel goals. Have some fun here. Imagine there are no limitations. If you had all the time or all the money in the world, where would you travel to? Let your imagination go. There are many beautiful and exciting places to visit.

Community goals. Do you want to spend more or less time involved in community events? By setting a time frame, I was able to become involved in a fulfilling, satisfying community activity.

Material goals. Remember our shopping spree? Do you have any other items you would like to add? Now's the time.

Financial goals. From the Harvard–Yale study of 1953–73, researchers found that the 3 percent of students who wrote down their goals set on the average 1-, 2-, 3-, 5-, 10-, and 20-year financial goals. They wrote down what they wanted to earn in 1953, 1954, 1955, and so on. Remember that these were the people who 20 years later had accumulated great wealth. I am going to recommend that you do the same. Set 1-, 2-, 3-, 5-, 10-, and 20-year financial goals. Based on what you are earning now, what are realistic financial goals for you? Set some savings, investment, and retirement goals in these same time frames.

Take seriously that fantastic financial advice of the great philosopher Yogi Berra, "If you don't know where you are going, you'll probably end up there." Over and over again I hear this 3 to 5 percent figure. Only 3 to 5 percent of people actually set and achieve their goals on a consistent basis; only 3 to 5 percent of people who read a book, attend a seminar, or learn something that excites them actually put what they learned into action; and only 3 to 5 percent of the people in the United States, the richest country in the world, will retire financially independent. It comes back to the old truth that if you fail to plan, plan to fail. The exercise of writing down your financial goals will go a long way in getting and keeping you in the top 3 percent. Just do it!

Productivity goals. These are the relevant goals you wrote down and then reviewed with your supervisor. These goals might be in the number of phone calls per day, appointments per week, proposals and new sales per month, or other high-impact areas. Make sure you are putting your attention where you are going to get your greatest return. Add to your original list as appropriate.

Career goals. Where do you want to be in one, two, five years from now with your company? If you want to become the president of the company, what promotions will you need to progress toward the presidency? In what time frame? Do you have career goals outside your current employer? Do you wish to start your own business? What do you have to do, what actions do you have to take to start moving yourself in that direction? What studying do you have to do now to prepare yourself for these higher positions of responsibility?

Emotional goals. Where is some improvement needed? It could be to be more patient, to be a better listener, or to show your appreciation and love more clearly to those important in your life. These emotional goals can definitely be made specific and measurable.

Social goals. These include goals with friends and goals around your hobbies. I literally set myself a goal to have more friends. I had neglected my friends and realized that none of them were calling me. So I set some goals around contacting these friends before it was too late. The goal-setting procedure certainly saved several of my friendships.

Spiritual goals. Write down any private, family, or congregational goals that you have.

TAKE FIVE

I am going to ask you now to take five to do something you may have never done before or may not have done in a long time. I am going to ask you to take out five uninterrupted minutes from your day. Sounds like an oxymoron, doesn't it? Uninterrupted minutes? (An oxymoron is two successive words that seem to be direct contradictions of each other. Some classic examples being: military intelligence, sweet sorrow, pretty ugly, jumbo shrimp, or death benefits.)

Your oxymoron will actually be experiencing five minutes of uninterrupted time. You need to take this time now or you run the risk of never getting started in the goal-setting process. At my public or in-house seminars, I actually lock the doors and patrol the halls to make sure no one interrupts this precious part of the seminar. At other seminars I have attended, the seminar leader would say that the first thing to do when you get home is to write down your goals. Your intentions are the purest, but something comes up that night and you promise yourself that the first thing the next morning you'll write down those goals, but again something unexpected comes up and before you know it nine months have come and gone and still no written goals.

Put everything else aside for now and take five minutes for yourself that can have a very profound impact on the rest of your life. Here is what I want you to do during these five minutes: I want you to inventory your dreams. Keep your pen moving, writing down those stretch goals under the 12 categories. Don't worry about the specific and measurable part of these goals since this five-minute portion will lead us to part two of goal setting. Then we will make our goals both specific and measurable.

It's not necessary to set goals in every category. The 12 categories are there to give you some focus, to act as guidelines.

For instance, one or two family goals may come to mind. Write them down. If nothing else surfaces, go to the next category where you may have no goals, or maybe six goals or more. The category headings serve as mind joggers. You may have many goals in any one area or you may have none. Unlike those wonderful college SAT exams, you are allowed to go back to sections you have already completed. Just time the five minutes, loosen your imagination, have fun, and you will be amazed at how much you can accomplish in such a short time.

Now, take and time five minutes!

As in our earlier exercise, you may have listed many or very few goals. It really doesn't matter. Either you have a lot of the goals already accomplished or you're still unclear as to what it is you want out of life. You will soon get your answer. Let's now use the results of your five minutes to get us to part two of goal setting.

Look at all the categories and all the goals you just listed and pick out the five most meaningful goals you want to accomplish. It can be five from any of the categories, and all five can come from one category. It doesn't matter. Just pick out the five that turn you on the most. We're going to use these five to give you some practice on how easy it is to identify goals.

The KISS principle goals ideally are a set of one-liners, easy to write, easy to understand, and easy to read. There are three points to cover in writing your goals. A goal statement should be:

1. Personal. Somewhere in the goal statement have the words *I, me, my, our, us,* and any word that personalizes the goal and makes it relate to you. After discussing the three sections of a goal statement, I will give you several examples.

2. Positive. State it in a "can do" phrase instead of a "won't or don't do" phrase. A classic example of this is a baseball story. In a crucial World Series game, Warren Spahn was pitching to Elston Howard. Spahn's manager came out and told him, "Whatever you do, don't throw this guy a high and inside pitch." Of course, all Spahn could think of at this time was high and inside. He made the mistake of throwing the next pitch high and inside and sure enough Howard hit a game-turning hit. A more effective approach by the manager would have been to tell Spahn to throw pitches only low and away.

3. The third part of a goal statement is to make it in the present tense. State it as if it were already accomplished. Not "I'll try . . . " or "I will . . . " but "I have . . . " "I do . . . " "I earn . . . " "I am . . . "

The goal statement in the present tense is a nice, clean, and direct message to yourself. This is what I want and this is what I am becoming. Some examples of personal, positive, present tense goals are:

"I earn $100,000."

"I weigh 160 pounds."

"I drive a Lexus LS 400."

"I am a master prospector."

"I am excellent at asking for and getting commitment."

"I make 15 new prospect calls a day."

"I have 15 appointments a week."

I promised you some practice. Take the five goals you decided are the most important and write them now as personal, positive, present tense goals.

1. _____

2. _____

3. _____

4. _____

5. _____

This is how to write goals. Keep it short and simple, a series of one-liners or two lines at the most. Following are three exercises that will drive your desire and faith deeper. Then we'll talk about when and where to set goals and wrap it all up with the glue that holds this system together.

Take three separate pieces of paper and put one of the following headings on each (see some examples on pages 143 and 144):

- What I want to accomplish during my life.
- The reasons why I want to achieve my goals.
- The obstacles that stand in my way.

The first exercise is something I learned from listening to an audio-tape by Lou Holtz, the great Notre Dame football coach. Early in his career, Lou received some excellent advice after a very disheartening setback. A friend suggested that to keep from wallowing in his depression, Lou should make a list. The philosophy was that when you're feeling listless, make a list. This list was to become a constant inspiration of his continual growth and development. On his list were items such as be a football coach, be the head football coach, be the head football coach of Notre Dame, coach a team to a national championship, and be invited by the president of the United States to breakfast. His initial list had 110 items. Over the years he has accomplished more than 90 of those original goals while adding to his dreams for further and higher achievements.

This list can be for you, as it was for Lou Holtz, a source of continual motivation and the spark for constant movement upward toward the quest for success.

The second exercise is based on the philosophy that "reasons are the fuel in the fire of achievement." This is a quote from the classic by Napoleon Hill, *Think and Grow Rich*. If you have one or two reasons for striving toward your goals, this will give you some motivation, but filling your mind and heart with 30, 50, or 100 reasons why you want and need to reach your goals will definitely turn your life on fire. I recommend you post these two lists where they can be a constant reminder of why you need to discipline yourself to do the things you need to do.

Think of these lists as an advertisement to yourself. All of us need constant reminders. And that is what advertising does. It reminds and influences us. These lists staring you in the face day after day will encourage you to stay focused, to stay on track, to remember why you're doing what you're doing.

Another good idea is something called *poster boarding*. Cut out pictures of things you desire and post them on one or several poster boards. Select beautiful pictures of places you want to visit or things you want to buy. It's a great motivator and fun.

The third exercise deals with overcoming and handling obstacles. Write down those obstacles that stand between you and your success. It might be lack of contacts, or poor presentation skills, or not knowing how to be effective on the phone. The golden attitude to take is that obstacles come to us to instruct us, not to obstruct us. There is a lesson to be learned from everything that may be holding us back. When we overcome this obstacle, it will speed up our progress and form us into stronger and better people.

One sign of growing maturity is how well you manage disappointment and setbacks. Successful people quickly learn from disappointments and put them behind them. Unsuccessful people run the setbacks over and over again in their minds.

How often should we be setting goals and are there any recommended forms? I suggest that you set goals on a monthly basis. A month is an easy time frame to plan for. It's easy to have a good idea of what you want to accomplish during a month. Many people get discouraged about goal setting because they think they need a clear vision of what they'll be going after in three months, six months, or 1, 5, or 10 years from now. If you take proper care of your month-to-month responsibilities, the longer-term goals will start to form more clearly in your mind. Essentially, this entire goal-setting process boils down to 15 to 20 minutes of planning a month.

Take your month-at-a-glance calendar, or whatever type of system you use for keeping your promises and commitments (appointments), and set goals around some of these future engagements. It could be a goal around an upcoming appointment: "XYZ Corporation puts me on an annual retainer for $40,000." For the opening of a new account: "The initial order is delivered to ABD with no problems leading to a second order that is 10 percent larger and ordered by 9/30/94." After looking at the schedule that is already in place, take a look at your daily "to do" list.

Goals might be something like this:

- "I have an appointment with Core Systems."
- "A follow-up decision-making meeting is set up with Green Corporation."
- "Initial proposal is received by NCT by 1/1/95."

Set goals around those activities that must be acted upon. Approach your list with this thought, "When I complete all of the actions I have committed to and reach these goals, it will maximize my results for the month."

Then continue the process for the next month. Set new goals and carry over those that need to be continued into the next month. This habit gets easier and easier. At first it might take you 15 to 20 minutes, but over time you'll probably get it down to 10 to 15 minutes. It will keep you productive, focused, and successful.

Use the forms shown in the end of this chapter. The four-part form is for your month-to-month goal setting and the smaller "no whining" form is for your goals that are beyond the one-month period. Many of the goals that you wrote down during your five-minute exercise of inventorying your dreams would be put onto this form. After listing your goals on the four-part form, using the back if necessary, trifold the form, after cutting one-quarter part out, and then put the folded goals into the "no whining" form.

GETTING RESULTS

Here are several suggestions that will intensify your positive results.

Look at and read your goals at least three times a week. Remember, they are advertisements about your success. This will help minimize anything falling through the cracks. Seeing the goal still undone will motivate you to take action. So carry your goals around with you. It will help you make productive use of downtime. While standing in a line, or while waiting for someone, or when stuck in traffic, you can pull out your goals and quickly review them.

Track your accomplishments. Let's say you have 10 goals that will change from month to month. I do not recommend any more than 10 goals in a month, but we are all different and the demands on us will change from month to month. Some months we'll have 10 or more, while other months we'll focus our attention on three to five goals. The guideline is whatever will maximize our results.

For this tracking example, let's say you have 10 goals for the upcoming month. Measure and track which goals were achieved. You may hit one goal fully and another goal 50 percent. You may experience a little frustration at first because you'll find them hard to measure and not specific enough. But as you continue the process, your goals will get more and more specific and measurable. And here is where the management of disappointment becomes so critical.

When I first started the goal-setting process, I found myself hitting about 30 to 40 percent of my goals. It was very discouraging. Remember, the number one reason people do not set goals is the fear of failure. The accumulating months of not hitting most of my goals began to wear on me, and I considered not writing my goals because it was becoming so painful. But I took my own advice and persisted. Slowly but surely, I started hitting 50 to 60 percent of my goals. After four years of consistent goal setting and finding my goals becoming more and more specific and meaningful, I started hitting 80 to 90 percent of my written goals, and this trend has continued for the last couple of years. This is why the "no whining" is on the goal forms. No whining when sitting down to set goals, no "I don't want to do this," and no whining when seeing how you did. Just do it! And continue doing it!

Accountability! The two biggest reasons people do not consistently achieve their written goals is that (1) their goals are not specific enough and (2) there is no accountability. Accountability means sitting down with someone and reviewing what you did and did not do. Without accountability, there is the tendency to adapt a "so what" attitude. "Hey, I didn't achieve my goals, but what does it matter? No negative consequences." Well, of course, the negative consequence is lack of results, but if the individual thinks he or she can live with this lack of results, so be it. But when accountability is attached to goal setting, there is a greater chance you will take your goals more seriously and see them through to completion.

Put some teeth into your goals. Find a coach, someone who will encourage and support you along the way. This person can be your immediate supervisor, a boss from the past, a fellow worker, someone in a similar business, a business associate, a friend, a significant other, or a spouse. You will get together with this person on a regular monthly basis to review what you said you were going to do and what you actually did. You'll be motivated to accomplish your goals for the "bragging rights," or you'll be motivated to accomplish your goals because you don't want to embarrass yourself. Either way it works, you accomplish your goals.

This monthly meeting should take no longer than one hour, preferably less, especially when it occurs where you work. Review your previous month's goals and come to the meeting prepared to discuss your upcoming month's goals. You and your coach will discuss what's working and what needs to be improved. Your coach is someone who will give you a pat on the back when you deserve it and will also give you a boot in the pants if that is what is needed. If your coach does not work in your company, meet with him or her over breakfast, lunch, or dinner. Set a one-hour time limit for the goal discussion. It will keep your conversation tight, specific, and to the point.

Only 1 to 5 percent actually will use this information to get the results they want out of life. *Become one of the few who do!* Your persistence and determination is your belief in yourself. It takes time. There are no magic bullets or quick fixes. *Goal setting is one of the most important things you can do to assure you will be successful.*

Now you're ready for time and territory management. Without goals, you don't need time management. No priorities? No sense of urgency? Hey, use your time any way you see fit or unfit.

Here again are the three questions from the Harvard–Yale motivational study: (1) Do you have goals? (2) Do you write them down? and (3) Do you have action plans for their accomplishment? We have addressed the first two questions; now let's direct our attention to the third.

Keeping to our KISS theme, action planning to me means working at least with a month-at-a-glance and a things-to-do list. *Look at your goals and start assigning actions and dates/deadlines that will effectively move you toward your goals.* Start with these two basics, and from here you can get as sophisticated as you wish. But these two simple forms, the monthly and daily, should do it for you.

Time management is priority management. The essence of time management is organizing yourself and executing around priorities. That's it. Planning your work and working your plan.

A Baker's Dozen of Time Management Tips

1. Accept the fact that *you* are the cause of many of your time problems. Make the decision to find some solutions.
2. The number one time saver: Thinking in advance and planning, goal setting! Plan your day with these three essentials: What are my goals? What are my priorities? What does my ideal day look like? Nothing is more powerful than a written plan with deadlines. *Write it down!* Take 10 minutes at the end of the day to plan for the next day.
3. Start your day with your top priority first. Setting clear, specific goals equals more time. Develop the skill of concentrating on real priorities. Don't leave important jobs for the last minute.
4. *What gets written gets done.* Be in the habit of taking notes. Don't rely on your memory.
5. Use a complete "all in one place" time system organizer with:
   • Annual calendar.
   • "Things to do today" list.

- Place to take and retrieve notes.
- A–Z tabs for key phone numbers and addresses.

6. Get away from the excuses, "I can do it better and faster myself," and "I work best under pressure." Delegate more. Make a "to delegate" list. Allow people to grow. Avoid perfectionism. Rule of thumb: If you know somebody who can do it 70 percent as well as you, have them do it. If you do not, you will end up doing everything, which leads to lower productivity and ineffectiveness. When you delegate, monitor people's progress. Delegation gets the job done and motivates.

7. Learn to say no.

   - Listen.
   - Say no.
   - Give reasons.
   - Suggest alternatives.

8. Expect delays and interruptions. Build in safety cushions. If you expect something to take 45 minutes, schedule an hour.

9. Fallacy: The more meetings you attend, the more important you are. Reality: Most meetings are too long and waste too much time of too many people. A lot of them should not be held at all. Solution: No meeting without a written agenda, with time frames for each topic.

10. Eighty percent of paperwork in your in box can be handled once and be done with. Use the four Ds: drop (a person's best friend is the wastebasket), delay (put into an appropriate "to do" file), delegate, and do.

11. Recognize that a stacked desk can be a major interrupter. Can you concentrate at your desk? Can you easily find things? If not, you need to fight clutter's last stand. Use the above four Ds again. Don't be a stuffer, stacker, spreader, saver, or slinger.

12. Have a "things to read" folder. Scan, tear, skim, highlight, and underline.

13. Know your prime time. Use your most productive time, when your energy is highest and your mind the clearest, to do your most important/productive work. Keep a quiet hour, with the door closed, for making and taking calls and for those high-impact, must-do projects.

Some of these ideas will work some of the time for some people. Please don't have an all-or-nothing attitude. Pick out the ones that will work for you, using the time management contract from the end of this chapter, and disregard the rest.

One other suggestion: read *The Time Trap*, by Alec MacKenzie (New York: Amacom, 1990). This book is filled with practical time management tips. It is the best book I have ever read on time management.

Now, go do it!

What I Want to Accomplish during My Life

Note: Make up your own additional sheets. The sky's the limit!

The Reasons I Want to Achieve My Goals *(The more reasons you have, the more you will be motivated.)*

Note: Make up additional sheets. Go for 30, 40, 100 reasons you want, need, *must* achieve your goals.

Time Management Contract

I agree to commit to using, over the next four weeks, the three following time management strategies to improve my efficiency and effectiveness.

•

•

•

I will report my results to_____ during the week of
_____.

_____   _____
Name   Date

My Monthly Goals

For the month of _____ 🚫Whining

Personal Goals

_____

Family Goals

_____

Business Goals

_____

_____

_____

_____

_____

_____

_____

_____

_____

_____

_____

_____

My Monthly Goals

For the month of _____ 🚫Whining

Personal Goals

_____

Family Goals

_____

Business Goals

_____

_____

_____

_____

_____

_____

_____

_____

_____

_____

_____

_____

My Monthly Goals

For the month of _____ 🚫Whining

Personal Goals

_____

Family Goals

_____

Business Goals

_____

_____

_____

_____

_____

_____

_____

_____

_____

_____

_____

_____

My Monthly Goals

For the month of _____ 🚫Whining

Personal Goals

_____

Family Goals

_____

Business Goals

_____

_____

_____

_____

_____

_____

_____

_____

_____

_____

_____

_____

My Goals

Personal Goals

Family Goals

Business Goals

Whining

Human Resources

UNLIMITED

Mark Riesenberg ▽ President

10 Tips to Stop Whining and Start Winning

1. Know when you're whining and decide to stop
2. Create a mission
3. Set goals
4. Write down your goals
5. Become unstoppable
6. Take action/take risks
7. Believe in what you're doing
8. Have a "can-do" attitude
9. Be focused
10. Conquer fatigue

© 1993 Human Resources Unlimited

Chapter Seven

The Art of Listening

Roni Abrams

The wise person listens and learns. The fool hears nothing but knows it all. In sales, listening is a powerful tool.

Salespeople tend to speak more than they listen. It is ironic, because the effectiveness of the spoken word depends on how people listen. Your ability to discern what you are really listening to will impact the actions you will take. Your business dealings and personal life will reflect your level of skill as a listener.

A SALES TALE

Purchasing agent:

"An account representative gave me a standard sales pitch. I told the rep what the company needed. The rep repeated the exact same pitch, and I stopped the meeting."

Account representative:

"I gave the presentation of a lifetime. The purchasing agent didn't understand."

Analysis:

The purchasing agent perceived the rep was not listening. The account representative perceived the agent was not listening.

Moral:

If no one is listening, you cannot close the sale.

In this chapter you will learn how to:

1. Engage in two-way communications.
2. Be an effective listener.
3. Apply the benefits of listening to business and personal relationships.
4. Develop listening into a sales tool.

You will discover how to be an effective communicator, develop an awareness of the communications process, enhance interpersonal skills, refine interviewing skills, and create trust and understanding.

Listening is an essential component of the communications process. Listening, speaking, reading, and writing are the four uses of language.

The narrowest definition of language is "that which is produced by human vocal organs and received by the hearing organs." In this chapter, the broadest definition of language will be used—an interchange of meaning, a transfer of significant concepts. This interchange of meaning can be accomplished through speaking, writing, gesturing, and pictures.

Listening is all-encompassing. You are receiving information through your five senses: sight, hearing, taste, smell, and touch. During a conversation, you are listening to and observing:

- What is being said.
- What is not being said.
- The speaker's body language.
- The environment.
- People other than the speaker who may be involved in the proceedings.
- Your interpretation of what is occurring.

Being aware of what you are seeing, hearing, and experiencing is key to being an effective listener. Masterful communicators learn to use this knowledge to produce extraordinary results.

If you were to log your daily activities, you would find that the majority of your time is spent listening. If you looked at those areas that are most problematic, such as a difficult prospect or account, or a disagreeable friend or family member, you would realize that the core of the hot spot is something you or the other person did not hear or perceived in a distorted way. Though we are taught to read, write, and to some degree, speak while we are in school, there is little or no training in listening.

Some individuals are born with a special talent. Most people require coaching to have their talents bloom and grow. It should come as no surprise that the same complaint can be heard in boardrooms, classrooms, homes, stores, factories, and between buyers and sellers, "You don't listen!"

How do you know when someone is or isn't listening? The answer lies in examining what works and does not work when we are communicating with prospects, clients, employees, employers, vendors, family, and friends.

What doesn't work?

Looking into space.

Interrupting the speaker.

Being disinterested in what the speaker has to say.

Giving your opinions before the speaker has finished talking.

Pretending to understand.

Being tense or threatening.

Beating around the bush.

Using technical jargon.

Allowing distractions.

Taking extensive notes.

Making or receiving telephone calls while the conversation is in progress.

Conversing with other people in the room.

Checking your watch.

Rearranging papers on your desk.

What works?

Making eye contact.

Drawing the speaker out.

Focusing your attention on the speaker.

Being nonjudgmental.

Asking questions to create clarity.

Having a sincere interest in what the speaker has to say.

Being relaxed.

Saying what you mean.

Keeping your emotions in check.

Summarizing points of agreement or disagreement.

Concentrating on key ideas instead of noting every fact and detail.

Keeping the conversation on track.

Eliminating distractions.

Sitting or standing close to the speaker.

These two lists outline many elements involved in the communications process. These elements can be called criteria for listening. The more criteria you have the greater your capacity to fully listen. If you do not have the above-mentioned criteria, you would have no way of determining whether someone was listening to you or not.

Imagine you are going for your annual physical. Your doctor orders a blood work-up. When the test results are in, your doctor invites you to examine a drop of your blood by looking at it through a microscope. What do you see? In all probability, you will have little or no idea what you are looking at. Your doctor will be able to identify between 20 and 40 specific items pertaining to your blood. Your doctor developed criteria by which he or she can analyze the blood sample.

It is crucial that you develop criteria for listening. This gives you a foundation that you will need to listen effectively. In addition, it is important that you fine-tune your powers of observation. Astute observers are aware of what they are looking at and listening for based on the criteria they have established.

Example: Precision Inc., Vincent Shields

Vincent Shields is an account representative for Precision Inc., a computer software company. He has been with the firm for two years. Shields has had three meetings with Foods Ltd., a major food distribution organization. His contact at Foods Ltd. is Ted Neil, vice president of operations.

Shields is going to meet with Ted Neil today. He is convinced Precision's product is just what is needed by Foods Ltd. and feels confident he will close the sale this afternoon. Shields even tells his sales manager he will come back with a contract.

During the meeting, Ted Neil tells Shields the software does not meet the very specific requirements of Foods Ltd. He goes on to identify what those requirements are and why they are so important.

Shields tells Neil the software is ideal for Foods Ltd. and his concerns are not warranted. Neil pushes back his chair and stands up. He takes on a stiff and formal demeanor and once again states what the software must be able to do. Shields repeats what he said before, "The software is ideal for you." Neil ends the meeting and tells Shields Precision software is not suitable for his company's purposes.

Shields returns to the office and his sales manager asks to see the contract. He looks dazed and says, "The prospect refuses to do business with me." The sales manager asks Shields to go over what transpired during the meeting, but Vincent can-not tell him anything. Without this information, the sales manager could not help Shields and Shields could not learn from the experience.

What happened?

Shields was convinced the sale was a *fait accompli,* and he stopped listening to the prospect. Shields thought he knew what was in the prospect's best interests. The prospect told him not once but three times Foods Inc.'s software requirements. Neil had already given Shields this information at their second meeting. The prospect realized he was not listening. Neil perceived this as (1) disinterest, (2) arrogance, and (3) lack of competence on Shields's part. What's more, if Shields represented the caliber of personnel at Precision Inc., Neil didn't want anything more to do with the company.

Shields let his opinion and attitude get in the way of his closing the sale. He was so busy listening to his own ideas that he blocked out everything and everyone else. Shields had forgotten that you either have an opinion or it has you. He became deaf, blind, and dumb to what was occurring around him. By focusing attention on himself instead of the prospect, Shields rendered himself ineffective.

Remember that being aware of what you are hearing, seeing, and experiencing is the key to effective listening. If you cut off those channels of information, you cannot effectively use or even access the criteria for listening you have established. Shields had no information markers along the way to alert him to the fact that his "done deal" was falling apart. He did not observe the change in Neil's voice tone and body language and his increasing impatience. If Shields had heard Neil's specific concerns regarding the software, he could have easily had the software adjusted. Shields was surprised at the turn of events. Without the tools of listening at his disposal, he was unable to turn a no-win situation into a win-win for all. His inability to listen cost him the sale.

It is important to recognize that one person who is not listening can cast a negative shadow over an entire company. The financial viability of organizations and employees rests on their ability to listen. Successful salespeople and companies listen to:

- Customers.
- Prospects.
- Market trends.
- Employees.
- Management.
- Social and cultural trends.

If you do not listen, you cannot learn. Acquiring information and knowledge enables you to make more educated decisions and take effective action.

Example: Best Furniture Corporation, Helaine Gordon

Helaine Gordon has been selling furniture to national department and specialty store chains for eight years. She works for Best Furniture Corporation, the country's leading wholesale furniture manufacturer, and is the top salesperson. Two years ago, Gordon had suggested the company offer discontinued items on a retail basis at discount prices. It would give the company an additional source of revenue and an opportunity to test-market new styles. After considerable research, the company has decided to open its New York distribution center to the public.

Mitchell Woods, president of Best Furniture, has asked Gordon to develop a sales strategy for this new venture. Management has come to trust and rely on Gordon's judgment. She has an uncanny sense of consumer buying trends. If the concept works in New York, the plan is to duplicate the success in many of the distribution centers across the country.

Gordon identified the competition and visited all their facilities to get firsthand knowledge of what and how they are selling their products. She was reorienting her listening and perspective in order to think and operate on two levels simultaneously: wholesale and retail.

Competitors made no attempt to display their furniture in an organized fashion. It was a jungle atmosphere where a potential buyer needed a machete to cut a path from one end of the warehouse to the other. Salespeople were scarce and service nonexistent. She observed customer frustration and few sales being made.

Gordon submitted a report to Mitchell Woods in which she suggested they make optimal use of their large distribution center by arranging the furniture by category as well as setting up model rooms to show customers how they could incorporate the merchandise into their homes or offices.

She recommended creating working relationships with manufacturers of bedding, tableware, window treatment, floor coverings, and electronics. This would serve two purposes: (1) enable them to feature fully decorated model rooms, and (2) enable them to cross-sell merchandise. Gordon strongly urged the company to select a highly trained sales force to help customers choose the furniture most appropriate for their needs.

Management gave Gordon full approval to organize the center as she had outlined in her report. She met with manufacturers and negotiated contracts with them that were beneficial to all parties concerned.

Best Furniture Corporation's New York experiment in retailing worked out extremely well. Gordon has been promoted to vice president of sales and is now planning the conversion of three additional distribution centers.

Why is Gordon successful?

- She is an effective listener.
- She is an effective speaker.

- She is open to learning.
- She is resourceful and inventive.
- She is committed to the project.
- She has a positive attitude.

Gordon knows she is more knowledgeable about selling whole-sale than selling retail. She does not perceive this as a stumbling block but as a challenge and a way to develop new areas of exper-tise. For Gordon to succeed in this endeavor, she will expand the cri-teria she has regarding retail selling by observing, asking questions, reading books and articles, and immersing herself in the various aspects of the business. The more criteria for listening she has, the more information she will have at her disposal.

Think of a project that required you to stretch beyond what you thought was possible. What did you tell yourself? "I can do it," or, "I cannot do it." By listening to the possibilities, you will improve your ability to produce results.

Gordon's ability to spot consumer buying trends and turn them into profits for Best Furniture earned her the respect of man-agement and a high salary. She does not use a crystal ball to predict trends. She has a highly refined network of criteria that she uses to help her listen for possibilities. In addition, Gordon understood her assignment and was committed to its success. She knows her likes and dislikes, opinions, perceptions, and points of view influence the way she listens. By riveting her attention to her commitments, she eliminates distractions and is open to possibilities.

Your likes and dislikes change all the time, but your commit-ments are unshakable.

Once you hear what is possible, your next job is to speak up to make it reality. Gordon had to gain approval of Best Furniture's top management. Then she had to present the concept to five manu-facturers and successfully negotiate separate contracts with each of them.

The following meeting occurred between Helaine Gordon and George Bard, president of Bard Electronics, Inc., after several tele-phone conversations.

Bard immediately opened the meeting by telling Gordon he was very interested in featuring his company's products in Best Furniture's New York distribution center. He was a proponent of cross-merchandising. He acknowledged Gordon for her clear and concise speaking and the enthusiasm she conveyed over the phone.

Bard asked Gordon to spell out the specifics of the project as it related to his firm. What merchandise was needed from Bard Electronics for the model rooms and when? Also, how much stock does Bard need to supply to the distribution center? They discussed computer systems to keep track of merchandise, percentage of sales revenue to be divided between them, and delivery costs to the distribution center.

Gordon had done her homework and answered all his questions to his satisfaction. She told Bard she initiated the project and was determined this venture be successful. Gordon said close communications between them was important and he would be able to reach her at any time through her beeper number. She said the only other people who have this number are the top management of her company. At the end of the meeting, Bard told Gordon to count his firm in and that he looked forward to a long and mutually rewarding relationship.

What happened?

Gordon's product knowledge, in-depth research, and personal inspection of competitors' facilities and selling practices gave her the information to present the concept and herself in the most effective way. It was clear to George Bard he was dealing with an extremely knowledgeable, capable individual. Since she created the project, it would have her full attention and energy.

Bard heard the commitment in Gordon's presentation.

- She was committed to the project's success and her enthusiasm was contagious.
- She was committed to developing a win-win agreement between Bard Electronics and Best Furniture. Bard would not work with Gordon if she was looking out only for her own interests.
- She was committed to full and open communications between them and gave him her private number.

To engage in effective two-way communications requires that there be a committed listener and a committed speaker. Committed listeners are willing to put aside their likes and dislikes, opinions, perceptions, and points of view long enough to hear what someone else is saying. Committed speakers are willing to get their point across to the listener not with words alone, but by conveying the spirit and intent behind the words.

Think of the last time you met an old acquaintance on the street. He says, "We have to get together." You concur. And you both know then and there that will never happen. Why? There is no commitment to do so on the part of either party. If the intention was to meet, a date, time, and place would be established.

The good news and bad news in life is that the moment you start speaking, people know a great deal about you. What can people hear when someone speaks?

Sincerity	Satisfaction
Insincerity	Dissatisfaction
Commitment	Trust
Lack of commitment	Distrust
Intention	Decisiveness
Competence	Hesitancy
Incompetence	Positive attitude
Confidence	Negative attitude
Lack of confidence	Stress
Enthusiasm	Anger
Lack of enthusiasm	Joy
Flexibility	Love
Inflexibility	Humor

The list is endless depending on your skill as a listener. Astute listeners can glean a tremendous amount of information in a short time. This gives you an edge over the competition. By quickly determining what motivates your prospect, you possess the information necessary to close the sale. Listening is a powerful sales tool.

Example: Medical Resource Corporation, Larry Long

Larry Long is an account representative for Medical Resource Corporation. The company manufactures medical equipment and supplies hospitals around the world. The company recently introduced a new piece of equipment to monitor heart rate and Long has been given the West Coast sales territory.

The purchasing agent for Worth Hospital, Ben Lloyd, has a reputation that is known throughout the company. He is the one purchasing agent no one can get along with and is considered uncooperative, cantankerous, and cold. Lloyd is Long's first sales call in Los Angeles.

Long called Ben Lloyd to arrange a meeting. He introduced himself and told Lloyd about the new equipment and its innovative technology. The meeting was scheduled to take place in two weeks.

Long did research on Worth Hospital and discovered it was expanding its facilities, hiring the finest specialists, and becoming one of the most prestigious medical centers in California. Ben Lloyd has been with the hospital for 15 years. According to newspaper articles about Worth Hospital, Lloyd was instrumental in convincing the board of directors to purchase state-of-the-art equipment.

Long went to the meeting with an open mind and with a commitment to sell this important piece of equipment to Worth Hospital. Lloyd did his best to intimidate Long. Long focused his attention solely on Lloyd and listened carefully to what he was saying.

Lloyd told Long he was determined to help make Worth Hospital not only the best in California but also in the entire country. He was always looking for equipment that could save more lives and increase the staff's productivity.

In a direct, clear, precise manner, Long told Lloyd about every aspect of the equipment. He spelled out the benefits and said it matched Lloyd's requirements for excellence. What's more, Long shared with Lloyd his reasons for being in the business. His younger sister had been ill and because of an innovative piece of equipment, she is alive today. He chose Medical Resource Corporation to work for because the firm strives to develop the most advanced equipment to help as many people as possible.

As the meeting progressed, Lloyd's attitude and manner changed. He was moved by what Long told him about his sister and by his commitment to excellence. Lloyd was interested in the equipment but was unwilling to commit himself. Long asked him what stood in the way of buying the equipment now. Lloyd said he would like some tangible evidence that it works as well as he says it does. Long thought a moment and made the following proposal. He would arrange to take him to New York, at Medical Resource's expense, to see the equipment in use. If he had all his questions answered and his concerns eliminated, he would agree to sign a contract then and there.

Lloyd said yes.

Since that time Ben Lloyd and Larry Long have become good friends. Worth Hospital has become one of Medical Resource Corporation's most loyal accounts.

What happened?

Long learned early in his career to decide for himself if someone was nasty or nice. Over the years, he has been able to work with people that no one else could. Long researched all the prospects and people he was going to meet. The more he understood what was important to them, the better he could tailor his presentation.

When Long found out Worth Hospital was expanding its facilities and staff and was considered a major medical center, he knew it would be an appropriate institution for this equipment. In addition, he read that Ben Lloyd was responsible for urging the hospital to acquire state-of-the-art equipment. It is unusual for a purchasing agent to be publicly acknowledged for his contribution to the growth of his hospital. This information about Lloyd was a signal to Long that there is more to this man than meets the eye.

Long went to the meeting without any preconceived notions about Lloyd. However, he did go to the meeting clear on his commitment—to close the sale. By staying focused on his commitment, he would not let himself be sidetracked by Lloyd's gruff behavior. Instead, he gave Lloyd his undivided attention and listened intently to what he was saying. Long discovered that Lloyd was a very committed individual who is deeply concerned about the health and well-being of people. He now had the insight to deal effectively with Lloyd as a caring human being and not as the ogre he was purported to be.

Long spoke to Lloyd as he would to a friend and discussed his sister's illness and his reason for working with Medical Resource Corporation. Lloyd reacted positively to Long's openness and saw that he was speaking with someone who had commitments similar to his own. From that moment on, Long and Lloyd developed a comfortable working relationship.

Long knew that Lloyd was a straightforward man and presented the facts about the equipment and its benefits in a clear, precise manner. Lloyd was interested in the equipment but was hesitant to place an order.

It is crucial that you find out why a prospect is saying no or maybe. Listen carefully to the response. The prospect will tell you what you need to know to turn no into yes.

Long asked Lloyd what was troubling him. Lloyd stated he has buying medical equipment a long time and has heard every type of sales pitch. He wants positive proof of its effectiveness. Once Long could determine the objection, he could find a way to overcome it. Utilizing the information he had acquired about Lloyd, Long took an educated risk and made his proposal to him. Long's ability to listen, his understanding of human nature, and his knowledge that people take action based on their commitments enabled him to develop a loyal customer and friend.

Everyone has experienced dealing with difficult people. It is how you perceive that person that will make or break the relationship.

In the above example, Long chose to see Lloyd as a humanitarian who shared his commitment to excellence in health care. If Long chose to see Lloyd as the most impossible purchasing agent on the West Coast to work with, he might never have closed the sale. Look and listen beyond a person's gruff demeanor. By doing so, you may discover a remarkable human being.

Salespeople must remain cool and collected regardless of the circumstances. Whether you are meeting with a prospect, renewing a contract with an existing account, or being interviewed for a new position, the moment you become tense, frustrated, or angry, you stop listening. When that happens, you lose your competitive edge.

Example: Alice Fields, Anthony Barnes

Alice Fields is an account representative for the engineering firm of Rice, Needham, Marks Inc. The company designs bridges, highway systems, and airports. Last month the firm was acquired by the Reed Corporation. The employees were notified that six departments would be phased out.

Fields was told by her manager that their department was one of the six. They had five months to close operations, and she should start looking for a job now. Fields went home that night very upset.

She had been with Rice, Needham, Marks for five years. She was not planning to leave, and ironically she was to be promoted the same month the department would be disbanded.

After the initial shock wore off, Fields made a list of companies to contact and started updating her résumé. She included in her list engineering firms as well as other organizations to which she could apply her specialized selling skills.

She was preparing to go on her first interview and found herself nervous and fearful. She recalled other interviews that she had gone on and what awful experiences they had been. She didn't think this one would be any better. By the time she reached her destination, she decided her chances of being hired were slim.

Fields met with Anthony Barnes, personnel director of the Johnson & Miller Engineering Corporation. This company, like her current employer, designs major infrastructure projects. Fields walked slowly into his office and sat down. Barnes told Fields about the company and the position that they wanted to fill. While Barnes was talking, Fields stared out the window. He asked her if she had any questions and there was no reply.

Barnes reached into his desk drawer and took out a photograph. He showed it to Fields and told her it was a picture of himself after one of the job interviews he went on. She laughed out loud. What she saw was a disheveled man carrying in one hand a briefcase and in the other a sign reading, "I may not be perfect but I sure can get the job done."

Fields told Barnes she had not been on a job interview in years, she was extremely nervous, and to make the situation worse, she was angry that she even had to look for one. Barnes said he understood and had been in a similar situation himself. He added that it took him a while to release all the anger he felt about being a casualty of downsizing.

They continued the interview. Fields was animated and told Barnes about the success she had in bringing business to Rice, Needham, Marks and that she could do the same for them. She mentioned that she had read that Johnson & Miller wanted to bid on the new airport to be built in Atlanta. She had long-established contacts with the appropriate government agencies in Georgia and it would be her pleasure to represent the company and help it win the contract.

The phone rang three times during the interview. Each time Barnes told the caller he was in a meeting and would call back. His secretary came in asking him to clarify how she should type the report he needed for that afternoon. He told his secretary he would go over the report after he completed the interview and to hold all calls.

Fields and Barnes spoke for an hour and a half. Barnes told Fields he would recommend her for the position. She would have to meet with the person she would be reporting to, Sharon Billings, vice president of sales. If Sharon Billings agreed, the job would be hers.

Why did Fields get the job?

The first step Fields took was to do research on the companies she was interested in working for. She narrowed down the list and concentrated on the organizations that were involved in projects where she could use her industry resources. The best way to get a new position or close a sale is to show the prospective company that you have a way to help it increase profits and productivity.

The second step Fields took was to update her résumé. To present her background and accomplishments in a powerful manner, she had to be able to adapt them to suit each company's requirements.

Fields's preparation regarding prospective companies and presenting herself was impeccable. However, she did not mentally prepare herself for the interview process. Instead of boosting her self-esteem by reexamining her accomplishments and how she achieved them, she told herself the odds of getting the job were negligible. If you say to yourself something will not happen, you are setting the stage for disaster. If you say to yourself something can and will happen, you are priming yourself for success. The message you are sending to yourself will impact the actions you will take.

Recall her entrance into Anthony Barnes's office. She was slow and fearful. He knew immediately something was troubling Fields. This was confirmed by her staring into space and not responding to his question. Body language is very revealing to a trained listener. It can confirm or contradict what you are saying. In Fields's case, it was what she was not saying.

It is crucial in a sales situation to be alert, observant, and listening. By doing so you can:

- Hear what is being said.
- View the environment.
- Determine if more information is needed.
- Ask for that information.
- Listen for possibilities.

Just like Fields, Anthony Barnes was prepared for the interview. He knew exactly the type of person the company was looking for and the skills needed to be successful in the position. He had spoken twice with Fields over the phone and had thoroughly read her résumé. She was extremely well qualified for the job. He thought her behavior was not consistent with his experience of her based on the phone conversations and résumé.

Barnes is a highly skilled interviewer and knows how to draw people out. He used humor to get Fields's attention and put her at ease. **Be inventive. Find a way to get and keep your listener's undivided attention.** If you do not have a committed listener, it is the equivalent of talking to the wind.

Barnes understood what Fields was going through because the same thing had happened to him. Fields transformed her perception of Barnes from an enemy to a friend when he told her this. **Whether you are the interviewer or the interviewee—be yourself.** People respond favorably to someone who is understanding and compassionate. Life is unpredictable. Tomorrow may be your turn to need a helping hand.

Fields told Barnes that she was angry. Anger is a powerful human emotion. It can block out everything and you will hear and see nothing. Her anger kept her so preoccupied she ignored Barnes. Once Fields told Barnes she was nervous and angry, she was freed from the debilitating hold on her emotions.

Many professional platform speakers will tell their audience at the start of their presentation they are nervous. The audience responds to this by:

- Perceiving the speaker as human.
- Wanting the speaker to do well.

Your emotions can divert you from your purpose. Acknowledging your fears and concerns helps to eliminate them. **Keep your attention focused on your commitment and not on yourself.**

Fields quickly regained her composure and self-confidence. She presented her qualifications and what she could do for Johnson & Miller with great enthusiasm. She told Barnes she wanted the position and she could start bringing in business from the day she starts. Her research on the company turned up the fact that it wanted to bid on the Atlanta airport project. She would utilize her long-established contacts with the appropriate government agencies in Georgia to help pave the way.

Barnes gave her his full attention. He had his secretary hold all calls and minimized outside distractions. This was an indication to Fields that he respected her time and ability.

Anthony Barnes's skill as an interviewer enabled him to pick the best person for the job. His strength lies in being:

- An astute listener.
- A masterful communicator.
- An understanding and compassionate individual.
- An excellent judge of character.
- A student of human nature.

To be an effective communicator, speak to the point and make certain the listener fully understands what you are intending to say. **You must be crystal clear when expressing yourself or else you leave your communication open to misinterpretation.**

There is nothing that creates more confusion, frustration, and anger then when someone:

- Says one thing and means something else.
- Perceives what is being said in a distorted way.

Example: Blue Diamond Appliance Ltd., Todd Hastings, Bernard Haas

Todd Hastings is an account representative for Blue Diamond Appliance Ltd., manufacturer of refrigerators, dishwashing equipment, washing machines, and clothes dryers. Hastings has been with the company four years and works with hotels, restaurants, and educational institutions.

His department has been reorganized and two salespeople have been moved to a different division. During a 10-minute meeting his manager gave him the territory left uncovered by the recent changes. In addition, Hastings was told to compile a year-end sales report on this territory and have a draft ready in one week.

Hastings left the meeting furious. There was no time for him to say anything or to ask questions. He was angry that his manager, Bernard Haas, had just dumped extra work in his lap without even discussing it with him first. To add insult to injury, he was supposed to do this with no salary increase.

Hastings walked around for days seething inside. With great resentment, he began working on the sales report. It became obvious to him the records had not been prepared properly and the only person who could help him was Bernard Haas. Hastings did everything he could to contain his anger and went in to speak to Haas. He was dealing with a crisis and could spend very little time with Hastings. Haas gave Hastings the paperwork he had on the accounts and told him to figure it out.

Hastings didn't understand why his manager was ignoring him. Haas was always very supportive of his sales staff and went out of his way to ensure their success. Hastings began to think Haas was displeased with his level of production and was trying to make his working conditions intolerable so he would leave.

The following week Hastings submitted a preliminary draft of the sales report to Haas. Haas called him into his office and said it was good, but he needed to make a few revisions. "This is the last straw," Hastings said to himself. "Haas can't even pay me a compliment without criticizing something."

Hastings became very upset and demanded to know why he was being treated so badly and being forced to leave the company. Haas was flabbergasted. He did not have any idea of what Hastings was talking about.

Haas asked Hastings to explain to him how he came to this conclusion. After Hastings recounted all the events and conversations to him, Haas walked across the room and looked him straight in the eye and said, "You are my best salesperson, and I gave you the additional responsibilities in order to secure your promotion to assistant manager. I thought you would be pleased. It had never crossed my mind that you would have interpreted my actions in a negative way."

Hastings and Haas spent the next hour discussing what occurred over the last two weeks. By the end of the conversation, their relationship was stronger than ever and Hastings was excited over his upcoming promotion.

What happened?

Whenever a company goes through a reorganization, the staff can become anxious and even fearful. The daily work routine has been shattered and the employees question the security of their jobs. Regardless of what management says or does, it is interpreted by employees through a filter of concern.

Change can be perceived as threatening. Change can also be perceived as opportunity.

Hastings perceived his additional workload as a burden and a penalty. Given the restructuring all the departments were going through, he thought he might be the next to leave. Why else would he be asked to take on this extra work without any appropriate compensation? His time and talent were worth nothing to the company. Hastings was only listening to his fear and anger. As a result, everything he heard had negative implications.

Bernard Haas had been honored as manager of the year for three consecutive years. During the last two weeks, he acted as though he had forgotten some of his most important management skills. The first 10-minute meeting set the tone for his new relationship with Hastings. He went from having two-way communications with him to having one-way communications. In short, Haas stopped communicating with Hastings.

He did not tell him:

- His job was secure to eliminate his fears.
- He considered him his best salesperson and had recommended his promotion to assistant manager.
- Upper management would make the decision based on his ability to effectively handle these additional responsibilities.
- He should require less supervision by him and exhibit more initiative.

Haas did not realize his actions were having an adverse effect on Hastings. He assumed Hastings would understand his motives and be pleased. **To avoid communication breakdowns, never assume the listener knows what you mean and your reasons for saying something. No one is a mind reader.**

Be responsible for what you say. Observe the impact you are having on the person you are speaking to. If the listener is angry and you feel he should be happy, your message did not get through. Find another way to convey your thoughts. **Remember, to engage in effective two-way communications, there must be a committed listener and a committed speaker.**

Hastings was unable to express his anger to Haas. He withheld what he needed to communicate and his rage grew. The stress and anxiety this created could have been averted if, right from the start, Hastings had asked Haas to clarify what was going on.

Once Haas explained to Hastings that he was being considered for promotion, everything fell into place. Hastings could relax. He was able to communicate what he needed to say to Haas and his anger dissolved. Hastings immediately began to reorient his listening and perspective to make the most of his new position and the opportunities available to him.

Many people say they are victims of circumstance. Events occur that are not under their control. In the face of life's unpredictability you have a powerful tool: the ability to listen.

Example: Pane & Weeks Financial Service Corp., Joyce Blake, Eric Tate

Joyce Blake is a financial planner with Pane & Weeks Financial Service Corporation. She has been with the firm three years and specializes in estate and retirement planning. Tomorrow she has an 8 AM meeting scheduled with Eric Tate, the company president, to discuss a seminar she will be conducting for a Fortune 100 company.

At 2 AM, a water pipe in her bathroom burst, flooding two rooms below. Blake was up all night trying to minimize the damage. At 5 AM, she still had not reached a plumber and knew she had to leave in an hour or she would not get to the office on time. The meeting was too important to miss, and she would come back in the afternoon to deal with finding a plumber.

To save time, Blake decided to drive instead of taking the train. While she stopped for a red light, a car plowed into the back of her car. Fortunately, no one was hurt. Blake's car was badly damaged, but she was able to drive it to the office.

She arrived 45 minutes late for her meeting. She apologized and said nothing to Eric Tate about the flood and car accident. Tate went over the specifics of the seminar such as the number of attendees, length of time, program content, and the fact that if this one is successful, they will be able to offer seminars companywide. Blake questioned Tate on things he had already mentioned. He had to repeat what he said twice.

After the meeting Blake's secretary reminded her she had a client conference scheduled with Diane and Al Gerber at 10 AM. Blake had forgotten all about it. This was an initial fact-finding session to enable Blake to get the information she needed to begin developing a retirement program for them. It is a time-consuming process. The Gerbers had many questions and Blake barely answered any of them. She tried to shorten the process by filling in some of the blanks herself. Blake constantly interrupted them, and they could not get their points across to her.

As soon as the meeting was over, she rushed home. She reached the plumber and he promised to be there by 2 o'clock. She called for a tow truck and they promised to be there by 4 o'clock. Neither one showed. Blake was furious. It took her another two hours to find a plumber and to get her car towed to the garage.

It is crucial that when you make a promise you follow through. If you have to revoke your promise, tell the other party as soon as possible to minimize the damage. You lose credibility every time you do not keep your word. In sales, a prospect is listening and watching everything you say and do. **The moment your prospects decide you are not capable or credible they will take their business somewhere else.**

The next morning Eric Tate asked her to come to his office immediately. Tate looked very concerned. He told Blake the Gerbers called him yesterday afternoon to complain about the way she had dealt with them. They told him she had been rude, disinterested in their needs, and rushed them out of the office. What's more, they did not trust her and refused to work with her. "You are one of our best financial planners. Is there something wrong?" Tate asked Blake. "If there is any way I can help, please let me know," he offered. Blake thanked him for being a friend and for his vote of confidence. She told him that stress, panic, and fatigue had gotten the better of her.

Blake apologized to the Gerbers. She told them she was overwhelmed by the circumstances. For the first time in her career, she acted very unprofessionally. She asked the Gerbers if they ever found themselves in a situation where they had to ask for a second chance. Al Gerber chuckled and said he had been around many years and would be lying if he said no. They agreed to meet with Blake again.

What happened?

It is virtually impossible to separate our personal and professional lives. Joyce Blake tried to do so. What's more, she locked herself into a particular way of thinking that prevented her from asking for help.

She always preferred to handle problems by herself. To ask for help was a sign of weakness. Early in her career she decided she would not discuss personal matters with business associates. She considered that to be unprofessional. Her fear of appearing weak and incompetent—coupled with wanting to be the consummate professional—made her a prisoner of her own listening. Trying to be superhuman does not always work.

It is important to question your attitudes, opinions, perceptions, and points of view on a regular basis to reevaluate their usefulness. Remember, what you are listening to will enhance or limit your ability to produce results.

Though Blake was tired from battling the flood, it never occurred to her to ask a friend or neighbor for assistance. Even after the car accident she would not call Eric Tate and request that the meeting be postponed. Blake went through the entire day not communicating her feelings to anyone. The pressure and stress she was experiencing inhibited her ability to listen.

Your ability to listen empowers you to:

- Crystallize your thinking.
- Organize your thoughts.
- Develop strategies to deal with the situation at hand.
- Quickly alter your strategy.
- Manage change.

If Blake had taken the above steps, she would have been able to effectively deal with the situation. She cannot control the circumstances, but she can manage the way she perceives what is happening around her. It is ironic that at the meeting with Eric

Tate, which she deemed too important to miss, Blake was physically present but mentally absent. Her level of distraction was so high she forgot she had a client meeting. Blake was consumed by her problems and could not concentrate on the Gerbers. Instead of being frank with them and rescheduling the meeting, she chose to proceed.

Blake did most of the talking and very little listening. She did not give the Gerbers the opportunity to tell her what was important to them. Every time they started to speak she interrupted them. Blake voiced her opinion before they had a chance to finish what they were saying. By doing this, she made the Gerbers feel she did not have their best interests at heart. In this environment, the possibility of developing a relationship built on trust and understanding did not exist.

Eric Tate has worked closely with Blake for three years. She is very knowledgeable and had become the company's senior planner. She is always alert and doesn't have to be told anything twice. Tate recognized immediately that Blake was not herself. He knew she had never discussed anything other than business with him. He assumed it would pass and thought nothing more of it until the Gerbers called him in the afternoon refusing to work with her.

When Blake heard his sincere concern for her well-being, she told him how stressed out and overwhelmed she was by the circumstances. Once Blake communicated this to Tate, she was able to take her attention off herself and begin to deal with the broken pipe, the damaged car, and the Gerbers.

Like other examples discussed earlier in this chapter, when Blake was able to be herself and tell Tate and the Gerbers she got caught in the act of being human, she began the process of relationship building. The Gerbers respected her honesty and they agreed to work with her.

SUMMARY

The importance of listening

- If you do not listen you cannot learn. Acquiring information and knowledge enables you to make more educated decisions and take effective action.

Listening and success

- Successful salespeople and companies listen to customers, prospects, employees, management, market, social, and cultural trends.
- Successful salespeople are effective listeners and speakers, open to learning, resourceful and inventive, committed to closing the sale, and holders of a positive attitude.

Language

- Listening is an essential component of the communications process. Listening, speaking, reading, and writing are the four uses of language.
- In this chapter, the broadest definition of language was used—an interchange of meaning that can be accomplished through speaking, writing, gesturing, and pictures.

Perception

- Listening is all-encompassing. You are receiving information through your five senses: sight, hearing, taste, smell, and touch.
- In the face of life's unpredictability, you have a powerful tool—the ability to listen. You cannot control the circumstances, but you can manage the way you perceive what is happening around you.

The communications process

- What doesn't work? Looking into space, pretending to understand, beating around the bush, using technical jargon.
- What works? Eye contact, being nonjudgmental, saying what you mean, asking questions to create clarity.
- Develop criteria for listening. This gives you the foundation you need to listen effectively.
- Fine-tune your powers of observation.

Effective listening

- What inhibits your ability to listen? Preconceived notions, stress, fatigue, likes and dislikes, opinions, perceptions, and points of view.

- What increases your ability to listen? Taking the focus of your attention off yourself and riveting it to your commitment, the speaker, and the situation at hand.
- Acknowledging your anger, fear, and nervousness to yourself and others frees you from their debilitating hold.
- Listening to possibilities will increase your ability to produce results. Once you hear what is possible, your next job is to speak to make it reality.
- Your ability to listen enables you to:
  Crystallize your thinking.
  Organize your thoughts.
  Develop strategies to deal with the situation at hand.
  Quickly alter your strategy.
  Manage change.

Two-way communications

- To engage in effective two-way communications requires a committed listener and a committed speaker.
- Committed listeners are willing to put aside their likes and dislikes, opinions, perceptions, and points of view long enough to hear what someone else is saying.
- Committed speakers are willing to get their point across to the listener not with words alone but by conveying the spirit and intent behind the words.
- Once you start speaking, an astute listener can hear if you are sincere, insincere, committed, uncommitted, competent, incompetent, enthusiastic, or unenthusiastic.
- Do your homework; base your presentation on what is important to the people or company you're meeting with.
- Your attitude can make or break the sale. Think negative and you are setting the stage for disaster. Think positive and you are priming yourself for success.
- Body language can confirm or contradict what you are saying.
- Skilled interviewers can draw people out. Be inventive. Find a way to get and keep your listener's attention.
- Give the speaker your full attention. Hold all phone calls and minimize outside distractions. This indicates to visitors that you are interested in what they have to say.

- Find out why a prospect is saying no or maybe. Listen carefully to the response. The prospect will tell you what you need to know to turn no into yes.

Avoid communication breakdowns

- Speak to the point. Be crystal clear when expressing yourself or your communication is open to misinterpretation.
- Communication hot spots:
  Saying one thing and meaning something else.
  Perceiving what is being said in a distorted way.
- Never assume the listener knows what you mean and your reasons for saying something. No one is a mind reader.
- Observe the impact of what you are saying on the listener. If the person is angry and you expected the opposite reaction, the message didn't get through. Restate your thoughts another way.
- When you make a promise follow through. If you have to revoke your promise, tell the other party as soon as possible to minimize the damage. You lose credibility every time you do not keep your word.
- Be yourself. Honesty and openness help build trust and strong relationships.

Chapter Eight

Negotiating for Success

Roni Abrams

Everything in life is a negotiation. You are negotiating something every day. In sales, negotiating is the key to success.

You negotiate a contract with your prospect. You negotiate with your boss that it is time for a raise. You initiate a new marketing program that must first be approved by upper management. You negotiate with your peers to develop a new sales automation system. You negotiate with your children who want to watch TV past their bedtime. You and your spouse negotiate over where to go for dinner.

In this chapter you will learn how to:

1. Prepare for a negotiation.
2. Be an effective communicator.
3. Develop relationships.

You will discover how to create win-win agreements; develop your own negotiating strategy; define, in advance, your options and terms; determine your risk levels and limits; and know when to compromise or stand your ground.

Negotiating means different things to different people. To some, the person who remains standing after both parties have beaten each other over the head with a club is the winner. Another view of negotiating is the completion of a transaction by meeting each party's conditions of satisfaction. The focus of the material in this chapter is on the latter, win-win negotiations.

Let us examine what works and does not work when we are negotiating with prospects, clients, employees, employers, vendors, family, and friends.

What doesn't work?

- Not caring about the other person's needs.
- Yelling and screaming.
- Inflexibility.
- Trying to take all the marbles.
- Having preconceived notions.
- Not listening.

What works?

- The ability to verbalize the other person's viewpoint.
- Staying calm.
- Being flexible.
- Creating a give-and-take environment.
- Maintaining an open dialogue.
- Listening.

PREPARATION IS ESSENTIAL TO SUCCESSFUL NEGOTIATIONS

Consider the following question. Would your enter the New York marathon or the Boston marathon without training? Chances are you would not, since it could prove disastrous to your health.

Preparation is essential to successful negotiations. You have to do your homework before you start speaking across a table to anyone.

First and foremost, you have to be *clear* about what it is you are negotiating. *Clarity* is one of the cornerstones for effective negotiations. If you do not know *exactly* what it is you want, it's virtually impossible to ask for it.

Example. Two brothers are fighting over a letter they received from Aunt Jane in France. Their father determines the boys cannot handle the situation on their own. Since the letter is addressed to both of them, he reads it aloud. The moment their father leaves, the boys start fighting again. He comes back and is perplexed that a fair solution is not working. He sits the brothers down and after a quiet discussion discovers that one wants the stamp and the other wants the letter.

If each boy had been asked to define his objective, his reply would have been, "I want the letter." But initially, neither one clearly identified what his conditions of satisfaction were and could have fought forever.

STEPS FOR CREATING CLARITY

1. Identify your objective. Ask yourself, "What do I want to accomplish?"
2. Determine your interests and concerns behind the objective. They can be referred to as your conditions of satisfaction, what you need to be satisfied, regardless of the circumstances. Be specific.

Example. John Jones is selling his house in Pennsylvania. His objective is to get $100,000 for it. Jane Smith offers $80,000. Jones and Smith could debate over the price for weeks. If Jones did his homework and determined his specific interests and concerns, he could expedite the negotiation.

Jones's interests and concerns are:

- He has been relocated to California by his company.
- He has six weeks to move his family.
- He has 24 rooms of furniture that he cannot take with him.
- He would like to buy some of the property on which his present house is located.

Smith's interests and concerns are:

- She has been relocated by her company.
- She has five weeks to move her family.
- She needs a large house in an excellent school district.
- She must live close to new corporate offices.

Smith offers Jones:

• Availability of the barn on the premises to store his furniture for up to two years.
• Buyback rights for up to two years on five acres of the property.
• Her ability to obtain a mortgage in one week.

An agreement was reached. Money is not always the issue. You and the other party are actually negotiating over interests and concerns. It is crucial that you identify them, yours as well as the person's you are dealing with. To do this requires that you utilize your interviewing skills to ask questions and listen to the answers.

It is important to gain as much information as you can about the people you will be dealing with. This knowledge could prove useful during the negotiation. Find out if the person is single, married, has children, owns a home, rents an apartment, and interests and hobbies. Explore the person's business responsibilities, years in current position, past positions and with what companies. Masterful negotiators put themselves in the other person's shoes.

Remember not to get locked into a position regarding your objective. Once you get locked into a position, it is very hard to move off. Inflexibility will not help you reach your goal.

If Jones insisted on only receiving $100,000 in cash and did not explore the options, it would have cost him at least $20,000 to ship the furniture cross-country. In addition, it could have taken him longer to find a buyer and he might have had to leave Pennsylvania before selling the house.

TIME FRAME

Time is a major factor in any negotiation. How urgent is the situation? Set the pace. Determine your time frame and the other person's time frame. Time is a tool that can accelerate or limit the negotiation. If you need something right away and the other party has all the time in the world, it's possible that party will try to wear you down. Use time to your best advantage.

OPTIONS

Develop an alternative. It enables you to negotiate from strength.
Devise your alternative plan by examining your options in advance.
An alternative plan recognizes the possibility that you cannot negotiate an agreement to your satisfaction. A backup plan helps you to
determine if an agreement would serve your best interests.

For argument's sake, say Smith needed two months to secure a
mortgage. Jones thought that was unacceptable and continued
looking for a buyer. He was unable to find one that could get a mortgage sooner. On the other hand, if Jones had no time restrictions,
two months may have been preferable.

What would Jones's alternative have been if he would not sell his
house? He might rent the house, tear it down and sell the property,
or have someone live in the house rent-free if he or she would maintain it for him. With his alternative plan in place, Jones can decide
whether it is to his benefit to wait the two months for Smith or make
other arrangements. An alternative plan is an excellent way to
gauge the effectiveness of a negotiated agreement.

Be knowledgeable about the product/service you are selling
and/or buying. Your familiarity with the variables can help you
make effective choices and decisions. Here are a few of the questions you should ask or be prepared to answer:

What are the benefits and features?

How can the product/service best suit our purposes?

Is it new?

Is it used?

Is it slightly damaged?

What is the markup? Is there room for movement up or down?

How soon can it be delivered?

How much discount?

*Learn to determine your objectives, interests and concerns, time frames,
and options in advance. These four elements examined from your and the
other party's point of view, coupled with product knowledge, comprise
your negotiating strategy.* **Your negotiating strategy will influence
the way that you speak and the actions you will take.**

Example.   A women's sportswear manufacturer was having difficulty with its fabric supplier. The manufacturer was designing a new line for the upcoming season. Buyers were coming into the showroom and the garments had to be ready for market week. There was no room for error: The future of the business was at stake.

The president of the manufacturing company called the fabric vendor repeatedly for assurance that the fabric would be delivered as promised. The fabric never came. The president, in desperation, asked the vendor the cause of the problem. He was told the drivers' union was on strike and no deliveries were being made.

The manufacturer saw a viable option and followed through. He hired and paid for outside drivers and trucks to get the fabric on time.

- What was the manufacturer's objective? To stay in business.
- What was the vendor's objective? To maintain the current level of revenue and accounts.
- What were the manufacturer's interests and concerns? To produce a new line of merchandise to show buyers during market week.
- What were the vendor's interests and concerns? To accommodate the customers during the strike.
- What was the manufacturer's time frame? Now.
- What was the vendor's time frame? Now.
- What were the manufacturer's options? To pick up the fabric.
- What were the vendor's options? He initially did not see any or he would have suggested an alternative solution himself.

The vendor was not able to suggest innovative ways to maintain operations and fill orders during the strike. This cost him future business. To make matters worse, the vendor stopped communicating with customers. No one has all the answers, especially in the middle of a crisis. If the vendor had immediately alerted customers to the impending strike, they could have developed a number of ways to deal with the situation together.

Your ability to listen to possibilities and create options depends on focusing on the objective and the interests and concerns. **It is important to separate what you are negotiating for from the people and events.** Otherwise, you merge what you want with your emotions, ego, and perceptions. This results in lack of clarity. You become part of the problem instead of the solution.

*The outcome of any negotiation is determined by how **you** think and how the **other person** thinks. You can be crystal clear on your strategy and yet be blind to what is possible.*

Example. Tom Wren is a senior account representative for a company that sells medical equipment. The firm's inventory and cash flow is low. Large contracts waiting to be signed depend on the company's ability to procure enough equipment to fill the orders. It is Wren's responsibility to get the equipment, no matter what.

Wren's negotiating strategy is (1) to get the best price possible, and (2) even more important, to get the most favorable payment terms. He plans to exert pressure on the pricing. When the vendor resists, Wren will use this to negotiate a longer repayment period.

Notice how clear Wren's strategy is. However, he has locked himself into a particular way of thinking. His choices and actions are based on being able to have either a good price or good terms. The possibility of having both doesn't enter into the picture.

If you say that something cannot happen, it will not happen. This occurs not because you are incapable of making things happen but because what you say will leave you open or closed to possibilities.

Wren's predecision would definitely impact the outcome. He had forgotten that it may be possible to have all his conditions of satisfaction met. **Remind yourself to stay open to all possibilities.**

POSITIVE COMMITMENTS

In most negotiations, there are areas of opportunity that enable you to accommodate customer requests.

Example. Karla Duke is negotiating with a client who is interested in purchasing a Christmas order of 600 to 1,000 wall plaques shown in last year's catalogue. Duke found out the item had gone up in price by $5, from $20 to $25. In discussing this with the client, she learned the $5 increase would put the client over its budget.

What is Duke's strategy?

- Duke's objective is to get the sale.
- Her interests and concerns are to satisfy her client and to continue a long, established relationship.
- The time frame is now.
- Her area of opportunity/possibility is to create compromise pricing.

The option she chooses to follow is to take advantage of her company's in-house manufacturing capabilities. She initiates a dialogue with the director of operations to explore a price range between $21 and $23. They agree the company will generate more revenue from the increased volume and offer the client a price he can work into his budget.

Many salespeople hear a request from a prospect or client, regardless of what it is, and say, "Oh, no!" The salesperson is setting the stage for an uphill battle. Watch what you say. Your speaking will make it so. You have a choice. **You can view the request as a problem or as a challenge.**

Duke was committed to maintaining the relationship with the client. Her *commitment* moved her to take action. It gave her the courage to contact the director of operations and find a way to accommodate the account. Tom Wren also operated out of his *commitment* to buy the medical equipment no matter what. People take action based on their *commitments*.

You need to determine if the parties involved in a negotiation are committed to seeing it through to a win-win conclusion. If they are not, the negotiation is doomed to fail. How can you make this determination? Listen to what people are saying.

Uncommitted speaking:

"I really don't want to bother."
"Call me next year."
"Let's handle it now or else call the whole thing off."

Committed speaking:

"We will find a way."

"Be patient. A solution is just waiting to be uncovered."

"We work well as a team."

With commitment, all things are possible in a negotiation. You can be empowered to bore through solid rock. Miracles happen every day and it is not by accident.

Duke recognized that relationships need to be nurtured to grow. She never forgets that she is negotiating with a human being who has feelings and emotions just like hers.

NEGOTIATE TO MAINTAIN RELATIONSHIPS

Always complete your negotiation so all parties leave in a good state of mind. Otherwise, you will not get them to go along with you again. They will be ready and waiting for you next time and will do to you what they think you did to them—a very difficult position to begin a negotiation.

Customers who are seeking special customer service and customized products often consider them to be more valuable than a discounted price. The salesperson must understand the prospect's interests and concerns to be able to detect if this is the case.

Example: The Real Issue. George Peters is the new vice president of sales for a national chain of toy stores. He inherited an automated sales system that has become obsolete in less than two years. The company is expanding operations into Europe, and it must have a computer system that supports its growth.

Peters contacted numerous firms and has narrowed his choice down to two. Both the Alpha Company and the Beta Company have had extensive meetings with him.

Peters's objective: To set up an automated sales system.

Peters's interests and concerns:

- To acquire a system that can expand to accommodate growth for the next five years.
- The system should be up and running before the summer.
- All appropriate personnel should be trained to use the system as soon as possible.
- Easy access to service and training personnel.

Time frame: It's now March 1. He wants the system operational
no later then May 1.
Options: Upgrade old equipment until a new system can be
installed to handle the European orders.

Alpha Company offers Peters:

- A system that can accommodate the company's growth.
- The system will be operational by May 1.
- Personnel will be trained by May 31.
- Service and training personnel available 9 AM to 1 PM Monday
  through Friday.

Beta Company offers Peters:

- A system that can accommodate the company's growth.
- The system operational by April 1.
- Personnel trained by May 1.
- Service and training personnel available 8 AM to 8 PM seven
  days a week.

George Peters chose to work with the Beta Company even though
he would be paying 30 percent more than the Alpha Company
would have charged.

The salesperson for Alpha Company met the requirements.
However, the salesperson did not hear Peters's main concern and
its urgency. He said, "This time, the company cannot afford to make
any mistakes." Price was not the issue.

There is no debate over the importance of service as a sales tool.
However, for some buyers, price is everything. To meet this challenge, a salesperson must be creative, willing to take risks, and open
to developing new markets.

TIME FOR LISTENING

Susan Clark is an account representative for a 35-year-old company
that manufactures gift clocks. She has been with the company six
years and sells to department stores.

Clark, a keen observer of trends, has tracked the buying habits of
middle-income families and sees they are infatuated with discount

stores. She believes her company would make a great deal of money if it opened up this market.

Clark took the initiative and discussed the idea with the vice president of sales and the company president. She got approval from the president to proceed and promptly got an appointment with the biggest discount chain store in the country. Clark presented the company's clocks and the buyer told her they were great but much too expensive.

The buyer made design recommendations so Clark's company could modify the clocks to meet the discount store's price requirements. He told Clark that if the company made these modifications, he would place a substantial order. In addition, the clocks would be featured in the chain's advertising for all stores coast to coast. Clark requested that the buyer put in writing the modifications he suggested and what he offered to do. He complied with her request.

Clark gave the president and vice president of sales a detailed report about the meeting. She showed them the letter of intent. Within one month of Clark's meeting with the buyer, management decided to proceed. All appropriate divisions of the company were then mobilized to design and market this new line of inexpensive clocks.

Clark's ability to listen for possibilities enabled her to spot a consumer buying trend that proved to be beneficial to the company and herself. She keeps herself well informed through books, magazines, newspapers, radio, television, movies, and networking with people involved in many industries and professions. Clark remains open to learning and looks for ways to apply her knowledge.

Her willingness to take the initiative on this project was a signal to the vice president of sales that she is ready and able to take on more responsibilities. She has demonstrated that she would be a valuable asset to the management team.

Negotiations are not reserved for prospects and clients only. Successful salespeople negotiate with peer groups and management as well.

Clark had been involved with three separate negotiations, each interrelated. She had to solidify the forces within the company to get the go-ahead. Then she had to sell the national discount chain store buyer. The following outlines the objective,

interests and concerns, time frame, and options for each of the
three negotiations.

Meeting with vice president of sales

Clark's objective: To open the discount store market.

Clark's interests and concerns:

- To gain his support in her concept of opening up the discount
  market.
- To explore the potential of creating an inexpensive product
  line.
- As a team, to present the idea to the company's president.
- To be promoted to manager of discount store sales.

Time frame: Now.

Options: Continue to sell exclusively to department stores.

Meeting with company president

Clark's objective: To open the discount store market.

Clark's interests and concerns:

- To get his support in the concept of opening up the discount
  market.
- To explore the potential of creating an inexpensive product
  line.
- To get approval to proceed.
- To be promoted to manager of discount store sales.

Time frame: Now.

Options:

- Present suggestions to cut costs.
  1. Manufacture product in another country.
  2. Acquire an existing company that has an inexpensive
     product line.
- Work with other discount store chains.
- Explore other markets.

Meeting with national discount chain store buyer

Clark's objective: To develop a major new account.

Clark's interests and concerns:

- To open the buyer's eyes to the product's potential.
- To determine the price range and modifications of the product if necessary.
- To obtain a letter of intent to buy.

Time frame: Now.

Options:

- Arrange meeting between buyer, company president, and vice president of sales.
- Present product to other discount stores.

Many salespeople back away from taking the initiative out of fear that they have more to lose than to gain. Clark clearly did not see it that way. Here is her "risk list" and how she perceived the project.

Negative risk factors

- Idea rejected by vice president of sales.
- Upper management disapproves.
- Laughed at by peers.
- Lost time and effort.

Positive risk factors

- Substantial increase in income.
- Upper management will respect her ideas.
- Promotion.
- Become a role model in the company.
- Develop new industry contacts.

Risk taking can be interpreted as leaving yourself open to be damaged. Risk taking can also be interpreted as a creative act that requires courage and conviction.

All the possibilities represented by Clark's options and positive risk factors would not exist if she did not try to be an innovator.

In a negotiation, taking a risk based on a whim can be dangerous. However, taking an educated risk based on your negotiating strategy, product *knowledge, and an understanding of the other party's viewpoint and needs could **turn a difficult situation into a win-win.***

Tony Leeds has been negotiating with Rice Inc. for three months to print its annual report and stationery. Rice is internationally recognized for conducting medical research. The company has facilities in 15 countries around the world.

Leeds has worked with Sam Perry, Rice's purchasing agent, for 10 years. This year Rice has spent millions developing a new corporate image. The annual report and stationery will be the first printed matter to reflect the changes.

After endless meetings, Perry still refuses to sign a contract with Leeds. Perry believes Leeds can cut corners and give him a better price. Leeds's knowledge of printing is legendary. If there is a way to save money he will find it. Leeds has already worked miracles for Perry. The price he has been given is the best price.

Leeds looked Perry straight in the eye and said the following. "I have always given you the best price and the finest quality printing. This job requires extra care to maintain the integrity of the design and the impact it is intended to make. To cut any more corners would destroy what the company is trying so hard to accomplish. As much as I want this business, I will end the negotiation now rather than do what I know doesn't work. Here is the contract. Sign it or feel free to find another printer."

Perry signed the contract.

Perry knew Leeds is committed to his company's success. They have had a mutually beneficial relationship spanning 10 years. He has always trusted his judgment, knowledge, and standards for excellence. Leeds has always given him the best prices and finest quality printing.

Leeds took an educated risk. His response to Perry was based on a relationship built on trust. Leeds wanted Perry to know he gave him the best price. To clearly make the point and give credence to what he said, Leeds informed Perry he would rather not have the business than do something that would hurt the company.

Leeds's intent was to support Rice in achieving its goals. Perry heard it that way. That is why he signed the contract. If Leeds had intended his statement to be a threat, the outcome of the negotiation would have been very different.

Leeds knew he had to be responsible for what he says. He was aware that once he introduced the possibility of ending the negotiation he had to be prepared for Perry to take him up on it. If you are not willing to end a negotiation, don't say so.

Self-knowledge, product knowledge, an understanding of human nature, and a fully developed negotiation strategy are tools you can use to determine your own risk levels and limits. With this information, you are empowered to know when to compromise, walk, or stand your ground.

TEAM NEGOTIATING

There is no rule that says you have to work alone. Team negotiating is encouraged by many companies. The advantages of a collaborative effort are maximum use of time and energy, a constant flow of fresh ideas, and partners to strategize with.

Linen Ltd. supplies towels, bedding, and tablecloths to hotels across the United States. The company has divided the country into eight regions, and each region has a negotiating team. The team that generates the most revenue is given a bonus and is honored at Linen's annual corporate gala.

The northeast team has been honored five years in a row. The team members are Carol Stevens, regional vice president; Bob Stone, sales manager; and Paul Ray, account representative. They attribute their success to in-depth preparation and effective communications skills. Most important, team members have learned to use their individual talents to strengthen the team.

Before any negotiation, the team meets to develop its negotiating strategy. Together the team members determine the objectivs, interests and concerns, time frame, and options. This ensures that they speak as one during the negotiation. United they succeed. Divided they fail.

Each member is responsible for gathering specific information about the prospective account and the people they will be dealing with. The more they know about the other party's needs and point of view, the better.

Nothing is taken for granted. They review all aspects of their products and services. Then they look to see how they can satisfy the prospect's needs.

They have regularly scheduled meetings to practice and sharpen their presentation skills. They know who will cover what topic and have created a system of signals that lets speakers know if they are going on too long or if someone wants to add something.

The commitment of the team is: close the sale! As a result, individual agendas and personal differences are resolved outside the negotiation room so they can focus solely on the negotiation. They will not have anything stand in the way of their success.

Stevens, Stone, and Ray are brainstorming over an upcoming negotiation. Ray tells the others that blue bedding is the only way to go. Stone says green would be as good or better. Ray interrupts Stone and insists that blue is best. They begin to argue over the choice of color.

Stevens intercedes and acknowledges both points of view. She thanks each of them for expressing their opinion. She says that until they talk with the prospect, a final decision cannot be made.

The fastest way to induce conflict is to speak as if your word is law.

Ray had forgotten that either you have an opinion or it has you. Once reminded of this, Ray can relax and listen to other suggestions. He no longer needs to impose his opinion on the other team members. Ray gets back in touch with his commitment to do what is best for the prospect and close the sale.

Stevens had indicated to Stone and Ray that she heard and understood their points of view. Whether she agreed or disagreed with either of them was not the point. She gave credence and respect to what they were saying. She did not enter the debate. Stone and Ray no longer had to continue trying to convince Stevens or each other.

Let the other person know you understand him or her and be sure that person understands you. Otherwise the negotiation will not move forward.

Stevens, in an appropriate, responsible manner, let Ray know he has a right to his opinion and that it is *only* an opinion. Everyone is entitled to opinions. In a negotiation, all parties must be mindful of keeping their opinions off the table or it will collapse under the weight.

Stay on purpose. Do not let your likes and dislikes sidetrack you from producing results. Catch yourself reacting to the people and events around you. "He is too tall." "She is too skinny." "Her clothes are terrible." "The weather is getting me down." "The conference table is the wrong size." Your opinions, preferences, and emotions change all the time. Your commitments are unshakable.

Stevens, Stone, and Ray have another commitment that enables them to work so well together as a team. It is their *commitment to relationship*. They have built a strong foundation for their relationship based on mutual trust and respect. By developing the same type of relationship with their prospects, they can turn them into long-term accounts.

Trust is one of the key ingredients in establishing successful relationships. The question is: How do you create an environment where all parties trust each other?

The Apple Hotel presentation. The northeast negotiation team has completed its preparation for a meeting with Edward Thomas, vice president of Apple Hotels.

Apple has acquired 35 facilities in New York, New Jersey, Connecticut, and Rhode Island. It is renovating the properties and reexamining all vendor agreements. Linen Ltd. has not worked with Apple Hotels in the past. The team is determined to add Apple to its family of accounts.

At the initial meeting, Stevens briefly introduces Linen's products and services. She asks Thomas to tell them about Apple Hotels so they can understand what is important to them. Each team member speaks with Thomas to find out Apple's exact interests and concerns.

Thomas requested that they tell him the feasibility and cost of having 100 percent cotton sheets instead of a blend. Stone said he would look into the matter and call him tomorrow at 3 PM.

Ray asked Thomas to go into more detail about the children's pool party promotion. Ray suggested that Linen Ltd. could supply towels featuring cartoon characters for the youngsters. Thomas thought the idea was great. Ray said he would get the specifics to him by the end of the week and would call Friday at 10 AM. The meeting lasted two hours and was considered productive by all.

A second meeting was scheduled for the following Wednesday to go over any additional requirements that Apple may have. Before Wednesday's meeting, Stone and Ray had obtained information on the sheets and pool towels and discussed it with Thomas.

At the second meeting, the team outlined the products, services, quantities, and costs for Thomas. He indicated there were no additional requirements. He was extremely pleased with the team's proposal. However, he wanted a better price. Stevens told him they would put their heads together to see what could be done. She arranged to call him Friday at 2 PM.

When Stevens called Thomas, she said the team went to bat for him. Top management believes Apple Hotels would be an asset to Linen Ltd. In fact, Apple could become one of the firm's largest accounts and a lower price based on volume would be in Linen's best interests. The price Stevens quoted worked for Thomas and an agreement was reached.

Right from the start, the team had focused on the interests and concerns of Apple Hotels. They had encouraged Thomas to do most of the talking. Because Ray was paying close attention to Thomas, he saw a way to support Apple's advertising and marketing campaign geared to children. By supplying pool towels with cartoon characters, Linen Ltd. offered a service that gave it an important competitive edge.

Questions that could not be answered on the spot were acknowledged and a specific person took responsibility for getting the answer. That person also set up a telephone meeting with Thomas stating a date and time for the call to give him the information he requested. Each team member called Thomas as promised.

Thomas made himself accessible to the team. He kept his word by being available for all scheduled calls and he was on time for all meetings. In addition, Thomas gave the team the the detailed information it needed to develop a win-win agreement.

Stevens, Stone, and Ray had to go the extra mile with Linen's management to get the best price for Apple. If they hadn't, the sale would have slipped through their fingers.

Both parties proved themselves to be trustworthy by:

- Listening to what the other had to say.
- Putting the other's interests and concerns first.
- Maintaining an open dialogue.
- Keeping their promises.

KEEP YOUR WORD

It is imperative that you keep your word in order to establish credibility with the other person. Follow up when you promise to do something. If you cannot fulfill your promise, notify the other party as soon as possible to minimize the damage. The prospect and/or account is allocating time, money, and resources based on your promises.

Barbara Mann is a senior account executive with an international electronics company specializing in calculators and watches. The company has an impeccable reputation for service. Most accounts have been with the company for over eight years.

Mann is responsible for selling merchandise in the corporate gifts division. This Christmas she closed more sales than in the last three years. However, her excitement was cut short. She started getting angry calls from customers complaining the gifts had not arrived on time. Mann told the customers she spoke with she would find out what happened and call them back that afternoon.

She immediately contacted the company's distribution center and was informed there had been a flood in the facility. The merchandise would not be shipped due to water damage. Mann and the vice president of sales came up with a plan to minimize the inconvenience being experienced by their customers.

As promised, Mann called each account back. She acknowledged the situation, apologized for the inconvenience, and offered to replace their order with a more expensive item at no additional cost. Nothing could change the fact that the gifts were not delivered on time. In an act of good faith, the company made this offer to accommodate its long-term accounts.

Because the customers had received years of excellent service, all was quickly forgiven. Not one account was lost. In the end, it was the company's credibility that enabled it to weather the storm.

Unless you have no intention of ever dealing with a prospect or account again—keep your word. Your integrity will make or break the relationship. Every time you don't follow through on a promise, you are diminishing your credibility.

Break your promise often enough and no one will take you seriously. In a negotiation, that is the kiss of death. Communications will break down because the other party will no longer speak to you in an open manner. People will not reveal their interests and concerns to someone they do not trust. Once you lose your credibility, it's almost impossible to get it back.

Effective communication is at the heart of all successful negotiations. A negotiation is simply people listening and speaking to one another to produce a result that is mutually satisfying to all parties. Masterful negotiators combine impeccable preparation with highly developed interpersonal skills.

DEALING WITH ANGER

Have you ever been angry with a prospect or client? Most sales-people say yes. Anger is a powerful human emotion that can block communications and stop any negotiation. Self-knowledge and an understanding of human nature are needed to manage your anger as well as someone else's. By itself, anger is neither good nor bad. *How* you deal with the anger is what makes the difference.

John Baron is a certified financial planner who works for Securities USA selling stocks, bonds, and mutual funds. He is going to meet with Tim Matts, president of High Tech Industries, to offer financial planning services to the company's employees. The only contact between them has been two telephone conversations.

Matts is on the phone when Baron enters his office. He continues the conversation for 10 minutes without acknowledging Baron. The instant he hangs up he yells at Baron, telling him this meeting is a waste of time and he has five minutes to give him. Baron doesn't know what he has done to get Matts so upset. He tries to defend himself and yells back. The situation deteriorates and Baron is asked to leave.

Your perception of what is going on around you will influence the outcome. Baron thought he had done something wrong to elicit such a response. By taking Matts's actions personally, he rendered himself ineffective. Baron allowed himself to be pushed off purpose by the circumstances. Instead of holding fast to his commitment to close the sale, he shifted the focus of attention to himself.

The moment Baron did this, he could no longer move the meeting forward. He became deaf, blind, and dumb in the face of Matts's anger. Since Baron felt he was being attacked, he responded in kind. The meeting became a war of words.

Communications between the two of them closed down. Neither one could hear what the other was saying. During a heated debate, no matter how accurately the facts are presented, the only thing the individuals involved perceive is that they are being attacked. It takes tremendous skill to remain calm and maintain your objectivity while someone is screaming at you.

It is almost impossible to communicate with someone who is consumed by anger because that person's ability to effectively listen and speak is greatly impaired. Wait until the initial wave of anger subsides and then speak. Do not permit yourself to be caught up in the other person's anger. Otherwise you stop listening and will not be able to determine when that moment has arrived. *To help defuse a volatile situation, you must know when to speak and when to remain silent.*

Take personal responsibility for managing your anger. Angry faces and words will not win friends or close sales. To prevent a confrontation from escalating, simply state what works and does not work for you. No one can argue with the way you feel.

If Baron had not taken what was happening personally, he would have been able to:

- Separate himself from the circumstances.
- Observe Matts's behavior.
- Immediately recognize there was a problem.
- Determine his conditions of satisfaction.
- Identify his options.

Baron could have analyzed the situation to come to the conclusion he had nothing to do with the upset. He could have examined the following facts:

- They hardly knew each other.
- This was the first time they had met.
- He had not spoken before Matts yelled at him.
- Matts would not have agreed to a meeting if he didn't feel there was a need for his services.

If Baron had been able to quickly identify these points at the start of the meeting, he would have initiated a new dialogue with Matts instead of being trapped into reacting without thinking. If Baron had remained composed and not taken Matts's actions personally, he would have been able to come up with at least two viable options.

1. End the meeting and reschedule it.
2. Redirect attention to the welfare of Matts's employees and continue the meeting.

ATTENTION GETTERS

To communicate with someone, you need the person's undivided attention. If you do not have a committed listener, you are wasting his or her time and yours. Be creative in getting another person's attention. Try the following:

- Say something outrageous.
- Say something funny.
- Do something startling or out of the ordinary.

For any of these strategies to be effective, be sure you have a clear sense of the person you are dealing with and what is appropriate given the circumstances.

Once you have the other person's attention, make the most of the opportunity. Ask questions to find out what is important and listen to the answers. Be well versed on the subject so you can speak in a brief, concise manner. Know what you want and ask for it. **Organizing your thoughts creates clarity for you and the person listening.**

Every negotiation is different. Even if you have given 300 presentations, no two are exactly alike. You are dealing with human beings, not machines, and people are unpredictable. Stay flexible and adapt to the changing environment. Your one-hour meeting with the purchasing agent could end up as 15 minutes with the company president. Whether you have five minutes or five days, learn to present your material in whatever time frame is available to you.

Keep in mind that the moment you start speaking, an astute listener is discovering a great deal about you. The listener can determine your level of competence, confidence, and sincerity by the way you present yourself and your product or service. If you are not believable, you will not close the sale.

SPECIFIC GUIDELINES PRODUCE RESULTS

It is extremely important that you make *effective* requests to the other party, members of your negotiating team, and your support staff. *The more specific your request, the more likely you will get what you ask for.*

John Baron asked his assistant to compile a list of case studies showing the benefits to companies offering financial planning services to their employees. Baron planned to use this information during his meeting with Matts.

Baron's assistant knew he would be traveling to four other branch offices and asked which office she should send it to. She asked him how soon he needed the list, and whether the material was for his own use or should be prepared as a formal document to be given to the prospect.

Baron left out three elements in his request: (1) where it should be sent, (2) the time frame, and (3) the format. Without these specific instructions he would not get what he needed. Fortunately, his assistant realized she was being given only a partial set of requirements and got the missing information.

Here is Baron's request restated to produce results.

- Please compile a list of case studies showing the benefits to companies offering financial planning services to their employees.
- I want this material in a presentation kit to be at the Chicago office next Wednesday morning at 9 AM.

STEPS FOR MAKING EFFECTIVE REQUESTS

Clearly state:

- What you need.
- What form you need it in.
- Where you want it to go and to whom.
- When you need it.

After you make a request, listen for a committed response. Be certain you are getting an authentic yes or no. It is difficult to negotiate with someone who does not follow through.

Listen for:

- Someone who says yes but means no.
- Someone who says no but means yes.
- Someone who refuses to commit one way or the other.

Do not proceed until you know what the other person has agreed or not agreed to do. Once this has been determined, you can take effective action. For example, Baron's assistant might not be able to fulfill his request. He is one of four financial planners she works for and she is overwhelmed with assignments.

She offers to ask if any of the other assistants could help him. Baron thanks her for the counteroffer. He tells her not to approach anyone else until he has spoken to his three associates. The other planners were amenable, and Baron and his assistant rearrange her work schedule. His assistant could then promise to have the list ready to meet his deadline.

When you have elicited an authentic promise, you can then establish a system to follow up with that person. Baron tells his assistant he will call her in three days to see how the list is coming. If she is unable to obtain the information, Baron has enough time to find another source or develop an alternative approach.

The way in which you state your request can help or hinder you in achieving the goal. People are listening beyond the words.

"I'm requesting that you sign the contract today. We have the best product to suit your needs. You will always have access to the company because I will service your account." The person is talking in a whisper, looking at the floor, and slumped over in his chair. He is saying one thing but conveying another.

FALSE ASSUMPTIONS

Janet Brooks is the senior account representative for ComputerView Ltd. The firm has developed a revolutionary software and hardware package designed to help companies streamline their operating procedures. Brooks believes the products would be very beneficial to government as well. She has arranged a meeting with 10 California state officials.

Brooks asked the officials to describe how their respective agency is organized and how they believed it could be run more efficiently. She then spoke in great detail about the technical aspects of ComputerView's products. "Are there any questions?" she asked at the close of her remarks. After a long pause, a single hand went up. The question raised was very elementary and she answered it quickly.

What was her next move? "Is anyone ready to start working with ComputerView?" she asked. The silence in the room was deafening.

Brooks repeated her request with some anger in her voice. There was no reply. Finally, a man stood up and said, "It is clear to all of us that you know *your* business. The problem is *we* don't know very much about computers."

Brooks thanked him for telling her. He had given her the opportunity to turn the situation around. "Everyone makes mistakes and with your permission I will rectify this one," she said. She gave them a fun, easy-to-comprehend overview of the firm's products.

Brooks did not indicate before the meeting that those coming should possess a certain level of technical expertise. She based her presentation on the assumption that the attendees would be knowledgeable about computers and software.

She went into the meeting with a preconceived idea about what the group knew about computers. If she had ascertained their computer literacy at the start of the meeting, she could have adjusted the presentation to satisfy the officials' needs.

Remember, your opinions and points of view can pull you off purpose, focusing attention on yourself and not on the prospect.

Brooks was not listening to or observing her audience. She always had lively question-and-answer sessions. The lack of participation and the fact that the only question asked was a very basic one should have been a red flag that indicated the group lacked a technical background.

It was courageous for that official to make his statement. Many people are unwilling to speak up during a meeting because they fear they will appear ignorant. They do not want to appear foolish to their peers; this is a powerful force that influences what someone will say or do in a group situation.

Once you lose your listeners' attention you are finished. They are physically in the room but mentally in Tahiti. To close a sale in this environment is almost impossible. Rarely will people tell you why they have stopped listening.

Brooks was given a gift. To her credit, she was quick on her feet. She acknowledged what had happened and took responsibility for it. She immediately got the group's attention and gave a presentation that was both educational and entertaining. She asked for their business again. This time 10 hands went up. She turned a no-win situation into a win-win for all.

SUMMARY

Negotiations

- Win-win negotiations occur at the close of a transaction that meets each party's conditions of satisfaction.
- Win-win agreements are generated by flexible, open, creative thinking.
- The opposite of this is to get locked into a position regarding your objective. Once you become entrenched in the position, it's very hard to move off.

Preparing for a negotiation

- Clarity is one of the cornerstones for effective negotiations. If you do not know exactly what it is you want, it's virtually impossible to ask for it.
- Identify your objective. What do you want to accomplish?
- Determine your interests and concerns behind the objective — your conditions of satisfaction.
- Find out about the people you will be dealing with, their backgrounds in business, their talents and hobbies.
- Know everything regarding your product and/or service.
- Establish your time frame. Is the situation urgent or do you have all the time in the world? Use it to your best advantage.
- Listen for possibilities and create options by staying focused on your objective, interests, and concerns.
- Develop an alternative plan as a backup if you cannot negotiate an agreement to your satisfaction.
- Identify the factors influencing and motivating the other party. Masterful negotiators put themselves in the other person's shoes.
- Learn to determine your objectives, interests and concerns, time frames, and options in advance. These four elements examined from your and the other party's point of view, coupled with product knowledge, comprise your "negotiating strategy."
- Self-knowledge, an understanding of human nature, and a fully developed negotiating strategy are your tools to deter-

mine your risk levels and limits. This information helps you to decide when to compromise, walk, or stand your ground.

Team negotiating

- The advantages of a collaborative effort include maximum application of information, efficient use of time, and a constant flow of fresh ideas.
- Before a negotiation, the team devises its strategy.
- The team's mutual agreement on strategy will ensure a single, unified voice during the negotiation.
- Team members should be well rehearsed in their presentation skills. They must know who is responsible for each aspect of the presentation and be adept at using a system of signals to alert the speaker if the presentation is running too long or if a team member wants to add a point.

Engaging in a negotiation

- Effective communications are at the heart of all successful negotiations.
- Maintain your objectivity by separating what you are negotiating for from the people and events. Otherwise you become part of the problem instead of the solution. Remember, you either have an opinion or it has you.
- Let the other person know you understand his or her point of view and be sure that person understands yours. Put the other's interests and concerns first. Listen more and speak less.
- Listen for committed speaking. People take action based on their commitments. Your opinions, preferences, and emotions change all the time. Your commitments are unshakable.
- Use your interviewing skills to discover what the buyer values most. To some, service and customized products are more important than a discounted price. To others, price is everything.
- Relationships are built on trust. Keep your word to establish credibility. Follow up when you promise to do something. If you cannot fulfill your promise, notify the other person as soon as possible to minimize the damage.

- Anger is neither good nor bad. It's how you deal with it that makes the difference. You are not usually the cause of another person's upset.
- Attention—once you have it, speak in a brief, concise manner. Organizing your thoughts creates clarity for you and those listening.
- Be specific when making a request. State (*a*) what you need, (*b*) what form you need it in, (*c*) where you want it to go, and (*d*) when you need it.
- Preconceived ideas and assumptions will limit your ability to listen and observe what is occurring around you. Instead, stay open, flexible, and willing to change direction.
- Masterful negotiators combine impeccable preparation with highly developed interpersonal skills.

Chapter Nine

Writing for Salespeople

Mel Haber

Writing is an integral part of every salesperson's job. Letters, memos, trip reports, and proposals are among the various types of writing that must be done often and effectively. While the writing must be persuasive, clear, and concise, it should not be overly time consuming. The less time salespeople spend writing, the more time they can spend in seeing prospects. In short, effective written communication can lead to increased sales.

Unfortunately, writing effectively is not easy for most people, and that includes salespeople. The two main problems most people have in writing are organizing ideas in a logical way and writing them in a clear, easy-to-read style. In this chapter, you will learn some helpful techniques for generating and organizing ideas for any type of sales writing. You'll also learn various ways of expressing these ideas in a clear and simple style. In addition, you'll be able, in the future, to produce this writing more quickly. Finally, we'll review certain punctuation marks that cause problems for most people. Let's begin with how to organize a piece of writing.

THE "PLUNGING-IN" APPROACH

If you are like most people, you go about writing in the worst possible way. That is, you think about what you have to write for a moment or two, you experience a sense of fear or panic, and you may even procrastinate for many minutes or hours. Then, after all this, you begin putting words down on paper or on a computer screen. This process of thinking about what you have to write and then writing it after only a short time is called the "plunging-in" approach. This process is characterized by little or no planning before you begin writing. Then, when you begin writing, you write sentence by sentence, without being sure of where you are going.

When you use this approach, several problems result. First—mainly because you have been writing without any sense of direction—you will spend too much time in the writing and revising process. Specifically, you will waste time in delaying, rearranging sentences and paragraphs, and doing many drafts. Those of you who are accustomed to making arrows in the margin and using the "cut-and-paste" approach know what I mean.

To give you an idea of how ineffective the plunging-in approach is, let's take several common situations for which all of us would do a good bit of planning before we began. First, if we were to take a trip by car to a place that we haven't been to before, most of us would consult a map before we started. We would plan the whole route before we left.

Second, rather than do a day's work without any schedule, many of us would first make a to-do list. That is, we would first list, in no specific order, all the things we thought we needed to do. Then we would prioritize these items. In this way, we would make sure we don't forget anything and we do the most important things first. We are creating a plan for the day before we start, very much like the route we plot before taking a car journey.

Finally, those of us who give sales presentations plot out what we are going to say before the presentation begins. Few of us would go into a presentation and merely wing it. The plan that we create before we give a presentation is, in all probability, an outline.

In all three examples, it makes sense to plan rather than plunge in, and most of us do planning of some sort. However, when it comes to writing, most of us do not plan; instead, we just plunge in, writing sentence by sentence without being sure of where we are going. The alternative to the plunging-in approach is to do an outline before you write. An outline will help you write more quickly, logically, and persuasively.

PLANNING YOUR WRITING

Planning your writing is necessary no matter what type of writing you need to do. As a salesperson, you may need to write a letter to a customer, a memo to your boss, and initial letters to leads and prospects along with follow-up letters. You also will need to write presentations, document trip reports, and respond to customer complaints.

Before writing any of these, you must consider the following five items: audience, purpose, subject, format, and thesis sentence. Let's consider each of these.

Audience

The person or people who will be reading your writing may be top management, peers, subordinates, or customers. Knowing who is getting your writing will affect both what you write and how you write it.

If you write to top management, you should be extremely concise, because top managers do not have the time or patience to read writing that is wordy and overly detailed. In addition, you must consider the level of technical knowledge of top management. If the executives do not know the technical jargon that you know, you must translate; that is, either use the technical term followed by its translation in layman's terms, or use the layman's term alone. Depending on your relationship with the executive you are writing to, your tone might need to be on the formal side.

If you are writing to a peer or a subordinate, you might need to be more detailed than when you are writing to top management. You probably can include more specifics and more jargon than in writing to top management.

In writing to customers, adjust the amount of detail depending on your goals and your customers' need for information. The extent to which you can use jargon depends on their knowledge level. Finally, you will probably want to be informal and friendly to establish a bond that will facilitate sales.

Purpose

You may be writing to inform, recommend (persuade, convince), evaluate, describe procedures, summarize, or request action.

Anything that you write will fall under one or more of these six purposes. To inform is the broadest of purposes. While all pieces of writing are intended to inform, some have informing as their sole purpose. For example, a memo that announces a meeting is strictly informational.

Subject

The topic you are writing about will be stated in a few words that clarify the purpose, such as "Sales visit to the XYZ Company." Most memos will have a subject line or the word *re.*

Format

The format of writing can be a letter, memo, report, or proposal. Letters are usually written to people outside your company. For example, when you write to a prospect or a customer, you will be using a letter format. Check with your secretary or a standard reference book for your company's policy regarding the format for a letter, memo, or proposal.

Thesis Sentence

What you are trying to show, state, or prove in your piece of writing is contained in the thesis sentence. This is an expanded statement of your subject and purpose.

The thesis sentence ought to provide the reader with a sense of what is to appear in the piece of writing and how the piece is to be organized. Unfortunately, many writers do not give readers this necessary assistance. The thesis, for instance, may be nonexistent, and then the reader will have little or no clue as to what the piece of writing is about. Or, if it does appear, let's say in a memo, it may appear at the end. We can justifiably call this a "mystery memo," because the reader will not know until the end what the memo is about.

Effective writers place the thesis sentence as the last sentence of the first paragraph. Sometimes, in a complicated piece of writing, when you have many discrete things to discuss, you may need to write more than one thesis sentence at the end of the first paragraph.

To understand more fully how the thesis sentence functions, we need to see it in a piece of writing and observe how it logically determines the structure, or parts, of the piece. Each part is a paragraph.

For illustrative purposes, let's look at a sample memo that consists of five paragraphs.

The first paragraph, by tradition, is the introduction. The thesis sentence appears as the last sentence. Preceding it are one or two sentences of background information. To help you formulate these sentences, try to image why you decided to write this piece. Are you, for example, responding to someone's letter? Did your manager ask you to write a memo to him or her? Are you reporting the results of visits made to prospects or customers? In the memo below, when you look at the first paragraph, you'll see background sentences followed by a thesis sentence.

TO: John Smith
FROM: Mary Jones
SUBJECT: Visit to the XYZ Co.
DATE: August 17, 1994

I recently returned from a visit to Peter Martin and Jane Doe of the XYZ Company. I was hoping to hear from them about how pleased they were with our company's newest widget, the PZ75, which they recently purchased from us in large quantities. Unfortunately, Peter and Jane informed me of three problems they have found in using it.

Note how in the introductory paragraph above, the first two sentences lead up to the thesis and explain the origin of the memo. Note, too, that within the thesis is a word that tells John Smith, the audience, into what parts or sections the memo will be divided. That is, John would realize that Mary, the writer, will be telling him about certain *problems*, three, to be precise.

The word that tells the audience and the writer into what parts the piece will be divided is called the *key word*. The key word is usually a noun, that is, the name of a person, place, or thing. Some thesis sentences will have only one key word, while others will have several. Keep in mind that every thesis sentence must have one or more key words.

If you write a thesis sentence, and you can't pick out the key word, your thesis is not a good one. Moreover, you will not be able to decide what the topic of each paragraph will be. For example, if you are planning a memo you know will be lengthy, and you write the following thesis sentence, there is really no key word in it:

I would like to discuss our company.

A close examination of that sentence will reveal there is no word in it that tells how the memo will be organized (i.e., into what parts it will be divided). Whereas some people might say *discuss* is the key word, you must realize that *discuss* is not a noun, and each paragraph is not about *discuss*. On the other hand, if you wrote a thesis such as, "I would like to discuss three reasons for using our company's services," you do have a key word in it—the word *reasons*.

Let's now look at the remainder of this five-paragraph memo and consider the concept of a paragraph. A good rule of thumb is that a paragraph is about one point. When you finish discussing that point, you move on to the next paragraph. So let's say you are Mary Jones. Based on your thesis and its key word, you know your plan is to mention and discuss three specific problems in detail. Therefore, what you would do is devote a paragraph to each problem.

The first sentence of each paragraph, which is called the *topic sentence*, must contain two things:

1. It would state the one point you will explain in the paragraph.
2. It should also contain a transition (or linking) word(s) to connect this paragraph to the previous one.

At the start of the second paragraph, you might have a sentence like: "One problem they mentioned was that half the widgets didn't meet their specifications." Note how the writer stated the problem she will discuss in the paragraph, that is, half of the widgets didn't meet specifications. Note, too, the use of the transitional expression "one problem." If this problem were the most serious, the writer could have written, "The most serious problem was . . . " The remainder of the paragraph will contain details explaining in what ways the customer felt the widgets didn't meet specifications.

The topic sentence for the third paragraph might read: "Another problem was that our widgets were shipped two weeks after delivery was promised." Note the transitional expression "Another problem." The writer could also have said, among other things:

"A second problem . . . "

"Second, . . . "

"In addition, . . . "

This third paragraph, of course, deals with late delivery, the details of which the writer would explain in the remainder of the paragraph.

Here is what the topic sentence of the fourth paragraph might look like: "Finally, Peter and Jane were upset by 25 percent of our widgets breaking after 15 hours of use." Note the use of "Finally, . . . " as a transition. You could also use such expressions as "Last, . . . " or "The final problem . . . " As in previous paragraphs, the remainder of the paragraph would contain details about the one point to be explained, in this case, widgets breaking down.

The fifth paragraph would conclude the memo. Not all letters or memos require a conclusion or summary. However, in cases where you want some action or response from your reader, a concluding paragraph would be appropriate. Often a conclusion is little more than a repetition of the main points stated within the piece of writing. In this memo, Mary Jones might want to request a meeting with her manager, John Smith, to discuss how to rectify their customer's problems. If so, a simple conclusion might be: "In conclusion, John, the above problems seem very serious to me. I'd like to discuss them with you. If you are free this Friday at 2 PM, let's meet in your office. Please call to confirm the meeting."

Most often, it is relatively easy to come up with a thesis sentence in the planning stage. It is especially easy when your manager gives you clear instructions for a piece of writing and explicitly mentions a key word(s) that will structure the writing. For example, if your manager asks you to give reasons for recommending something, or to describe new procedures for submitting paperwork, you are being given key words like *reasons* and *procedures*. If you can't, however, identify the key word(s) in your manager's instructions, the best thing to do is ask for clarification.

THE "BACK-DOOR" APPROACH

But what if you do not get an assignment from your manager? Instead, you decide on your own to write a letter or memo and, because it's complicated and lengthy, you can't come up with a thesis easily. In that case, you need to do the "back-door" approach.

The back-door approach is a method you can use to identify an elusive thesis by first deciding what you want to say in each paragraph and then basing your thesis on that.

It works something like this. First, put a four-paragraph diagram of a piece of writing on paper, using a bracket around each paragraph. Since you don't know what your thesis is, leave the first paragraph blank. Then go to the remaining paragraphs and think about one topic you want to write about in each.

Let's say, for example, you are going to write a memo to your manager. A customer has complained about receiving damaged merchandise. You know you want to relay this information to your manager and say something about what should be done about the problem. Moreover, you have some idea why this problem occurred. However, you are confused about how to organize these points into a memo format. After thinking about these ideas, you should decide:

1. Are these all the ideas you need to cover?
2. In what order should the ideas be placed?

One logical way to deal with these ideas is:

- Describe the problem.
- Discuss reasons it has occurred.
- Recommend some changes in the way the warehouse sends out merchandise.

If you are satisfied that this represents all you want to say, go back to your blank paragraphs in the diagram and insert a phrase in each paragraph representing the topic that will be discussed in it.

Once you have decided what you want to cover in each paragraph, you can easily write the thesis sentence. To do so, all you have to do is write a sentence including all three parts in the order in which they appear in the diagram. In that case, your thesis, which you would now insert in the blank space that is paragraph one, would read:

> I want to give you a description of the problem the XYZ Co. is having with damaged merchandise, several reasons why this problem has occurred, and some changes I recommend regarding the way the warehouse sends out the merchandise.

With the thesis as the last sentence of the first paragraph, your manager would know exactly what you're planning to cover.

By the way, it is not illegal, unethical, or immoral to use the back-door approach. Many people may use it without even knowing it. Sometimes, it is the only technique that will work to help you discover what your thesis is.

In summary, by coming up with a thesis and topic sentences—whether you use a front-door or a back-door approach—it will be much easier for you to write the piece and for your reader to understand it.

SEVEN STEPS IN ORGANIZING YOUR WRITING

Now that we have carefully explored what is involved in planning your writing, which includes identifying audience, purpose, subject, format, and thesis, we are ready to look at what comes next. Before you write, you need to follow seven specific steps. We'll look now at these and use each to construct an actual letter.

Step 1

On a notepad or a computer screen, identify your audience, purpose, subject, format, and thesis.

This is the step we have just finished discussing. Below is an illustration of how you would complete Step 1 if you were writing a letter to a prospect at the XYZ Company with whom you had spoken on the phone. This person has been using an old-style widget for a number of years in the manufacture of toasters. You learn he's moderately satisfied with the widget. But after asking him a few questions, you realize he could greatly benefit from buying your company's new and improved widget introduced a few months ago.

Audience:	Vice president of engineering.
Purpose:	To inform.
	To recommend.
	To summarize.
	To request action.
Subject:	Benefits of our company's newest widget.

Format: Letter.

Thesis: It has three benefits that you said were very impor-
            tant to you.

Step 2

Write the key word from your thesis on top of one sheet of paper, if
you don't need more than one page for supporting details. If, however, you need more than one page, and your key word is, for example, *reasons,* specify each reason on a separate sheet of paper, one
reason per page.

If you have more than one key word in your thesis, put each key
word at the top of a sheet of paper. This key word will represent
either one paragraph or one section of your piece of writing. If you
write with a computer, spacing adjustments are easy to make.

To follow Step 2 for the letter we are working on, one page would
be sufficient for all the points that need to be presented. On this
page, you would list the three benefits. Make sure to leave sufficient
room between each so you can fill in supporting details, which is
what Step 3 calls for.

Three Benefits

- Increase your productivity

- Reduce defects

- Reduce downtime

Step 3

On the page you've allotted for the key word (i.e., reasons)—or on
the pages where each specific example appears (e.g., to save money,
to increase productivity, etc.)—jot down details that support or
explain the reasons. Write phrases, and don't worry about the order
of the details. Write down ideas as fast as you can. This technique is
similar to brainstorming or making a to-do list.

This step, by the way, would be unnecessary if your piece of writing were very brief, let's say one or two paragraphs. However, when it is three or more paragraphs, you ought to use Step 3.

For the letter we are working on, we need to do Step 3. The letter cannot be merely one or two paragraphs long because we need to back up the benefits with details to be persuasive. Simply listing the benefits would not be persuasive enough.

As you brainstorm, which involves writing down each detail under a benefit, indent and put a (•) in front of each point. Then you must consider whether each detail requires further explanation. If not, move on to the next detail and write it directly underneath the one you've just written. If you did that, it would look like this:

- Benefit
  - Detail
  - Detail
  - Detail

However, if a detail requires some explanation, you can do one of two things. You can decide to elaborate on it immediately, perhaps because you are afraid of losing the ideas. If so, then indent just a bit and list each supporting point one under the other. If these supporting points require some elaboration, then do so by indenting and then listing the subpoints one under the other. Use bullets to set off each point more clearly just in case you list a detail that is so long it carries over to the next line. This hierarchical listing would look like this:

- Benefit
  - Detail
    - Supporting point
      - Subpoint
      - Subpoint

The other option is not to elaborate on a point until later, after you've written down all the major points you can think of. You make this choice if you are not afraid of forgetting subpoints, and it is more important for you to get all the major ideas first. Here you would put down a point under a benefit and skip a number of lines, leaving enough space so you can insert the necessary supporting information later. (If you are doing this work on a computer, it's not important if you haven't left enough space, because you can easily move lines down to make more room than you originally allotted.)

Let's see now how Step 3 works by going back to the three benefits and brainstorming under each. You'll see instances below illustrating the different degrees of elaboration just discussed. In some cases, some details were elaborated on, while in other cases, there is little or no elaboration.

Three Benefits

- Increase your productivity
  - Current productivity with your widget
    - Your widget produces only 20 toasters per hour
  - Productivity most important to you
    - Keep competitive edge
    - Make more money
      - More toasters per hour = more money
  - Our widget's productivity
    - New design
    - Increased productivity with our widget
      - Can produce 30 toasters per hour
    - Faster than your old-style widget
    - Latest technology incorporated in our design
- Reduce defects
  - Current widget
    - Causes 3 defects per 500 toasters
  - Our widget
    - Only 1 defect likely per 1,000 toasters
    - Information based on our research (enclosed)
- Reduce downtime
  - Information you gave me about your widget
  - Our research
  - Customer satisfaction
  - Our service policy and warranty

Assuming you now have run out of ideas in doing Step 3, the brainstorming step, you need to ask yourself if you have really finished. Running out of ideas does not necessarily mean you have done an adequate job in brainstorming.

The best way to decide is to consider whether you have given sufficient detail to prove your point *to your audience*. Specifically, if the amount of detail you have come up with is too little for your reader—even though you can't think of any more—you may not be persuasive. If you realize you need more details, but can't think of them yourself, you'll need to ask for help. Consult colleagues and ask if they can provide you with more information. Also, you may need to do a review of the literature (i.e., your company's own literature, or books, newspapers, or periodicals in the library).

On the other hand, you may realize you have written down too much information for your reader. In other words, if you include all the details, you would bore or maybe confuse your readers. The solution is simple. Eliminate those ideas that are not that important to your reader, and you'll be left with the necessary highlights.

Step 4

Organize the ideas into final form by considering:

  a. The order of the specific examples of your key word.
  b. The order of the supporting details.

Step 5

Eliminate ideas you don't need.

Step 6

Write a final outline. Steps 4, 5, and 6 actually occur simultaneously.

Rank the benefits. In doing Step 4, you'll have to decide which benefit comes first. Make your decision based on whether one benefit is more important than the others. If the benefits are equally important to your reader, then it wouldn't make a difference which came first. However, if one benefit is most important, it is a good idea to put your most important one first, followed by the others in decreasing order of importance.

The rationale for such positioning is that most readers expect the most important benefit to be first. Moreover, if you decide to place the most important one last (i.e., saving the best for last) you can run the risk of your reader getting disinterested after the second paragraph and never getting to your most important benefit at the end.

Supporting details often, but not always, serve as proof or examples. If it makes sense to put one detail after another, do so. If you can sense the logic of your ideas now, the writing that comes later will be much easier for you to do.

At the same time you consider the ordering of the details, you also will be considering which details can be eliminated (Step 5). This is something you might have done as part of Step 3, when you were brainstorming and eliminating certain points your audience will not need. In Step 5, you are taking a second look at what points you must include.

The culmination of all your thinking about the ordering of ideas is reflected in Step 6, doing the final outline. While it would be acceptable merely to put numbers next to each point to indicate the sequence, numbers alone are really not sufficient to convey the hierarchical order of your thoughts. To be more specific, you couldn't convey with numbers alone the difference between main points, supporting points, and their subpoints. You need a system that uses Roman numerals, capital letters, numbers, and small letters to designate each element in your hierarchy; in short, you need an outline.

A sample outline appears below:

OUTLINE FORM

    I. Introduction.
        A. *Thesis* (There are several advantages of offering an in-house writing program on a regular basis.)
   II. Participants could write faster.
        A. Will learn to get started more quickly via outlining.
            1. No scribbling.
            2. No procrastinating.
               a. Doing other work first.
               b. Saving writing until last.
            3. No false starts and crumpled paper thrown away.
        B. Will do fewer drafts.
            1. Cuts down on rewrites due to:
               a. Leaving out ideas.
               b. Rearranging order of details.

    C. Result is producing better writing in less time.
      1. Each person can double or triple output.
III. Improve image (main points).
    A. (Supporting detail).
    B. (Supporting detail).
      1. (Further support).
      2. (Further support).
    C. (Supporting detail).
    D. (Supporting detail).
IV. Clear writing cuts down costly errors.
    A.
      1.
    B.
V. Conclusion.

Notice that the thesis sentence appears under Roman numeral I, which is used to designate the introductory paragraph. Remember, the thesis is placed as the last sentence of the first paragraph, preceded by one or two sentences of background information. In the thesis presented here, you ought to be able to pick out the key word, which is *advantages.*

The three advantages chosen by the writer are each given a specific Roman numeral and are placed in the order of importance to the reader.

An alternative way to construct this outline is to put the word *advantages* on top of a sheet of paper or computer screen and split the page into three parts. Roman numeral II would go in front of the word *advantages.* Then each of the advantages (main points) would be preceded by the capital letters A, B, and C.

Returning to the sample outline, notice that under each advantage you have supporting details, each of which is preceded by a capital letter. Details that offer further support are preceded by small letters. That is to say, if you look at II A 2, you'll see the supporting detail "no procrastinating." Two subpoints explaining "no procrastinating" are preceded by small letters *a* and *b.*

In our letter to the vice president of engineering of the XYZ Company, we are going to set up the outline of benefits using the alternative approach; that is, we'll use one sheet of paper with "Benefits" on top and capital letters for each benefit.

Outlining (Step 6) should always be done initially on your brainstorming page. This gives you maximum freedom to change your mind as to the order of all your ideas. When you change your mind about the order of a point, you simply change the letter or number.

So let's go back to Step 3 and the points we listed under the three benefits. Below you'll see what the brainstorming page would look like, with lines through certain points that should be eliminated, the Roman numerals, capital letters, and numbers in front of the rest.

II. *Three Benefits*
   A. Increase your productivity.
      2. Current productivity with your widget.
         a. Your widget produces only 20 toasters per hour.
      1. Productivity most important to you.
         a. Keep competitive edge.
         b. Make more money.
            (1) More toasters per hour = more money.
      3. Our widget's productivity.
         ~~new design~~
         a. Increased productivity with our widget.
            (1) Can produce 30 toasters per hour.
            (2) Faster than your old-style widget.
               (a) Latest technology incorporated in our design.
   C. Reduce defects.
      1. Current widget.
         a. Causes 3 defects per 500 toasters.
      2. Our widget.
         a. Only 1 defect likely per 1,000 toasters.
            (1) Info based on our research (enclosed).
            ~~(2) see enclosed literature~~
   B. Reduce downtime.
      1. Info you gave me about your widget.
      ~~2. Our research~~

2. Customer satisfaction.

  b. Our service policy and warranty.

  a. Downtime is rare with our new widgets.

If the outline you constructed on your brainstorming page is neat enough to write from, then do so. If it's too messy or confusing, make a neat, new copy. Below is a neat version of the outline we just constructed on our brainstorming page.

II. *Three Benefits*

  A. Increase your productivity.

    1. Productivity most important to you.

      a. Keep competitive edge.

      b. Make more money.

        (1) More toasters per hour = more money.

    2. Current productivity with your widget.

      a. Your widget produces only 20 toasters per hour.

    3. Our widget's productivity.

      a. Increased productivity with our widget.

        (1) Can produce 30 toasters per hour.

        (2) Faster than your old-style widget.

          (*a*) Latest technology incorporated in our design yields new speed.

  B. Reduce downtime.

    1. Info you gave me about your widget.

      a. Your widget causes 30 minutes of downtime every week.

    2. Our customer satisfaction is high.

      a. Downtime rare, say our customers.

        (1) Average one minute downtime every six months.

      b. Excellent service policy and warranty.

  C. Reduce defects.

    1. Current widget.

      a. Causes 3 defects per 500 toasters.

    2. Our widget.

      a. Only 1 defect likely per 1,000 toasters.

        (1) Info based on our research (enclosed).

After completing your outline, and before going on to Step 7, the first draft, you ought to evaluate the outline. Just because you have an outline with Roman numerals, capital letters, and numbers doesn't mean it's a good outline. To evaluate your outline's logic, you can use the first part of the postwriting checklist below.

Postwriting Checklist

After completing your outline

1. Have you identified and written down your audience, purpose, subject, format, and thesis sentence?
2. Have you done a good final outline?
   a. At a minimum, do you have a thesis sentence and several Roman numerals that represent paragraphs or sections of your piece of writing?
   b. Do your main points (Roman numerals) support your thesis sentence?
   c. Are your main points separate and distinct from one another?
   d. Have you brainstormed as thoroughly as necessary?
   e. Do your supporting details (capital letters) support your main points? To verify if this is so, if you have three capital letters, for example, under a Roman numeral, ask yourself, "A, B, and C are three *what?*" You should be able to come up with one word that links all three capital letters. Often that one linking word will appear in the heading next to the Roman numeral.
   f. Do your numbers support your capital letters?

Let's look back at the outline for the letter and answer each of the questions in the checklist. If an outline has only two Roman numerals, as ours does, then you need not consider questions 2 *a*, *b*, or *c*. After answering question 1, go directly to question 2 *d*. The answer to all the question that are pertinent on the checklist should be yes.

Now let's look at each question. The answer to question 1 is yes. All five points have been specified when we did Step 1.

Regarding question 2 *d*, the answer is yes. Based on the writer's knowledge of the audience and the purpose of the letter, there is a sufficient amount of detail in the outline.

Question 2 *e* requires some explanation. To determine if A, B, and C in our outline support the main point that follows Roman numeral II, you have to put a bracket next to the capital letters and see if there is a word(s) that connects all three capital letters. About 90 percent of the time, there will be a connecting word(s) that links the elements. In cases where you cannot come up with a connecting word, it does not necessarily mean your outline is not good; in these cases, as long as you can determine how B follows A, and C follows B, then it's likely there is a good sense of logic and flow in your outline.

In our outline, then, if we put a bracket around A, B, and C and ask "A, B, and C are three *what?*" the linking word would be *benefits*. Note how this is the same word that appears in the heading next to Roman numeral II.

II. *Three Benefits*

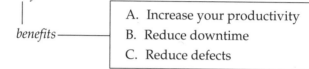

benefits ————
A. Increase your productivity
B. Reduce downtime
C. Reduce defects

The answer to question 2 *f* is yes. In our outline, there is no need to put brackets around the numbers under each capital letter because there is no linking word that will connect the numbers. However, there is a connection between these points. Under all three of the benefits, there is a contrast made between the relatively poor quality of the prospect's old-style widget versus the latest-style widget manufactured by the writer's company.

Step 7

Write the piece using the outline as an exact guide. Do not deviate from the outline when you are writing. If you are not satisfied with your outline, revise it before doing a first draft. Never write from a faulty outline.

With a completed outline that you approve of after using the postwriting checklist, you are ready to write a first draft, containing complete sentences that make up unified, coherent paragraphs.

For some writers, however, a prose narrative may not be needed. In cases where, for example, your manager asks you for a bullet list, you are essentially finished once you compose an outline. Once you have completed Step 6, you simply remove the Roman numerals, capital letters, numbers, and small letters and replace them with bullets.

WRITING STYLE

If, on the other hand, you do need to write a prose narrative, then you need to consider style. Style is the way you choose words and put them together to form sentences.

Often this choice is made with little or no thought, sometimes at a rapid-fire pace. Sometimes, though, we will get stuck and deliberate for minutes about which is the best or most correct word to use. If you are stuck, circle the word(s) or blank spaces and go on with your draft. Come back to these circled areas after you have finished writing and then make your decisions. Remember: Perfection is impossible, so don't even try. There is no such thing as the one "right" word.

Once you have selected your words, decide how to put them together to form complete sentences. Among other things, these sentences need to be clear and varied in both length and complexity. Moreover, they need to be logically connected to one another. Most important of all, they need to be understood by the reader. If your writing style is not clear, you and your company may lose business.

To help you get a perspective on what's a desirable style, look at the diagram below. It illustrates a wide range of styles, from overly simple to overly difficult. As with any range, there is a happy medium.

Range of Writing Styles

Dick and Jane Style (Too simple: 3–4 word, monotonous sentences)	Conversational Style (Write the way you speak)	Business or Academic or Government or Legal (Too difficult)

All salespeople should be concerned about making a good impression on their prospects, customers, and managers. Neither extreme on the above diagram is desirable. If you write in too simple a style, you'll be regarded as foolish. On the other hand, if you write as many people do, in a difficult style, you'll confuse people and antagonize them. To put it another way, few people want to pick up a letter, memo, or proposal and struggle to understand it; moreover, they may resent you for making it so hard for them to understand your writing and even for making them feel stupid.

The happy medium is the best way to write clearly and gain respect—and business—from your reader. In the above diagram, the happy medium is not one specific point exactly halfway between the two extremes. Instead, it is a wide rectangle, signifying a wide variety of conversational writing. Though you might express an idea in writing differently from a colleague, both of your versions could be equally acceptable, as long as the writing is easy to understand.

Listed below are several characteristics of difficult writing, along with a clearer version that would be easier to read. In addition, you will find a brief list of some of the most common errors in punctuation and ways to correct them.

Difficult writing	*Clear writing*
1. *Long sentences:* We are sorry you have not received the merchandise we sent you two weeks ago, merchandise we realize you needed a week ago to complete certain experiments, a delay that will result in considerable hardship, namely a loss of business that could be difficult to regain.	1. Break up a long sentence into two or more sentences. *Revision:* We are sorry you have not received the merchandise we sent you two weeks ago. We realize you needed it a week ago to complete certain experiments. This delay, we are aware, will result in considerable hardship, namely a loss of business that could be difficult to regain.
2. *Wordiness:* It is the opinion of this writer that the use of our product will result in a large number of benefits for those who work in your firm. (28 words)	2. Eliminate unnecessary words. *Revision:* I believe that by using our product, your employees will experience many benefits. (13 words) *Revision:* By using our product, your employees will experience many benefits. (10 words)

3. *Use of passive voice:* It would be appreciated by me if a call were to be made by you to Bob because he is known by you.

4. *Use of jargon (technical language)* when the reader does not understand it: Where appropriate, consortium entry for smaller banks may enable them to justify automated interfaces they could not support on a stand-alone basis.

5. *Use of uncommon words:* Your decision was a perspicacious one.

Revision: Your employees will benefit from using our product. (8 words)

3. Use the active voice. *Revision:* I would appreciate it if you made a call to Bob, because you know him.

4. Use jargon, and translate. Or don't use jargon. Use the translation instead. *Revision:* If small banks pooled their money, they could purchase automated equipment they could not afford alone.

5. Use common words. *Revision:* Your decision was a wise one.

Current Usage

Before turning to some examples of common errors in punctuation, let's look at a sentence that is not stylistically difficult. However, it needs to be changed because it contains four examples of outdated, trite expressions:

> Please be advised that we are in receipt of your invoice. Per your request, enclosed please find our check for $50.

The following are the four old-fashioned expressions that have been used for the last 50 years:

1. "Please be advised . . . "
2. "We are in receipt of . . . "
3. "Per your request . . . "
4. "Enclosed please find . . . "

These expressions were at one time in favor; their use was encouraged in business writing schools and texts. However, fashions change. Just as the length of hemlines and the width of ties change through the years, what is fashionable in language changes, too. The trend in writing, for at least the last 10 to 15 years, has been away from an artificial, impersonal style toward a more conversational, personal style. Even though most people are still using outdated expressions like the four above, more people are changing their writing styles to be personal. Writing personally is preferable for a salesperson because so much of selling is based on a personal relationship.

One revised version of the outdated sentence would read something like this:

> We received your invoice and, as you requested, we have enclosed our check for $50.

Punctuation

As a refresher, below are some of the most common errors in punctuation, along with the corrected versions:

Error   *Revision*

Commas

1. Since Joe forgot to call Bob will have to do it instead.

1. Since Joe forgot to call, Bob will have to do it instead.
   Rule: Use a comma after an introductory group of words like:

Since	Unless
If	During
When	Before
After	Because
While	Whenever
With	Though
regard to	Although
Until	

2. I plan to visit our plant in Georgia next week and

2. I plan to visit our plant in Georgia next week, and

then I want to take a long vacation in Mexico.

3. My manager Edith Bunker, is not very smart.

Punctuation with quotes

4. I think the scariest movie I ever saw was "Jaws".

Apostrophes

5. After eating that slice of pizza, he said its too bad that it's crust was not crisper and its' ingredients were not fresher.

6. Those customers's complaints are valid, according to Bobs' research.

Hyphens

7. That product has a two year warranty on parts.

then I want to take a long vacation in Mexico.
Rule: Use a comma when *and, but,* or *or* connects two complete thoughts.

3. My manager, Edith Bunker, is not very smart.
Rule: Use a comma before and after an identifying expression.

4. I think the scariest movie I ever saw was "Jaws."
Rule: Periods and commas normally go *inside* the closing quotation mark in the United States. This is true whether there is just one word inside a quote or a whole sentence.

5. After eating that slice of pizza, he said it's too bad that its crust was not crisper and its ingredients were not fresher.
Rule: Use *it's* as a contraction to mean "it is" or "it has." Use *its* to show possession. Never use its'; there is no such word.

6. Those customers' complaints are valid, according to Bob's research.
Rule: One use of an apostrophe is to show possession. If the owner is plural, put the apostrophe after the *s* (s'). If the owner is singular, put the apostrophe before the *s* ('s).

7. That product has a two-year warranty on parts.

Colons

8. Dear Mr. Jones,

Semicolons

9. I wish I could get John to
   continue buying from us,
   however, I'm afraid he's
   going to go to our biggest
   competitor.

Rule: Use a hyphen to connect two or more words
that function as an adjec-
tive and that precede a
noun.

8. Dear Mr. Jones:
   Rule: Use a colon in the
   salutation of a business
   letter. A comma is acceptable only in a social letter.

9. I wish I could get John to
   continue buying from us;
   however, I'm afraid he's
   going to go to our biggest
   competitor.
   Rule 1: Use a semicolon to
   connect two closely
   related sentences with the
   following connecting
   words between them:
   > However
   > Therefore
   > Moreover
   > On the other hand
   > Consequently
   > In addition
   > Thus
   > Nevertheless

   Rule 2: After any of the
   above connecting words,
   you must use a comma.
   Or, instead of using a
   semicolon, you can use a
   period followed by a capital letter for the next
   word.
   Example: I wish I could get
   John to continue buying
   from us. However, I'm
   afraid he's going to go to
   our biggest competitor.

Sentence errors: Comma splice

10. He said our price was too high, I told him that it was competitive.

10. *a.* He said our price was too high. I told him it was competitive.
    b. He said our price was too high; I told him it was competitive.
    c. He said our price was too high, but I told him it was competitive.
    Rule: A common splice is the error of putting a comma between two sentences that are not joined by the conjunctions *and, but, or,* or *nor.*

Run-on sentences

11. I just learned that I got a promotion I must say I'm overjoyed.

11. *a.* I just learned that I got a promotion. I must say I'm overjoyed.
    b. I just learned that I got a promotion; I must say I'm overjoyed.
    Rule: A run-on sentence results from omitting punctuation between two sentences.

Now that we've considered various writing styles and what's appropriate for salespeople, and we've seen some common errors in punctuation, it's time to write the letter. We'll follow Step 7 now and use our outline as a guide.

August 27, 1994

Mr. James Smith
Vice President
Engineering Department
XYZ Company
123 Main Street
Anytown, NY 15029

Dear Mr. Smith:

I enjoyed talking to you on the phone about your company's production of toasters and your heavy reliance for many years on the ABC Company's Model 45 widget. However, as I briefly told you on the phone, our company has recently introduced a new and improved widget that we believe is far superior. It has three benefits you said were important to you.

The most important benefit is that our new widget would increase your productivity. I recall that you told me it is crucial for your company to increase productivity. By doing so, you would maintain the competitive edge you've worked so hard to achieve. Moreover, your profits would increase if you could produce more toasters to meet the large public demand. Here is where our new widget would help. Whereas you now can produce only 20 toasters per hour using your current widget, with our widget you'd be able to produce 30 per hour. Production is faster because our widget is now made by laser technology.

Another benefit is that with our new widget, you would be able to reduce downtime. According to the information you gave me, your widget causes 30 minutes of downtime every week. By using our widget, downtime would be much less. In fact, many of our customers have told us how satisfied they are with the minimal downtime when they use our new widget. They have written to us reporting an average of only one minute of downtime every six months. In addition, they have told us how satisfied they are with our service policy and warranty.

Finally, our widget will reduce the defects you are getting with the Model 45 you are currently using. Now you get three defects per 500 toasters. With our new widget, only one defect is likely per 1,000 toasters. I have enclosed some research to back up our claims, as well as product information on our new widget.

I plan to call you again next Monday and see if we can meet to talk further. I am sure that in this meeting, I can explain more fully the benefits I have just touched upon in this letter and answer any questions you may have. I am looking forward to speaking to you then.

Sincerely,

Mel Haber

Once you complete a first draft, turn to the remaining parts of the postwriting checklist to evaluate the organization and style of your writing. Specifically, to evaluate the organization, ask yourself the following questions:

After doing your first draft:[1]

3. Have you followed your outline in doing your first draft?
4. Have you put your thesis sentence in your first paragraph?
5. Does each paragraph have a topic sentence taken from Roman numerals or capital letters that:
   a. Tells what the paragraph is about?
   b. Contains a word or words that relates to the previous paragraph?
6. Do you have good transitions between sentences in each paragraph so that your writing flows?

Style

1. Are your sentences reasonably short and clear?
2. Have you varied the structure of your sentences to avoid monotony?
3. Have you chosen words that:
   a. Will help you achieve your purpose?
   b. Will be clear to your reader(s)?
   c. Are commonly used?
   d. Are concrete and specific?
4. Have you avoided outdated, trite expressions?
5. Is your style close to being conversational?
6. Have you eliminated wordiness?
7. Have you used the active voice (putting the actor before the verb) when appropriate?
8. Have you proofread your writing for spelling and punctuation errors?

These questions summarize everything you have learned so far in this chapter. The answer to each question should be yes. If it isn't, you'll need to do some revising. Don't despair, however. Most good writers normally revise a first draft.

---

[1]There were two initial questions on page 208, which you asked yourself to evaluate your outline.)

SUMMARY

- Effective writing is an important skill that all salespeople need to master. It should be done regularly and well in order to attract customers and keep them.
- A good piece of writing is helped most by the plan you prepare before you do a draft.
- Especially for a letter or memo that is three or more paragraphs long, you'll need to construct an outline before you do a draft, using the "Seven Steps in Organizing Your Writing."
- When you write your draft, remember to write in a clear, conversational style.

While the process that has been described requires a good deal of thought and effort, using it will make you a better writer, a faster writer, and a better salesperson.

Suggested Readings

The books listed below are just a few of the many on business writing. Each is different and has its virtues; no one is the "best" book on writing.

Dumaine, Deborah. *Write to the Top: Writing for Corporate Success.* New York: Random House, 1983.

Fielden, John S., and Ronald E. Dulek. *What Do You Mean I Can't Write?* Englewood Cliffs, NJ: Prentice Hall, 1984.

Flesch, Rudolph. *On Business Communications.* New York: Barnes & Noble, 1972.

Lanham, Richard A. *Revising Business Prose.* New York: Charles Scribner's Sons, 1981.

Roman, Kenneth, and Joel Raphaelson. *Writing That Works.* New York: Harper & Row, 1981.

Sabin, Williams A. *The Gregg Reference Manual.* 7th ed. Lake Forest, IL: Glencoe, 1992.

Strunk, William, Jr., and E. B. White. *The Elements of Style.* 3rd ed. New York: Macmillan, 1979.

Venolia, Jan. *Rewrite Right.* Berkeley, CA: Ten Speed Press, 1987.

Zinzzer, William. *On Writing Well.* 4th ed. New York: Harper Perennial, 1990.

Chapter Ten

Developing Ethical Boundaries

Louise Korver

"Always do what is right. It will gratify most of the people, and astound the rest."

Mark Twain

Whenever I am asked what subject I teach to sales professionals, I always get the same smart remark: "You teach ethics to sales-people? Isn't that an oxymoron?" They always laugh and then wait for my response. My response is always the same: Somebody's got to do it. It is actually much more interesting to me than teaching "probing" and "handling objections." Am I an expert in ethics? Certainly not. There aren't any—except maybe a few role models like Abe Lincoln.

We all have the same problems in business. Solutions are unique to our sense of right and wrong, and to our perspective on the trade-offs we are negotiating. There aren't any right answers, just seasoned judgment and instinct. Sometimes we do not even realize we are involved in an ethical issue until somebody else makes us aware of it.

Mostly, I enjoy conducting classes on the subject because all you can teach are reflexes. You usually have only *a minute* to figure out what you are going to do in an ethical dilemma. This chapter is not about life and death situations. Rather, it is about the turning points in the daily office politics of every American businessperson. Ethics, after all, is not about the product you are selling; it is about the fragile spirit of the business relationship. Ethics constitutes the unwritten and unenforceable laws that allow us to get along with each other.

WHO CARES?

Ethics is all about mundane business negotiations that you find yourself in, each with their own set of trade-offs and consequences. Don't let anyone kid you about how tough these decisions are, especially if you are new to sales. It is a terribly tedious chore to figure out what to do, and the problem is made worse by all the mental exhaustion over whom to tell or to whom you should turn for advice. There is a lot of lost productivity over ethical dilemmas and no one has yet attempted to measure that.

According to a 1990 study by two Columbia University business school professors, the average business school graduate faces about five ethical dilemmas annually. Public exposure of prominent business czars and their unethical behavior has heightened our awareness of what ethics is. Because of events such as the Hill–Thomas hearings on sexual harassment, we are beginning to define the ethical issues in the context of our daily living.

While the first course in ethics was offered by Harvard Business School in 1915, one recent estimate placed the number of courses being taught on business ethics at 500. Ninety percent of the country's business schools teach the course. In addition, the Center of Business Ethics at Bentley College in Waltham, Massachusetts, found that 45 percent of the 1,000 largest US companies have ethics programs and workshops on their curriculums. This number is up from 35 percent in 1986. It is perhaps one of the current seminal issues of leadership.

The bottom-line results of leadership decisions are always more visible than the means by which they were obtained. The same is also true in sales results. In the field sales environment of most organizations, sales managers need to trust the salesperson and provide some latitude for error. This leaves sales managers without a real method for monitoring the ethical performance of people assigned to them. Sales managers cannot know in detail the exact results of their delegation. However, the field sales manager can manage the ethics of performance through coaching and policy formulation, rather than leaving it to the "corrosive environment of unprincipled competition."

There aren't any quick-fix solutions to reverse the problems caused by unethical sales practices though. Golden parachutes, hostile takeovers, downsizing, and "management by best seller" have all taught employees to be cynical. Self-preservation has become the norm. The workforce is also much more sophisticated. They believe what they see. They don't believe leaders who don't "walk the talk."

Employees watch for subliminal messages, and sales managers need feedback to be sure they know what messages their behaviors are sending. Unintended and inadvertent messages from silence, glances, and quick retorts are all possible behaviors that could steer a sales rep into an unethical situation, all with the belief that this is an activity that will help the company, or worse, that the company will condone the individual for or protect him from the unethical behavior.

When you consider that research found that from 1976 to 1986 roughly two-thirds of America's top 500 largest corporations had been involved in varying degrees in some form of illegal behavior, it isn't hard to see that most employees are caught in a system that condones some level of unethical behavior. What we see isn't easy to deal with because the daily choices we face may seem trivial compared to the headliners. Does that make our choices less important? Certainly not.

Who creates most of our ethical dilemmas? Surprisingly, most of the awkward, gut-wrenching situations that we describe as creating ethical problems for us are caused by well-intentioned co-workers and superiors who—without meaning to—make our choices difficult. Even the sales incentive system often creates problems.

WHAT EXACTLY *IS* ETHICS?

If you need a definition to help you recognize an ethical dilemma, let me run a few past you: reporting educational expenses as T&E, making exaggerated product benefit claims, working a "special deal" for a customer off the price list, quota pressure causing you to book a sale 24 hours before the books close and reversing the sale in the new year, inviting a friend to lunch on the company's credit card, bootlegging software, duplicating commercial videos, being MIA from a training class, blowing off a meeting and forgetting to call to cancel, and on and on.

Reading this chapter is not going to teach you to be ethical. Rather, it will force you to examine the assumptions and behaviors of your company and yourself. It will openly test the values that guide your daily business practices. At the end of this chapter and the discussions you will undoubtedly engage in with colleagues, you can expect a clarification and categorization of your own ethics and methods for comparing and measuring the differences between your own value system and that of your company's in daily situations. **The bottom line will be that you will know for sure when an action that is designed to achieve a certain business objective is going to violate a professional standard that you cherish as an ethical value.**

Your obligations and accountabilities to yourself are first, and then you can consider the trade secrets you protect for your employer and your customers. The confidentiality of information in this rapidly changing, high-tech information age is probably the most challenging aspect of ethics, with the possible exception of the biomedical issues facing those equipped with DNA-replicating medical devices. Your job and the contracts, agreements, and practices that you enter into that can cause a conflict of interest all combine to set the parameters around the five key issues in business ethics: professional standards, property ownership, confidentiality of information, practices, and the employment relationship.

MANAGEMENT ISSUES

In business, maximizing profits is the second goal. The first is ensuring a business's survival. Any company that believes it can ignore the active management of ethical business practices probably hasn't embarked on the total quality movement in the sales department or business process reengineering. For companies that have been forced to examine their sales practices, it has been a sobering experience for senior management.

One such company came to me a year ago with the results of a six-month field study of vulnerable sales practices. The study had identified 12 unethical practices that were so serious that senior management was willing to embark on a $100,000 initiative to train the entire 16,000-member sales function (top to bottom). The division's president was resigned to the fact that the initiative would take about three years to complete. From a well-appointed boardroom on the top floor of his New York office building, he bemoaned, "This didn't start overnight. It will probably take years to eradicate the abuses."

Eleven months later, the business press was reporting a class action suit by this company's customers charging that misleading sales practices had created confusion for vulnerable female customers. For this company, the important action of getting the program started and making sure the sales force was being taught the right things was clear. The president knew some abusive sales personnel and their managers would have to be singled out as examples.

What can a company do if it wants to change its culture? In addition to conducting a study, as in the example cited above, new policies and practice guidelines can be developed that address the subtleties and temptations known to exist for the sales force. Senior management needs to communicate the new guidelines, as well as the consequences of infractions. They also have to be a role model for these guidelines. **Training for management and the sales force to reinforce the responsibility and benefits of ethical business practices is the next step. In the final analysis, only the health of the monitoring system will keep everybody honest.**

Underlying the entire ethics debate is whether business has a social responsibility beyond its responsibility to make a profit. Corporate evolution in the postindustrial era has been swift. Profit-maximizing behavior has not been replaced by trusteeship behavior. Companies are still caught in the battle between corporate values and the quality of life for the planet. This social discussion in a few boardrooms has eclipsed some of the debate among executives who drive for financial success alone. There is growing evidence that American businesses are feeling the trusteeship and quality of earth life pressures at the operating management level.

For a quick glance backward at where we were, take a look at the remaking of Russia in the post-Communist economy. The legal, financial, political, and cultural supports of the society are all being rebuilt. There is a high price for temptation in Russia of 1994. Bribery is rampant—and it is just as illegal there as it is here.

TESTING THE LEGAL LIMITS

The financial and business aristocracy of capitalism faced a crushing defeat in the post-1980s Wall Street ethics cases. Laws have evolved to remedy the most egregious, common, and damaging abuses. A transformation of corporate social responsibility is taking hold. Industrial aristocrats' divine right to run vast monopolies however they pleased (the public be damned) has been restricted. Some business leaders believe this change of heart is attributed to the 60s idealists coming to power in the hierarchy.

Whatever its cause, not everyone can be a Wayne Silby, investing in only socially beneficial, early-stage companies that recycle tires, produce biological pesticides, and create new market niches with their products. Many more businesses, however, are reviewing and revising their policies for expense reporting, accepting gifts, documenting who owns company property for telecommuters, all with an eye toward defining the ethical values of the business. Who reads these policies? How often are they updated? Does senior management demonstrate serious regard for ethics? Is ethics a standard management tenet or is it a part of the mission of the business? Cynically, few companies have found ways to engrain ethics into the mission. Once again the moral ambiguity is present.

Of more recent interest to the consumer is the invasion of privacy practiced by direct marketers who buy lists from everyone they can, including the US Postal Service and the mail-order supplier. Electronic point-of-purchase terminals are capturing our buying behavior to an extent never before possible. The retailers are selling this data to the manufacturers. It is such a new practice that marketers have even coined a new term, *synchographics,* to embody the marketing practices of acting on this new data.

Now you can be marketed to on a timely basis because you fit a pattern—for example, getting free diapers delivered to your home on the birth of your first child. But is it ethical if that same data reveal that a member of your immediate family is about to enter the hospital for surgery and an insurance company tries to sell you life insurance?

The ethics debate rages in the ecology sector as well. Does anybody trust a company that wants to help? Is cynicism warranted? What about Exxon, Thiokol, NASD, and Stew Leonard's? We each have our favorite story, I am sure. Time is running out for companies that aren't on the ethics bandwagon these days.

GETTING PERSONAL

So do you know what your code of ethics is? Do you know how you acquired your value set? When it comes to sales, are you ever in doubt of the difference between your product knowledge and persuasive skill and lying? Have you ever lost a deal because someone didn't think he could trust you? Have you ever felt fraudulent with your product knowledge? Do you really get enough training from your company to know the difference between an objection and a product defect?

Are you propagandized by your management, or do you really have a healthy skepticism about new products you are asked to launch? Is it acceptable to you that new products aren't test-marketed anymore because it is too costly? Is it costing you your credibility when your sales territory constitutes the test market? Is it OK for the new product process to include "not ready for prime time" launches? Is it ethical that your bonus is tied to the success of these new products?

Testing ethics and value systems is a difficult chore without a framework for organizing your beliefs. We can offer you a few such frameworks. The first is a screen using the five key ethics issues as a sieve to sift through a situation to pick out the categories of issues facing someone. Use the key in Figure 10–1 as a code to label key issues:.

The second framework is a checklist adapted from the work of John McLeod, PE, chairman of the Ethics Committee for the Society for Computer Simulation in La Jolla, California. The checklist, shown in Figure 10–2, asks six basic questions, the answers to which will identify potential ethical dilemmas.

FIGURE 10–1
Five Key Ethics Issues

PS   Professional standards, such as obligations and accountabilities
PO   Property ownership, such as in trade secrets
CI   Confidentiality of information
P   Practices: such as contracts, agreements, and conflicts of interest
ER   Employment relationship

Testing Your Ethical Boundaries

In a situation described below, we will ask you to apply both the screen and the checklist. You will have three assignments. First, read the situation and underscore the key issues that crop up using the codes provided in Figure 10–1 (PS, PO, etc.). After completion of this assignment (where you code the situation with the five key issues), use the checklist in Figure 10–2, coding your answers yes or no based on how you would answer the question if you were the sales representative in the situation. Worksheets are provided at the end of the chapter to help you with this assignment (see page 260).

When you have completed the two assignments, go back and count the number of dilemmas inherent in this situation. If you found less than 35, reread the situation to see what you might have missed. An answer key is provided on page 261. The third assignment is detailed on page 248.

The Truth or Consequences Case

Friday, 7:45 AM

You woke up this morning humming a tune that only after a few minutes you realized was "Oh What a Beautiful Morning." You really feel on top of the world today. It's Friday and after next week's well-deserved vacation, you are starting in *your* territory with IRC Technologies.

As you make the bed, you notice that your boyfriend, Dave, has left a large folder of materials on the nightstand. Picking it up, you realize Dave is involved in researching another acquisition. Your

FIGURE 10–2
Ethics Checklist

1. If your actions were made public, is there anyone important to you who could take offense with your actions or could be ashamed in any way?
2. Are you being trustworthy? Could you be found to break any promises, or could your actions be found dishonest by anyone involved in the transaction?
3. Could anyone or anything get hurt by your actions?
4. Is there any way this action could be seen as an ulterior motive for something else?
5. Are you really able or skilled enough to carry out the situation? Is it possible that "trying" won't be good enough, or might be harmful?
6. Is it prudent and a good use of productive resources?

Source: Adapted from John McLeod, PE.

mind races back to the last deal Dave was working on. He had to do due diligence on the deal for three weeks—night and day—in the Bay area. God, you hope this deal isn't out of town. What are the chances?

As you pick up the file, a few pink phone slips drop out and you can't help seeing that your boss's name is on one of them. What *is* this file? Is your new company for sale? You can't resist wondering why your boss would be in contact with Dave. You have got all day to read Dave's file—unless you call Dave and run the file over to his office. Maybe you should wait until he calls to see if he left the file at home, then you can feign ignorance. Otherwise, he might suspect you've read the file.

You've never had a discussion about confidentiality with Dave before, but then, professional privacy has never been close to home before either. Why wouldn't Dave have said something if your new company were for sale? He wouldn't have let you take this job knowing it might have a career risk—would he? You decide to leave the folder by the top of the stairs and go take a shower. You'll think about it there, then decide what to do.

You have been fortunate to have started your job with two solid weeks of field "ride-withs" in the territory of the most successful sales representative with IRCT. What an eye opener it has been. Your previous company would never had condoned some of Greg's behavior, but IRCT is different. You're going to have to learn the politics of this place (and fast) to fit in.

It strikes you as funny that two companies in the same industry could be so different in their field sales practices. But then, maybe that's what sets IRCT apart. After all, it created this market and it is the biggest volume producer. It's a tough market, and IRCT has really won it through solid product performance. Nobody can beat it.

As you shower, your mind dances, reflecting back on the last couple of days in the field. Boy, those sales managers know how to keep a rep motivated! You had free tickets to the game, a great dinner with Frank, your sales manager, and his wife—all compliments of IRCT. What a company!

Thursday 4:20 PM *(the next week)*

Your stomach just tightened: Monday's too close for comfort. You've got to call Jane Clark, your best friend. Jane will understand your lack of confidence. All of sudden it just swept over you: "What the hell do I know about the CT market?" She'll get you back on track. Maybe you can get together for drinks tonight. After all, Dave called to say he wouldn't be home until at least 7:30.

After your discussion with Jane you felt a lot better. It convinced you it was the right thing to do to bring your sales database with you from Consytec. It is about the only way you can be sure to break the barrier in the new business quota you've been handed. You aren't sure yet whether the sales contact software you also bootlegged is going to do you any good, but you think it was a good idea to have it—just in case. Besides, you rationalized, the database is worthless without the software. Nobody said anything about maintenance of a database during your interviews with IRCT, nor did Greg when you were in the field with him for two weeks. This may be one area where Consytec might have been more advanced than IRCT.

Sunday, 2 PM *(two weeks later)*

What are the chances that a new rep with a company books a $600K order in the first two weeks on the job? Really, you just can't believe it, and somehow in the pit of your stomach you feel like you must have forgotten to describe some of the features or something. The sale just went down too easily. What's wrong? Jane thinks you're just paranoid. After all, she reminded you, the reason you were recruited into IRCT in the first place was because of your well-regarded competitive marketing skills. After all, they literally bought you—with expense account privileges, company car, tuition assistance for an executive MBA at a top school, a terrific territory, and a shot at national account rep by this time next year.

What are you worried about? Is this the plague of all new sales reps—or female sales reps? This sudden, "Did I really sell that? Did I demo that stuff enough? Did I really uncover all the needs? Did I describe the delivery systems?" It's all opening night jitters. Bottom line for you: It was just too easy. Your gut tells you that this deal is going to make a left turn before the contract is inked.

Dave has suggested you take the time to think it all through. "Maybe there *is* a glitch," he said. "A lot of confidence you have in me!" you said, as you slammed the door to your home office in Dave's face! Boy, are you touchy about this deal. That wasn't fair to Dave, and you know it. You're going to have to apologize. But not now. Let him back way off. Maybe it's coy, but Dave still hasn't said anything to you about the deal he's working on. Maybe this will make him think over whether he's got some competitive information from the acquisition he's working on that would help you sort this out. "Let him stew about it," you decide.

Friday 5 PM (end of week three on the new job)
On your way home from work today, you have decided to finally stop at the luggage store to return that Mont Blanc pen you bought yourself with the new briefcase, portfolio, and matching purse paid for out of your sign-on bonus. You haven't been able to find the ink refills and you are really upset about that. With the weekend coming up, you've also got to stop off at the ATM to get some cash. You remember that the bank has an ATM kiosk in the shopping center next to the luggage store.

Thinking back over the week, you calculate that you should still be able to get about $200 out of the ATM because your mortgage payment shouldn't clear until next Tuesday—it has to clear through Delaware, and that usually takes five days. Monday's payday. Of course, you're dead meat if the mortgage payment clears early and you've taken this $200 in cash. Oh well, what's a few hours of kiting when the bank knows you so well? The bank's branch manager will probably call you before the bank bounces anything. You really should apply for overdraft privileges one of these days.

At the luggage store, the original salesclerk is available, so you explain to him that you really want to return the pen. He is very cordial and takes the pen back without any complaint, taking your sales ticket to prepare a credit on your charge card. A few minutes later he returns with a red face and your card. Apparently he never charged you for the pen, and therefore, he can't give you a credit.

You and he both think the same thing you bet, "Too bad. This Mont Blanc was free!" Unfortunately, neither of you can do anything about it. You've given it back because you said you didn't want it. He's accepted it back. The transaction complete, you've just got to take your credit card and leave. You kick yourself all the way home thinking about the $200 pen you just gave away! You wonder if the clerk is going to put the pen back in inventory or keep it for himself.

Saturday

It's time to kick back and relax. You and Dave have decided to take a quick trip over the weekend to Calvister, your favorite little hideaway about three hours away. You have rented a room at the Calvinist Inn, and you're going to get back to nature for a while. You and Dave decide to leave at 7 AM to get a jump on the weekend traffic.

Your first stop is the Donut Shoppe at the gas station. Two coffees and two croissants and you'll be on your way. After you got back in the car, you realized you just made some money on the transaction: Instead of getting change for the $10, you got change for a $20. You and Dave looked at each other and just laughed. Dave's only remark was, "The Shoppe just bought us mimosas at the Inn!" and he put the car in gear and sped out onto the highway toward Calvister.

Wednesday PM *(five weeks later)*

Well, you're on your way to a great career with IRCT. You crashed the first month's quota with that $600K sale to Virtutec. Your sales manager, Frank Ziewski, even gave you special recognition. He also invited you to attend the big game with him and the executive vice president of worldwide sales. On the way to the game, after he picked you up, he stopped to put gas in his wife's car.

You noticed with interest that he used the company's gasoline credit card to do it.

You used the opportunity to ask Frank about some of the expense account privileges. You asked if it was standard operating procedure in the field to write off drinks with the other reps when you were traveling together. You didn't want to squeal on Greg, but he seemed to liberally write off all the expenses you two had during your ridewith. Frank took an interest in your story about the lunches and suggested you figure that one out on your own as you get used to the IRCT systems. Then he laughed and changed the subject.

Monday

The following Monday you finally got the phone call you were waiting for from Virtutec. Your $600,000 buyer has asked to see you as soon as possible. He suggested you stop by after work tonight. When you arrived at 6 PM, your customer greeted you in the lobby and was very cordial. But instead of inviting you into his office, he informed you that he had made 6:30 dinner reservations at a "lovely little French restaurant on the east side of town."

You were outraged, but couldn't show it. He didn't even bother to *ask* if you were in a position to join him, but instead told you his wife and children were visiting his in-laws and he hated to dine alone. He said, "I think we can discuss some of my concerns about the E-57K order over dinner just as easily as in the office," then he smiled wryly and held the door for you to leave the office with him.

On the way to dinner you kept thinking, "How can I get out of this?" About the only thing you were able to do right was to lie about this restaurant being "on the way home" so you could have your car. God *forbid* this guy puts the moves on you over dinner. What if he did? What are the chances that he won't?

The Virtutec order is the single biggest order in the company so far this quarter. Frank Ziewski already made such a big deal about your ability to close this business in your first month with the company. Your mind searched through the details of the business. You know the customer signed the contract, and you processed the paperwork for the sale just this week. The order probably hasn't made it out of the regional sales office yet. Can this guy back out? Is there any way he can renege at this point? Well, all you know is that the check isn't in the mail yet.

If only you could just turn around and make a beeline for home. Sick to your stomach, you reach for your cellular phone to call Dave and explain what's happening—well, at least to let him know you aren't going to be home for dinner. Somehow you have to make it sound to Dave like this is an expected and formal dinner that you forgot to tell him about. Otherwise he'll make matters worse by making you feel like you don't know how to handle yourself.

Could this really be happening to you? What are you going to do if this creep puts the contract on the line? What are the chances he's not going to? It's just too perfect a situation for him. What would Ziewski think of you if you lost this order over a proposition?

As you pull into the restaurant parking lot, Dave answers the phone. "Hello, Dave? I'm going to be home late tonight. Yeah. I forgot all about this dinner with the people from Virtutec. Yes, I think it is a celebration dinner. We're going to probably be until 9:30 or so."

THE ETHICS DEBATE

Four basic bodies of knowledge influence our ethics: scientific, metaphysical, religious, and secular values. In the scientific or metaphysical realm, we are concerned mostly with "what is real." What is right and valuable usually is dictated by our psycho, social, secular, and religious upbringing. What is *true* comes from our same roots in religious and secular training.

American history has developed secular values, which includes some of what we consider to be basic rights: freedom of speech, liberty, pursuit of happiness, and justice. We are now adding the employment relationship to those values, and include the right to work in a place free from hostility (sexual harassment and discrimination). Legislation and protection of our inalienable rights as workers is entering a new era.

As religious and familial ties break down in our society and the economy matures, the corporate sector has developed this odd secular role of defining what is valuable (right) and what is true. If you doubt this, think about who you believe when there is an oil spill or other ecological disaster. Also, ask yourself if the US government can be trusted to tell the truth when there are elections at stake.

The main problem facing new entrants into the business world in the late 20th century is that standards of conduct are no longer an adequate measure of *business* ethics. Daily newspaper and television stories tell of conflicts of interest ranging from female DEA agents' protection of Nicaraguan drug kingpins because they were sexually involved, to suppression of government cover-ups in toxic waste cleaning efforts, to the disgraceful practice of the Veterans Administration doctors covering up the cancers caused by chemical warfare. The stories are so common they have lost their power to shock.

Herein lies the problem of developing an ethical value system: The boundaries have blurred to the point of ambiguousness. Pollution, bribery, racial discrimination in lending, under-the-table deals, all spread disrespect for the law and yet, just as many ethical challenges deal with unlegislated issues.

The morality of the situation is what is at risk. The conscience is always there. When you ignore your conscience, it just goes subconscious. People have reported that repressed guilt, and the psychological and physical consequences of it, have been caused by not acting on their conscience about an unethical situation.

The tough part about business is that a person with a well-developed conscience will be at a disadvantage in business until the drive for success is balanced against some personal ethical policy. The type of conscience we are referring to is the one that can make the trade-off between an entrepreneur taking advantage of an opportunity to make a buck and making a decision not to do business and weakening the company's finances by turning down a piece of business. A deteriorating social and economic condition will create moral pressure to do just the opposite. Can a sense of right and wrong transcend the economic basis of business?

After all his research into the subject with heralded business icons such as the late Chester Barnard and A. A. Berle, Jr., Albert Z. Carr said, "No company can be expected to serve the social interest unless its self-interest is also served, either by expectation of profit or by the avoidance of punishment." Are each of us so different than the collective wisdom of business?

At the core of unethical actions is a private rationale that "I deserve this," or "I'm entitled to do this." Is there a temporary lapse from responsibility or obligations to others? Is there an exemption from guilt due to a self-permissive act?

Consider a debate, for example, in your view of the "Truth or Consequences Case." Did you side with the sales representative when she found the need to pressure Dave to reveal confidential information or trade secrets? Did you think she was within her bounds of being right when she lied about where she lived, rather than ride with the customer to the restaurant for dinner on the eventful night? If you felt a certain "So what?" about the decisions facing the rep in our story, you will need to dig deeper to connect yourself with your moral code.

COMPARATIVE ETHICS: THE SPIN DOCTOR

Do you deal with ethics in your personal life differently than you would in business? Do you think women have a different ethical value structure than do men? Do you think your values would change if you changed employers? Do you know the difference between discretion and politics? Do you believe ethical standards have gone through paradigm shifts since the turn of the century?

Every sales representative and sales manager finds himself or herself with time pressures, quotas, and proprietary information that can cause dilemmas. There are relatively few ways to cut the data to solve the problem. We can try to solve ethical problems by considering the degree of visibility and difficulty of the suggested decision.

The model described below offers one such data collection device. Figure 10–3, which is described as a payoff matrix, is a tool for data collection.

To clarify the visibility measurement, consider whether the action you take will be visible right away or later or maybe never. To understand how to apply the difficulty measurement, consider whether the action is going to take a long time to implement. This could make it difficult to do. Another consideration of difficulty is the extent to which you can operate independently in taking the action. Obviously, if you can do it by yourself, it makes it much easier because you don't have to explain it to anyone else. Use this payoff matrix to examine a few of the issues that faced our Truth or Consequences sales rep. This is assignment three. Then, try using

FIGURE 10–3
Payoff Matrix

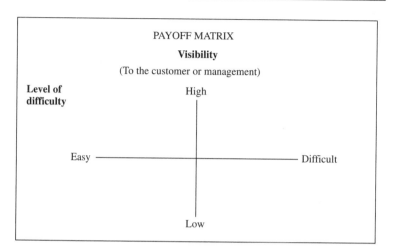

PAYOFF MATRIX

Visibility

(To the customer or management)

Level of difficulty

High

Easy ———————————————— Difficult

Low

this model to help you solve problems created by ethical dilemmas in your own life.

What might this payoff matrix have looked like when Ford decided not to recall the Pinto or when Thiokol executives decided not to act on the information about the O rings that caused the Shuttle disaster? Everyday management teams make decisions that are calculated risks of getting caught, and each time the trade-off of whether—even if they do get caught—the cost of a lawsuit they would settle out of court is worth the profits they will collect in the meantime.

POWERLESS?

If your enthusiasm is dampened just a bit from the thronging crowds at the end of the bonus race, consider that you can do something even though your sense of social responsibility will undoubtedly be shaped by the company that employs you.

How to Spot a Pattern

On the way to helping you develop a clear ethical boundary for yourself, let's see if you can spot patterns of unethical or borderline practices. Let's revisit Truth or Consequences to see what patterns you observed and what actions you can learn to take to ameliorate the ethical dilemmas were you to be placed in similar situations.

For those of you who think "I've seen this movie before," bear with the exercise. See what you can learn about yourself as you put the sales rep from the case under the magnifying glass.

First, does the rep in the case seem to deal with ethics differently in her personal life than she does in business? It would seem so. She sees it as wrong, but potentially harmless, to feign ignorance about Dave's file folder on the dresser and fib about the customer dinner having been planned. How might this affect her ability to perceive the drift of Frank Ziewski? How will she read his snide remark and chortle? Chances are she thinks her new company, IRC Technologies, plays by different rules than she has become accustomed to and she will need to learn some new politics.

Second, do you think her gender has anything to do with her natural ethical stance? Are women supposed to be coy? Is this a native female value? Many women would argue, including me, that being coy is a developed skill—and will not be content with it being labeled as a "female" character defect.

And what of entrapment? Does she feel differently toward entrapment when it is happening to her (as with the customer) as compared to how it felt when she did it to Dave?

Entrapment, it would appear, is a neutered issue. No one likes to feel like a caged animal. However, the probability of an attack as a natural reflexive action (once your back is in the corner) is considerably more typical of dominant male behavior than it is female.

When she felt the power "pinch" of being faced with the possibility of a sexual advance versus the loss of the business, she gave in to the situation. This lack of assertiveness in seemingly assertive women confounds most male colleagues. But it is much more typical than many would think.

The term *whimping out* is an apt description. The female's natural, reflexive reaction to power plays needs much more development. It is the subject of a number of new training programs.

Another pattern that appears as frequently in men as in women is bootlegging software and videotapes. Our rep did it with the sales contact software and the database. It is stealing, and it is as typical in the daily life of a professional as is lunch.

The fact that no one can really police individuals means this is left to be managed at the "collective conscience" level by the company. While I can't think of anyone that hasn't copied a disk illegally, the consequences of that action haven't been effective. It's like tearing the "do not remove" labels off of pillows—it has become a joke.

Changing political systems is another tricky pattern we saw emerge in our case. Have you experienced this? Do you think your values would change tomorrow if you changed employers? No, probably not overnight. But, given one to two years of constant weighing and balancing your options, discussions with colleagues and superiors, and a healthy dose of watching what happens when somebody reads the signals wrong, chances are good that you will be affected. For some of us, that is good—because the company may improve our perspective on watching out for the other guy or simply make us more socially responsible. For others, the opportunity to learn how to lie and when to withhold information becomes a shocking learning experience. I know, I faced it myself.

My first real job involved working in the training department of a major bank. My boss, a PhD in organizational psychology (no less), asked me to send a box of videotapes out for duplication. He had just accepted the position as director of human resource development for the bank, coming from an out-of-state company. Allowing for how tight our training department budget was, he wanted to save the bank the expense of buying tapes he already used at his previous company.

I was dumbfounded. Not only was I horrified to learn he had asked his former assistant to ship the tapes to us at his former employer's expense, but also he wanted me to go along with his request to duplicate the videos. I said no. He laughed. Then he asked someone else who didn't know any better to do it. It was a big joke to him. But he never asked me to do anything illegal again, even though I had a few more run-ins with his ethics (over sexual favors and colluding over large moving expenses that were a violation of company policy) before I quit the company.

I went straight from that employer into a small consulting firm, where I was confronted with an even bigger problem. One day I found out the man I was writing checks to for "referrals" was the client. It seemed he couldn't afford Gucci loafers and nice suits on his salary and asked that every consultant cough up 10 percent of their annual retainer just for the right to do business with his employer. Nice deal for him. Every consultant they had put him on the "dole roll."

I refused to write the checks. But the president of the consulting company, fearing reprisal, wrote the checks himself. One day the guy got transferred to Transylvania. Everybody wondered why. I knew somebody had to have fingered him. No. It wasn't me.

I think I know the difference between politics and discretion. Some things you just do not talk about. Not to anyone. We saw that several times in our case study. The biggest example in the case never did play out: Would she or wouldn't she tell Frank Ziewski about the client's dinner behavior?

On a smaller scale, the rep had a perfect chance to ask her new boss about the acquisition, but didn't. She also could have read Dave's file. But that would have been a breach in the confidentiality of Dave's information. She didn't do that either. How many of you could have put that file back on the dresser and left it there, unread?

Is nosiness a gender issue? I think not. There are a fair number of both sex who would think nothing of reading Dave's file if given half a chance. After all, she could keep his knowledge a secret. Discretion, as called for in this situation, would mean knowing when to use that kind of information to political advantage.

Conflict Resolution Skills

If you are looking to build skills to deal with the conflicts the previous scenarios presented to you, what do you need to learn? The basic sales skills will hold you in good stead. The basics in handling ethical dilemmas shown in Figure 10–4 are listening, probing, paraphrasing, redirecting, and selling the long-term benefits versus a short-term, quick hit.

At the end of the chapter there are sample situations that will test your skill in quickly spotting the dilemma and determining how to respond. If you have someone working with you to whom you can pose the questions or role-play the scenarios, you will soon develop quick reflexes and some standard lines that can help you keep your cool in conflict-laden situations.

Developing Ethical Boundaries

Do you think ethics have changed since the turn of the century? Most Americans would agree that our ethics have slipped at an

FIGURE 10–4
Skill Model Listening

Probing
Paraphrasing
Redirecting
Selling the long-term benefits

---

individual level, but most would also agree that the collective con-science of our country is making a comeback. The problem really is, how can we reconcile global issues with our own individual per-spective that allows us to fudge T&E expenses, pay tips with cash and the bill with our charge cards, write off charitable donations we don't make, break promises to our kids, miss appointments or show up late, and bootleg videos?

If you've read Stephen Covey, then you know his answer is using the "Seven Habits of Highly Effective People." In a nutshell, he talks about developing principles. If you can make the leap with me that building principles leads to greater productivity (a.k.a. "more effec-tive people") then the bottom line for stronger ethics is success. The real issue seems to be being able to unravel the complexity of things. People can get the work done with a minimum amount of difficulty if things are simple. Political organizations thrive on complexity. Hence, most businesses are less productive than they could be if they could get back to some of the basic principles of clear commu-nication. Then empowerment might work.

Covey's work differentiates between what he calls "personality ethics" and "character ethics." He defines personality ethics as a strongly held belief that if you have the right personality, behavior, attitude, skills, and image, then you will be a success. He contrasts this with the character ethics—integrity, humility, fidelity, temper-ance, courage, justice, patience, simplicity, modesty, and the Golden Rule.

Another important distinction, according to Covey, is that prin-ciples are external, while values are internal. This helps us in our search for personal ethics in the political environment within which we work. Covey believes principles are natural laws and values are subjective and arguable. Covey would probably argue that a com-pany that has unethical business practices will, in the end, go out of business. The natural laws will take care of it.

One of the showstoppers for me was Covey's statement, "You can't talk yourself out of problems that you behaved yourself into." You have to behave yourself out of ethics problems, too. The way to develop an ethical social system in a company, according to Covey, would be to build policy and tasks that end up producing the desired results. Over time, people would adapt their character to these choices of work habits.

Covey presents the work of a noted sociologist, Emile Dirkheim, in a recent interview. In Dirkheim's view, "Laws are unnecessary when mores are sufficient. When mores are insufficient, laws are unenforceable." That about sums it up: Our laws seem to be unenforceable.

The Role of the Customer

Getting back to business, our discussion of ethics would be incomplete without an exploration of the changing role of the customer–supplier relationship that exists today. To put ethics into the perspective of the customer, you have to think of ethics within the client relationship management process. Ethical choices begin the minute you start identifying the customer's needs, and they extend right through to the delivery of the required product and the service that complements it.

Could you or your company stand up to the ethical scrutiny of your major customers today? The question is not whether buyers and sellers lie to each other, but to what extent they do. To what extent does the sales force stretch the truth for a customer in order to get its own company to deliver what the salespeople know they can sell? How fair is sales management in dealing with performance issues? Is ethical behavior rewarded? Is profit the company's only objective? At what cost? These are the fundamental building blocks from which ethical choice is derived.

Never before in the postindustrial era has the customer had so much power. Today, the customer keeps computerized records of purchases and inventory usage and can pretty much dictate to a manufacturer when to ship and at what price. In the food industry, the power of the retailer changed so much in the late 1980s that sales training courses were being developed to deal with the power imbalance.

It would appear that the balance is also changing in the pharmaceutical business. A paradigm shift has developed where pharmacists, nurses, and doctors have had it with useless trinkets and slick golfing videos that introduce new products. They want hard facts and education. These professionals want to understand, they want to stay on top of the latest in molecular technologies. It will not be long before some companies start to realize that what is needed is trust building and a strategic partnership with these buyers. When that happens, there will be a major new role for the sales professional as the marketing strategy undergoes a major realignment to these new realities.

How does the power void affect you? Well, if part of your role was or still is devoted to forecasting expected customer demand, you can expect that duty to go away if your customers computerize their requirements systems. Why? Well, they don't need you to guess at when they are going to purchase when they can time their use of your product to their manufacturing process.

This is equally applicable to service businesses. If you are in need of examples, how about the timing of credit requirements or more generally, cash flow management. Companies with sophisticated treasury MIS systems do not give their lending officers much profit. Another example: If you know any auditors in a public accounting practice, you know they probably bore the full brunt of the power of the megabusiness mergers of the 1980s. Suddenly all those mergers created fierce competition among rather complacent accounting firms. All the "cushy" audit jobs on retainer for decades quickly became the whipping boys for the best package of public accounting services for the newly formed company. This rewrote a lot of contracts and, unfortunately, cost a number of accountants their jobs.

However, it created a new role in public accounting: the marketing functioning. Not that all these marketing types were welcomed with open arms. Remember, sales and marketing people haven't always had the most savory reputation in the eyes of accountants. It was an unholy alliance for the better part of 7 to 10 years as the marketing people learned the ethics of marketing professional services. It has really created a new niche for marketing people.

Other service businesses, including lawyers and designers, have all had to rely on marketing savvy to build their practices. The skills do not always come naturally to people who never thought they would have to promote their services to obtain work. But as the competitive marketplace became more vicious, everyone from chiropractors to printers have had to become experts at selling themselves.

Some of us can even remember the day when the only type of lawyers who advertised were fly-by-nights, and the only people who needed to sell their services in a promotional way were people who could not get business any other way. Today, it is a common practice made as professionally important as learning one's trade. Are ethics playing a bigger role as these professionals advertise and sell their services? You bet.

Ethics is also a major determinant of success of some newfangled organizational systems that blur the lines of distinction between supplier and customer. Some say it's because of ISO 9000, or total quality initiatives, or the latest "virtual organizations." But a day may come when your honesty and trustworthiness as a sales professional will spell the difference between your company's becoming a preferred supplier or becoming another has-been looking for a new market niche.

To say the least, businesspeople will find themselves with many more potential conflicts of interest. The reason is simple. More information on both sides of the table will be shared earlier in the buying process than ever before. Sometimes that information will not be treated confidentially. Trade secrets and professional standards for protecting those secrets will be tested over time.

As the customization of products proliferates and companies find themselves niche players in several markets simultaneously, you may find the sales practices (and the ethics of those practices) differentiated by market. What does this mean? The product may sell differently in different markets. The product may also face different competitive advantages in different markets. So your sales and marketing approach will adapt to the circumstances. That may mean your change in behavior or sales practices may feel like ethical dilemmas as you shift markets. Professional standards (the obligations and accountabilities) of competitors may vary market to market. So may the types of contracts used in trade and the potential conflicts of interest. Even the employment relationship between the supposed supplier and salesperson may be different in different markets. For example: In one market, direct sales channels may be the norm, while in others, independent contractors may be more typical.

WHEN TO SPEAK UP

All along there has been an undercurrent in this chapter about accepting responsibility for your own actions. At what point do you have an obligation to speak up about someone else's actions? Potentially, even you and your boss may have ethical differences.

We have counseled a number of senior executives. In one example, it meant calling in federal agents over a senior management scam that cooked the books. Our client, who was investigating methods for improving the documentation of the files, was told by those senior managers (and board members) to find something else to occupy his time.

He was desperate to make the right choice. For him, it was a career liability to be in a position of knowing what he knew. It was also a health risk, if you know what I mean.

And for him, the likelihood of being involved as a withholder of information that affected the profitability and legality of business deals meant his chances for working for a publicly traded company ever again were mincemeat if he got caught as a colluder. In the end, he called in the feds. But only after what I remember to be many long distance calls between the client and my partner.

Just how do you make the choice of speaking up? First, if you have a set of ethical boundaries, you will know pretty well when someone crosses them. Second, you need to judge for yourself the risk you—professionally and personally—are in with access to the unethical conduct. Third, you need to assess the size of the damage and who is being damaged by the suspected abuse.

After this three-point assessment, if you believe it is in the best interests of yourself, your company, and/or your customer to speak up, make sure you do it with the right person. If the boss is the one who is behaving in an unethical manner, then be prepared to skip one or two levels up for a discussion. And as you escalate the dialogue, be sure you have evidence, or your name will be mud.

Consider who else may also be knowledgeable about the practice(s) in question before you proceed to the next highest level. Just as in the Michael Milken case (Drexel Burnham Lambert), everybody knew something about what Michael was doing, and many employees privately (and not so privately) commented, "He will get his due." In the end, very few were ignorant of his actions, although I think the case uncovered even deeper abuses than most were even aware of.

At the end of the day, you and your conscience are the final judge. If you cannot sleep at night, seek some counsel. If your company does not yet have an ethical hot line or a grievance process for handling this type of situation, call the top human resources professional.

Typically, HR professionals come across all manner of seedy information about the goings-on in the companies they serve. For what it's worth, not much you say can shock them. In fact, you may have the missing piece of data they need to nail someone who has been observed and suspected of abuses that no one can document.

Even if you do not see any immediate action from your complaint, you can rest at night knowing the responsibility for acting is now in the hands of competent professionals. If you don't think you can trust the competence of the HR department, go straight to the top. Just be prepared to have your personnel jacket pulled and sifted through. Be sure you can stand up to the scrutiny of a strong light. If you have had any shady practices or run-ins with people in the past, your report may have less credence. Which is one more reason not to cry "wolf!" unless you know your proverbial skirts are clean.

CONCLUSION

The study of ethics is ethereal and some say too theoretical for practical use by the sales profession. I think that's wrong. You can handle the theory just so long as you have some opportunities to practice what you have learned. After all, think of some of the difficult technical discussions you get into with clients. You didn't learn to be good at that sales pitch overnight. It took practice, and it paid off. In the long run, applying yourself as diligently to setting boundaries for yourself ethically will pay off handsomely.

The chapter has given you the history of the debate, tried to help you define ethics, and has suggested that ethical practices will be taking on more importance as our competitive business environment and society change. Other trends have swept the business environment, and so have fads. Sometimes it is hard to tell the difference. **It is my belief that ethics is a trend, not a fad. Certainly you cannot lose anything by learning how to make ethical trade-offs.**

In closing, there are two key learning points I hope you have gleaned from this chapter: (1) learn to set personal boundaries, and (2) learn how to skillfully defend them. Using the material at the end of the chapter, you can test your principles for living and working, and that can help you become a more effective, competent sales professional.

We encourage you to photocopy the survey at the end of this chapter and send it back to us for tabulation. We expect that anonymous students responding over the next several years will help us to understand your educational needs because of the ethical dilemmas you face in the profession. As we understand more about your needs, we can build more effective courses to help you become more successful.

PRACTICE EXERCISES

Ranking

Rank the following items from most to least severe. After individual work is complete, ask table teams to present findings.

_____Taking office supplies home for personal use.

_____Not performing quality control on a proposal.

_____Sharing proprietary information over a beer after work.

_____Getting competitor information by dating a sales rep from a competitor.

_____Keeping inaccurate travel logs.

_____Receiving excessive gifts.

_____Giving excessive gifts.

_____Offering a kickback.

_____Accepting a kickback.

_____Engaging in insider trading.

_____Abusing drugs.

_____Drinking on the job.

_____Engaging in sexual harassment.

_____Having sex with a customer to get the order.

(continued on p. 262)

Ethics Checklist

(You may copy this worksheet for use in the assignment given on page 240.

Truth or Consequences Case Issue	Issue Type (Use the five issue codes: PS, PO, CI, P, ER)	Yes, this situation would present an ethical problem for me.	No, this situation would not present an ethical problem for me.
1.			
2.			
3.			
4.			
5.			
6.			
7.			
8.			
9.			
10.			
11.			
12.			
13.			
14.			
15.			
16.			
17.			
18.			
19.			
20.			
21.			
22.			
23.			
24.			
25.			
26.			
27.			
28.			
29.			
30.			
31.			
32.			
33.			
34.			
35.			

Source: Adapted from John McLeod, PE.

Answer Key for Assignment 1

(You may copy this worksheet for use in the assignment given on page 240.

Truth or Consequences Case Issue	Issue Type (Use the five issue codes: PS, PO, CI, P, ER)	Yes, this situation would present an ethical problem for me.	No, this situation would not present an ethical problem for me.
1.	CI		
2.	TS		
3.	CI		
4.	CI		
5.	ER		
6.	P (conflict of interest)		
7.	P		
8.	ER		
9.	PS		
10.	PO		
11.	PO		
12.	ER		
13.	PS		
14.	CI		
15.	P		
16.	PS		
17.	PS		
18.	P		
19.	PS		
20.	P		
21.	PS		
22.	P		
23.	PS		
24.	P		
25.	PS		
26.	P		
27.	ER		
28.	PS		
29.	PS		
30.	P		
31.	P		
32.	PS		
33.	PS		
34.	ER		
35.	P		

_____Showing favoritism in hiring.

_____Abusing expense account (cheating by making false expense claims).

_____Discriminating against women and minorities.

_____Evading income tax.

_____Marketing unsafe products.

_____Discharging untreated toxic waste into the environment.

_____Falsifying company invoices to support request for larger budget.

_____Lying to defend your boss.

_____Not showing up for an appointment because you forgot.

_____Taking another person or a couple on the company sales incentive trip as a "friend."

_____Cashing in first-class tickets for coach seats and pocketing the difference.

Discussion questions:

1. How would the ranking of your list need to be modified if you stood to make an additional $25,000 this year in bonus if you achieve your sales/budget target?

2. Try to classify the ranked list as: (*a*) against company policy, (*b*) illegal, (*c*) immoral.

Case Situations

To practice selling skills in an ethical dilemma, several case studies are presented below. Select a practice partner to take the role of the aggressor, so you have the opportunity to develop a comfortable, confident approach strategy for the type of scenario presented.

Rely on the skill model on page 253 for a guide on how to structure the response to the aggressor.

Case 1. The regional vice president is allowed to buy first-class tickets and then cashes them in for coach, pocketing the difference. You watch this and want to know if this is company policy.

Case 2. The vice president of sales tells the district manager to send someone to a training class and reimburse the participant by putting down an entertainment expense on the expense account so they don't have to go through any red tape in HQ Training and Development to get the person into the class.

The sales representative also submitted overstated telephone calls, auto mileage, and doctored a few meal receipts in the same expense report. You are the district manager. What should you do?

Case 3. The sales manager of an automobile dealership is informed that several customers have car repair problems that the regional office is well aware could be the next major recall of the line. In one case, the faulty mechanical problem caused a failure so significant that it endangered the customer's life and the customer was understandably unnerved by the experience. The sales manager values the customer's business and gives them the phone number of the customer service complaint line at regional headquarters. Pretend you are the sales manager. What should you do when the next customer approachs you about this same problem and asks you if this is a serious malfunction in the car?

Case 4. During performance appraisal, upward feedback to the manager is sought. You are an "honesty is the best policy" person, and you don't want to be dishonest, but you fear reprisal if you tell your district manager what you really think of her management skills. What should you say?

Case 5. You have deliberately overdrawn your account knowing your paycheck will be deposited tonight. The branch manager calls you in the morning and asks you if you know your account is overdrawn. What should you say?

Case 6. You have made a deposit and are withdrawing money at an ATM. You know you shouldn't be able to get any more cash today, but the machine gives you $500, which is $200 over your daily limit. You try the machine again and get another $500. It is 10:30 PM. What should you do?

Case 7. You are doing ride-withs with another representative who has been covering the territory to which you are going to be assigned. On a sales call during the ride-with, the other rep introduces information about a competitor's product that you believe to be hearsay. You have not been able to substantiate the claim yourself, and you can see the suspect information has had a dramatic effect on the customer.

After the sales call, you approach the sales rep to find out what he knows that you don't know. You learn he is no better informed than you are, but also heard through the grapevine that this feature was bogus on the competitor's new product line. You are vitally concerned that as a consequence of the previous sales call your new customer may have a faulty understanding of the competitor's product. What should you do?

Case 8.   You have been asked to set up a home office. The company has purchased you a PC and your wife, who is a graphic designer, has asked to use the computer for some freelance work at home while you are on the road. What should you tell her?

Bibliography

Andrews, Kenneth R. "Ethics in Practice." *Harvard Business Review,* September–October 1989, p. 99.

Carr, Albert Z. "Can an Executive Afford a Conscience?" *Harvard Business Review,* July–August 1970.

DeMaio, Harry B. *Information Protection Review.* Deloitte & Touche.

"How to be Ethical and Still Come to the Top." *The Economist,* June 5, 1993.

Gellerman, Saul W. *Harvard Business Review,* July–August 1986, p. 85.

Hager, Bruce. "What's Behind Business' Sudden Fervor for Ethics," *Business Week,* September 23, 1991.

Hammer, Michael. *Reengineering the Corporation.* In this best seller, he coined the term *business process reinengineering.*

"Interview with Wayne Silby: Making a Difference by Moving Money." *Business Ethics* 6, no. 6 (November/December 1992), pp. 28–30.

Kelly, Marjorie. "Musings: Business and the Decline of Kings." *Business Ethics* 7, no. 5 (September/October 1993).

Levine, Michael. "Guerrilla PR." IABC *Communication World.* New York: Harper Business, March 1993.

Manning, George, and Kent Curtis. *Ethics at Work: Fire in a Dark World.* Cincinnati: South-Western Publishing Co., 1988.

"Q&A with Stephen Covey." *Training,* December 1992.

Scharf, Cynthia. "The Wild, Wild East." *Business Ethics* 6, no. 6 (November/December 1992).

Thompson, Brad Lee. "Ethics Training Enters the Real World." *Training*, October 1990.

Trend Watch Column. "Marketing: Getting to Know All About You." *Business Ethics* 7, no. 5 (September/October 1993).

Mail-in Survey

To the reader: We are interested in an examination of the ethical values and practices of sales professionals who are participating in the IASP certification program. We value your input into this longitudinal study of ethical business dilemmas. Using the list below, we would like you to rank the items several times according to the scale explained below.

Directions: Using the scale, rank the item in the table on pages 267–268 for each of the four areas. You may assign different scores for the same item as you examine its frequency, perceived difficulty in dealing with it, your need for training in how to handle it, and your perception of how severe this ethical breach is according to your ethical standards.

There are *no right answers.* We are interested in surveying a random sample of participants in the IASP certification program to learn more about their educational needs and ethical practices.

It should take you 30 minutes to complete this survey. When you are finished answering all questions, please mail it in a plain envelope to: Corporate Learning & Development, 1139 East Putnam Avenue, Riverside, Connecticut 06878-1141 USA. If you prefer, you may fax your response to (203)637-8133. Thank you.

Scale: Please rate each item according to the following seven-point scale:

Frequency

1 Happens more often than once a day
2 Once a day
3 Once a week
4 Twice a month
5 Once a month
6 Once every few months
7 Once a year

Difficulty

1 The toughest issue I have to face
2 Big deal problem for me to deal with
3 Difficult to deal with
4 Hard, but not impossible to deal with
5 It used to be hard, but I figured out how to deal with it

6 It is no big deal for me to deal with this
7 Really easy to deal with

Training

1 Need heavy-duty training on this
2 Need training
3 Need some coaching
4 Would like to know more about this
5 Some training would be helpful
6 Some coaching would be helpful
7 No training needed on this

Severity

1 This is illegal, I think
2 The most wicked problem I know of
3 Big deal issue
4 Tough issue, but not the worst
5 Large issue, but not severe
6 Sort of a problem
7 Mildest form of ethical abuse

Rank each item four times, corresponding to the four different points of reference: frequency of occurrence, perceived difficulty in dealing with this type of ethical dilemma, your need for training in how to deal with it, the severity of this ethical breach in your perspective.

Abusive Practices Ranking

	Frequency of Occurrence	Difficulty Perceived in Dealing with it	Need for Training	Severity Rating
1. Taking office supplies home for personal use				
2. Not performing quality control on a proposal				
3. Sharing proprietary information over a beer after work				
4. Getting competitor information by dating a sales rep from a competitor				
5. Keeping inaccurate travel logs				

6. Receiving excessive gifts
7. Giving excessive gifts
8. Offering a kickback
9. Accepting a kickback
10. Engaging in insider trading
11. Abusing drugs
12. Drinking on the job
13. Engaging in sexual harassment
14. Having sex with a customer to get the order
15. Showing favoritism in hiring
16. Abusing expense account (cheating by making false expense claims)
17. Discriminating against women and minorities
18. Evading income tax
19. Marketing unsafe products
20. Discharging untreated toxic waste into the environment
21. Falsifying company invoices to support request for larger budget
22. Lying to defend your boss
23. Not showing up for an appointment because you forgot
24. Taking another person or a couple on the company sales incentive trip as a "friend"
25. Cashing in first-class tickets for coach seats and pocketing the difference

Demographic Questions:

Sex:	Age group:	Years in sales profession:
Male ____	Under 25 ____	0–5 ____
Female ____	26–35 ____	6–10 ____
	36–45 ____	11–16 ____
	46–58 ____	17+ ____
	59–72 ____	
	73+ ____	

Chapter Eleven

Stress Management

Sandra Fisher

WHY STRESS MANAGEMENT IN A BASIC SELLING SKILLS BOOK?

You get the new sales numbers. Your quota is up. Again. Your head pounds; your stomach tightens and burns. You reach for the industrial-size antacid container. It's empty!

"I never see you. You're working too hard!" complains your spouse when you accidentally run into each other grabbing for the morning coffee. Everything suddenly goes red. You explode!

Stress! Stress affects every part of your life.

The purpose of this book is to help you master the basic skills of selling. Although managing stress is not a specific selling skill, *how you handle stress can make the difference on whether you make or lose a sale.* Every sales skill you have learned in this book can be affected.

Think about it. If you are under too much stress, do you:

- Think clearly?
- Meet your deadlines?
- Listen to objections in a sales call?
- Concentrate on preparing a sales presentation?
- Speak pleasantly to colleagues?

Or do you

- Procrastinate doing paperwork?
- Yell at the support staff?
- Twitch when the phone rings?

- Make mistakes in the sales letter?
- Not return phone calls?
- Complain to anyone who will listen?

You Can't Sell if You Feel Like Hell!

How you handle stress is essential to attaining and maintaining health, productivity, peace of mind, life satisfaction—*and to becoming a peak sales performer!* In this chapter, you will learn:

- What stress is and how it affects your health and sales performance.
- How to recognize stress in yourself, and your prospects, clients, co-workers, friends, and family.
- How you are currently managing stress.

You will also learn stress reduction techniques:

- Coping skills:
    How to take control of your life.
    Time management.
    Assertiveness.
    Turn negatives into positives.
    Develop support systems.
    Cultivate a sense of humor.
- Lifestyle skills:
    Healthy lifestyle.
    Balance your life.
    Follow a high-energy, nutritious diet.
    Shape up for success.
- Relaxation skills:
    Your personal stress reduction plan.

WHAT IS STRESS?

Stress has become a popular buzzword to express a multitude of people's feelings, body reactions, and conditions. It is frequently fingered as the culprit that causes "whatever it is that ails you."

But it is something specific that happens within a person. Imagine this scene.

You are driving down the highway at a fast clip, hurrying to the sales appointment that has taken six months of perseverance to get.

Off to a late start because the car had a flat tire, you're thinking about the sales presentation and reviewing how to handle all the objections the prospect might have. You glance in the rearview mirror. Oh no! A police car is behind you flashing its lights, signaling to pull over. You come to a halt on the shoulder. The officer gets out of his car and advances toward you . . .

What are you thinking, feeling, and experiencing? What changes have occurred in your body? Perhaps something like this:

"Oh damn, I can't afford to get another ticket. How can I talk my way out of this?" Or, "If he writes the ticket fast, I can still make the appointment." Fear and anxiety grip you. Your head pounds, neck tightens, jaw clenches, clammy hands clutch the wheel, sweat breaks out, mouth goes dry.

You just experienced stress, also called the *stress response.* The stress response is an internal set of nonspecific responses to any perceived or real external or internal demand placed on you. The demand is often referred to as a *stressor* and can be caused by personal and business frustrations, family obligations, and financial concerns. Your internal response to any stressor is called a stress response. You might have heard it called "fight or flight" because it physiologically prepares a person to survive a perceived "dangerous" or "threatening" situation.

The body handles all stressors, good and bad, the same way. It treats all threats as if it were facing a physical attack and responds with chemical reactions so you can physically and mentally handle the situation. You are able to fight—defend yourself—or flee—run away fast. This fight or flight response was necessary to help us reach the 20th century, but we no longer need to, and most often cannot, fight or flee, which results in the chemical hormones building up to toxic levels in the body.

This is what happened to our errant sales rep when stopped by the police for speeding. Unable to fight or flee, the chemicals released into his bloodstream remain at high levels.

THE STRESS RESPONSE: WHAT'S HAPPENING INSIDE YOUR BODY

Let's look at precisely what happens to you during a stress response. *Every time your body is stressed, this physiological chain reaction phenomenon occurs—immediately.* The stress response can be mild to severe, depending on the demand or stressor. How often and to what degree you experience this physiological response, and whether it builds up in your system, can make the difference in your short- and long-term health—and performance!

Environmental stressor
↓
Brain perceives stressor and alerts
↓
Central and autonomic nervous systems
Endocrine system
↓
Hormones released into blood stream
ACTH, catecholomines
(epinephrine, norepinephrine)
↓
Raises blood pressure
Raises heart rate
Raises blood sugar levels
Stops digestion
Helps resist noxious stimulants
Strengthens, tenses, and contracts muscles
Restricts blood flow to veins and peripheral muscles
Increases blood flow containing extra sugar and oxygen to muscles,
heart, and lungs

THE STRESS RESPONSE: WHAT YOU MAY EXPERIENCE, FEEL, AND THINK

- Hair stands up.
- Pupils open wide.
- Sweat appears.
- Nostrils flare.
- Mouth goes dry.
- Jaw clenches.
- Hands feel cool, sweaty.
- Blood clots fast.
- Blood flows less.

- Lungs work harder; rapid, shallow breathing.
- Muscles contract.
- Heart beats faster, harder.

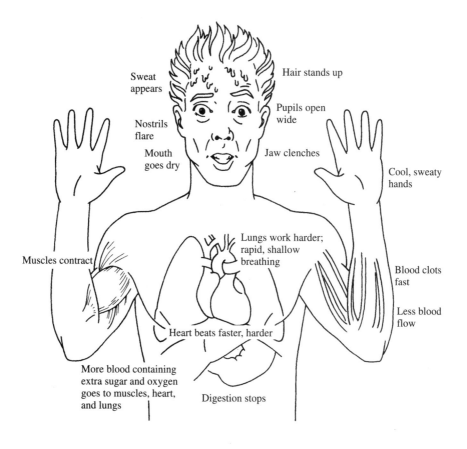

Sweat appears

Hair stands up

Nostrils flare

Pupils open wide

Mouth goes dry

Jaw clenches

Cool, sweaty hands

Muscles contract

Lungs work harder; rapid, shallow breathing

Blood clots fast

Less blood flow

Heart beats faster, harder

More blood containing extra sugar and oxygen goes to muscles, heart, and lungs

Digestion stops

HANDLING STRESS ON A SALES CALL

You're about to enter the office of the director of purchasing for Hot Shot, Inc. He is known in the industry to be a tough customer who drives a hard bargain. For days you have been preparing for this sales call. Suddenly you get a case of nerves: You're sweating, your mouth feels like cotton, your normally mellifluous voice goes up an octave, and you feel anxiety welling up in you. You must reverse this stress response immediately. Now what should you do?

1. Breathe!

This is the quickest way to start a relaxation response. When stressed, you take *shallow* breaths, depriving your body of oxygen. Unobtrusively (don't start heavy, noticeable breathing—the guy will think you're nuts), take a few deep, slower, quiet breaths. Inhale and exhale through your nose, as usual. As you exhale, feel the tension leave your body.

2. Positive Self-Talk

Say to yourself: I feel calm. I am prepared for this call. I can handle him. Slow down and concentrate on the job to be done. You're ready to sell!

YOUR BODY SPEAKS; ARE YOU LISTENING?

What are your stress points? Whenever you have pain or discomfort, such as backache, headaches, constipation, it's your body's way of communicating an important message to you. It's saying, "Help! Give me a break. You're pushing me too far, too fast. Lighten the load. Stop behaving this way. Too much drinking, smoking, caffeine, drugs. Fighting with your spouse, working too hard." Or your mind stumbles into mental blocks and misjudges situations.

It can be any of these things. But when they happen, take these symptoms seriously, and decide how you can decrease the pressure.

Think of any part of your body that is currently giving, or in the past has given, you problems when you experience stress. Note the ones that have caused you to take medication, have an operation, or go to the physician.

List the early symptoms that you experience when under stress.

1. _____
2. _____
3. _____
4. _____

List the symptoms and conditions that you experience when under chronic stress.

1. _____
2. _____
3. _____
4. _____
5. _____
6. _____
7. _____
8. _____

Of course, if you don't want to listen to your body, there's always denial. That's a defense mechanism when you tell yourself that nothing is wrong. "I can handle it." "I'm not upset." "No problem. Just having a bad day." "I'll work it out." Then see what happens to you!

CAN STRESS AFFECT YOUR HEALTH?

You bet! Up to 80 percent of complaints to doctors are due to stress-related illnesses.

After a stressful event, ideally the body returns to normal: muscles relax, blood pressure stabilizes, the stomach unwinds, breathing and heartbeat steady. But what day in the life of a sales rep has but a single demanding situation? When each day swirls in a tornado of ceaseless demands, stress begins to accumulate. And you suffer, physically and mentally.

Stress accumulates from major life events, such as divorce, personal injury, and the birth of a baby, to the daily hassles of a frenetic schedule. Your body begins to break down. Research shows that the adrenal glands, the body's prime reactors to stress, become exhausted, and you get sick—ranging from a minor, annoying cold to a devastating stroke. You must allow your immune system to rest, revitalize, and repair the body.

Otherwise, look for these common stress-related disorders in your life:

Heart disease	Allergies
Atherosclerosis	Pain
Hypertension	Injury-prone
Gastrointestinal disorders	Accident-prone
Irritable bowel syndrome	Change in appetite
Nervous stomach	Anxiety
Backaches	Depression
Neck aches	Paranoia
Shoulder aches	Renal failure
Dermatitis	

Let's take a look at how stress can affect personal and business life.

Ann is an experienced sales rep who has always performed in the top 25 percent of the sales force. Her job involves 50 percent travel, often working 10-hour days juggling a tough territory with countless problems. Last year Ann's mother was diagnosed as having cancer and has been undergoing chemotherapy and struggling with extensive pain. Her brother lost his job on Wall Street six months ago and is hinting that he might have to move in with her. Her best friend, with whom she spoke almost every evening on the phone, moved to Hawaii to pursue the "good life." Even though Ann has always prided herself on being well organized and able to handle everything, she's been feeling very tired and not wanting to get out of bed in the morning. At work, she is snapping at the service department and hardly listening to what sales prospects are telling her. Work used to be exciting, but now it feels like a drag. After working long days, followed by visits or calls to the hospital, she usually collapses in front of the television and relaxes with a few glasses of wine. Weekends are spent catching up on her household chores, caring for her parents, and stopping off at the local pub to have a few drinks with "the gang."

Is Ann under stress?
How do you know?
How is she handling it?
If she continues this way, what effects will it have on her?
What would you recommend that she do?

John is a sales rep with four years' experience on the job. Known as a high-energy go-getter, John was sales rookie of the year his first year. He prides himself on seeking every opportunity to learn how to be a better salesman and placed in the top division for the first three years. Recently, he ran into an old sports buddy who ribbed John about the new 25 pounds added to his middle and inquired how things were going. At first, John said everything was OK, but then added that during the last six months, he had gotten married; been transferred to a new, tougher territory; moved to a new community; and no longer had time to work out and play sports. Evenings and free time were spent fixing the house, catching up on paperwork, or plopping in front of the TV with his spouse and a few beers. His sales numbers were still going down, and he noticed he just didn't have the energy he used to. Getting old . . . settling down . . . you know how it is!

Is John under stress?
How do you know?
How is he handling it?
If he continues this way, what effects will it have on him?
What would you recommend that he do?

HOW DO YOU CURRENTLY MANAGE STRESS?

Here are many positive lifestyle behaviors and thoughts to help people reduce stress. How are you doing?

How Often Do You . . .	Never	Hardly Ever	Sometimes	Often
1. Have optimistic thoughts about your life.	0	1	2	3
2. Look forward to work.	0	1	2	3
3. Relate well to your spouse or lover.	0	1	2	3
4. Enjoy affection and physical intimacy.	0	1	2	3
5. Spend time with valued friends.	0	1	2	3
6. Assert your needs and wants at home and work.	0	1	2	3
7. Exercise aerobically 3 times a week (30 minutes each).	0	1	2	3
8. Eat breakfast.	0	1	2	3
9. Maintain your proper weight.	0	1	2	3
10. Eat a balanced diet.	0	1	2	3

	Never	Hardly Ever	Sometimes	Often
11. Get 7–8 hours' sleep at least four nights a week.	0	1	2	3
12. Participate in sports, recreation, and hobbies.	0	1	2	3
13. Play and have fun.	0	1	2	3
14. Take private, peaceful time for yourself.	0	1	2	3
15. Discuss concerns with a supportive person.	0	1	2	3
16. Speak openly about your feelings when angry or worried.	0	1	2	3
17. Consult health care professionals as needed.	0	1	2	3
18. Organize your time efficiently.	0	1	2	3
19. Accomplish a task you planned to do.	0	1	2	3
20. Get strength from your spiritual beliefs.	0	1	2	3
21. Define and achieve goals.	0	1	2	3
22. Keep your finances in order.	0	1	2	3
23. Practice a relaxation technique for 5–10 minutes daily.	0	1	2	3
24. Feel good about your accomplishments.	0	1	2	3
25. Believe you control most of your life.	0	1	2	3

Add up the scores. A score of 65 or above shows you are managing stress very well. Between 45 and 64, you can improve. Below 50 is poor. Examine all those you scored as 0 and 1, and consider how you can do them in your life, and those you scored as 2, how you can do them more frequently.

HOW MUCH STRESS ARE YOU UNDER?

How Often Do You Have . . .	Never	Hardly Ever	Sometimes	Often
1. Aches in shoulders, back, head, and/or neck.	0	1	2	3
2. Stomachaches, gas, nausea, or indigestion.	0	1	2	3
3. An illness that keeps you from working effectively.	0	1	2	3
4. Several things to do at once.	0	1	2	3
5. A feeling of exhaustion or fatigue.	0	1	2	3

6. Difficulty relaxing.	0	1	2	3
7. Little interest in physical intimacy or sex.	0	1	2	3
9. A desire to overindulge in alcohol.	0	1	2	3
10. A desire to indulge in mood-altering substances.	0	1	2	3
11. An urge to overeat or not eat enough.	0	1	2	3
12. Feelings of anxiety and worry.	0	1	2	3
13. Difficulty falling or staying asleep.	0	1	2	3
14. Feelings of depression, being stuck.	0	1	2	3
16. Feelings of being overstimulated or wound up.	0	1	2	3
17. Poor work performance.	0	1	2	3
18. Problems focusing and concentrating.	0	1	2	3
19. Worries about financial stability.	0	1	2	3
20. Arguments with family, friends, or co-workers.	0	1	2	3

Add up the scores. A score of 20 or lower indicates a low degree of personal stress reactions. A score between 21 and 39 reflects a moderate degree. A score over 40 indicates you are experiencing a high degree of stress in your life. Consult your physician as to whether you have a health problem that requires medical attention.

Common symptoms exhibited by people under too much stress:

- *Physical effects:* shallow breathing, numbness, tingling, cold hands and feet, queasy stomach, tight muscles, back and head pain, dry mouth, sweating, backaches, stomach upsets, headaches, hypertension, heart disease, immune disorders, and others.

- *Emotional effects:* anxiety, anger, boredom, depression, fatigue, frustration, irritability, moodiness, tension, nervousness, self-criticism, worry.

- *Mental effects:* difficulty concentrating, poor task performance, confusion, defensiveness, focus on details, sleepiness, mental blocks.

- *Behavioral effects:* smoking, over- or undereating, loss of appetite, drug abuse, alcoholism, impulsive or aggressive outbursts, crying, complaining, accident proneness, restlessness, blaming others, withdrawal and isolation.

- *Organizational effects:* job burnout, low morale, absenteeism, poor performance, mistakes, high job turnover, job dissatisfaction, lawsuits, sabotage, high use of medical facilities, accidents, poor working relationships.

CAN YOU RECOGNIZE STRESS IN OTHERS?

In each area, take one person you know who shows symptoms of being under a lot of stress. Briefly describe their symptoms.

Customers/clients: _____

_____

Co-workers: _____

_____

Spouse/lover: _____

_____

Children: _____

_____

Friends: _____

_____

SOURCES OF STRESS

Stress is a fact of life—sales goals, product launches, deadlines, presentations, heavy travel schedules, and performance objectives, not to mention balancing one's time between work and family. It can be caused by family concerns, job worries, financial obligations, personal expectations, and frustrations—almost anything.

"If I don't sell, I don't eat," said a sales rep with an educational training company. Another sales rep identified her major stressor simply: "Producing the required corporate numbers." *Making quota* is the most often reported cause of stress among sales reps I have interviewed. Also stressful is the chronic uncertainty of a salesperson's life. You never know what's ahead, and if you'll make the numbers.

Here is a list of common sources of stress reported by sales-people. Check your sources of stress:

Your job in sales

❑ Performance expectations.
❑ Making sales quotas.
❑ Constant rejection.
❑ Deadlines.
❑ Paperwork.
❑ Territory management.
❑ Never being caught up.
❑ Information overload.
❑ Working longer hours.
❑ New or difficult boss.
❑ Little recognition.
❑ Little or no feedback.
❑ Endless travel.

Your organizational environment

❑ Major changes in the workplace or industry: downsizing, restructuring, merger.
❑ Conflict between job and personal responsibilities.
❑ Insufficient income and benefits.
❑ Poor lines of communication.
❑ Fear of job loss.

Dealing with new technology

❑ Rate of change.
❑ Computers, faxes, e-mail, voice mail, cellular phones, and more to come.

Personal sources of stress

❑ Health problems, your own or family.
❑ Meeting family and household responsibilities.

❑ Poor relationship with spouse or lover.
❑ Lack of social life.
❑ Financial worries.
❑ No time for self.

Write down the major current sources of stress in your work and personal life. Separate them into chronic, a condition occurring on a daily basis, or occasional occurrences.

		Chronic	*Occasional*
On the job:	1. _____		1. _____
	2. _____		2. _____
	3. _____		3. _____
	4. _____		4. _____
Personal:	1. _____		1. _____
	2. _____		2. _____
	3. _____		3. _____
	4. _____		4. _____

STRESS REDUCTION TECHNIQUES

Now that you understand your stress symptoms, their sources, and causes, you're ready for the remedy! Let's look at a variety of mental and physical techniques that offer a way out of the quagmire you find yourself in and let you see the light at the end of the tunnel. Not all of them will work for you, but after trying some, you will soon know which ones give you the best results.

Stress is a challenge; how you deal with it means the difference between success and failure.

Coping Skills

Take control. Feeling in control is most importantly associated with good mental health. A person who feels in control is someone who takes charge and handles stressors positively. Rather than be passive and overwhelmed—"I can't do anything about it!"—instead . . .

The Stress Cycle

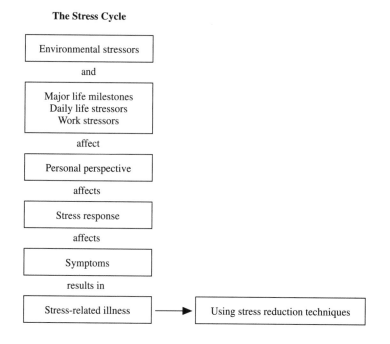

Become aware of symptoms, feelings, and stressful situations you are now experiencing.

Assess what's really going on. Step back from your feelings and mentally evaluate and analyze what is happening. Be realistic. Determine what choices you have to alleviate the situation.

Act, rather than worry. For example, you are exhausted and tired because you haven't had a good night's sleep in days. Cancel the dinner engagement, forget the ball game, and hit the sack early. Or you find out the company has been bought by a "mean and lean" international corporation, and your job is in jeopardy. Rather than sit and get anxious, update your résumé and make five calls to start networking in your industry.

Alter the situation. A "hit and run" lunch gives you indigestion, so brown-bag it in a quiet, comfortable place and really enjoy your lunch.

Avoid the situation. You're at a sales meeting, the gang is going out for some late-night partying, but you want to maintain your early morning jogging routine and weight loss program. Bow out gracefully, retire at your usual time, and wake up ready for the run.

Accept what you can't change. You're sad that a promising relationship fizzled out. Don't waste your energy. Let go when you
have to. You have done your best.

Time Management

There are just 24 hours in a day, so what you do with them
makes the difference. Trying to do too many things at once over-
whelms you, and puts you on a collision course. First, track how
you spend your time now, hour by hour, day by day, and see
where you waste time and where you can put it to better use.
Use your time planner system for both professional and personal
life. Start with your goals—what you want to accomplish, feel,
and experience. Then write down all the things you must do to
achieve them during this month, week, and day. Prioritize in
order of importance.

- Simplify your life.
- Keep only one "to do" list. Do away with little scribbly
  notes.
- Cut down on telephone time.
- Be realistic. If it's the end of the quarter sales blitz, don't take
  on the leadership of the community project.
- Create time-savers. For example, always keep your keys in
  the same place.
- Plan ahead. Put your clothes out the night before.
- Take a time management course.

Assertiveness

Ever get a headache by sitting on your feelings? Or the words get
stuck in your throat? Rather than clear the air, you sulk, take it out
on the kids or some poor hapless soul, all because you can't speak
up for yourself. Many of us are assertive in some situations and passive in others.

Assertiveness means you speak up for your rights, needs, and
wants, while not stepping on others. It does not mean you get your
wishes, but you have the right to ask. Yes, believe it. For example,
your manager consistently calls you late in the evening to discuss

the day's progress. Politely, but firmly, tell him that you need to discuss these matters at a more propitious time. Set boundaries on your time. Consciously decide what is important to you, and find ways to get what you need. Learn to say no.

Pent-up feelings are destructive. If you have a situation where you want to speak up, but you can't express what you want, it helps to role-play with a close friend or associate. Do away with the "shoulds." Let guilt go (never easy).

As you learn to become more assertive, you will learn to relax and lay claim to time that is rightfully yours.

Turn Negatives into Positives

Negative feelings and situations drain you of energy and turn a healthy body into a sick one. Our own minds are our most severe critic. We are too hard on ourselves. Here is one way to turn negative self-talk into positive language:

Take a stressor that you find particularly difficult to handle. Deal with your inner critic: I'm too old. I'm too fat. I'm not smart enough. Why does this always happen to me? I'm not a good . . . The negatives can be endless. Stop putting yourself down. *Apply some attitude adjusters. Replace the negatives with realistic positive thoughts. I can do this. It may be difficult, but it is possible.* The power of positive thinking. It's true—what you visualize comes true.

Another attitude adjuster is to ask yourself: What is the worst thing that can happen? Saying it out loud—being fired, losing $2,000, whatever it is—releases some of the pent-up fear and allows you a new perspective.

Develop Support Systems

You've had a bad day. All sales appointments ended in zilch. The quarter is ending and your manager is breathing down your neck.

Now's the time to call on your support systems, both at home and at work. Discussing your frustrations with a trusted colleague, close friend, or family member helps alleviate a lot of stress. It is essential to health and well-being to feel connected to other people. Studies show that if you feel isolated and detached, stress is much harder to bear.

Your first line of defense is your family. The second line is to make and retain your friends. Supportive relationships have to be developed and nurtured. It is important to have at least one close business associate whose opinion you trust and value to provide support through difficult times. Support is a two-way sharing process; both of you benefit from the give-and-take.

A Sense of Humor

Sales seems to attract outgoing, people-related personalities who enjoy quick verbal thrusts, jokes, and schmoozing.

Research shows that laughter causes physiological changes in the body, similar to aerobic exercise. According to one expert, laughing 100 times is like rowing for 10 minutes. Laughter stimulates the endocrine system to produce endorphins, diminishing tension in the central nervous system.

Just for laughs, try doing 30 seconds of nonstop belly laughter and notice how much better you feel. Everything tingles. Stress can make you very serious, boring, and unable to see beyond your own nose. Laughter helps foster creativity, wit, and maintain a better perspective. When you are around witty, humorous people, you will become more witty and humorous yourself. Laugh at your own mistakes. Be playful, take yourself lightly. Don't suffer from "terminal seriousness."

At a national sales meeting of a company facing a major crisis (plummeting sales), management hired an improvisational comedy team to present the serious issues facing the reps in a humorous way. Poking fun at their dilemma and placing the difficulties into a different perspective helped break the tension and loosen up the audience. Everyone slept better, at least for one night!

"RDLA" stands for recommended daily laugh allowance: 15 hearty laughs a day! It takes 72 muscles to frown and only 14 to smile. They who laugh, last!

SOS on Stress

Recognize the danger signs—don't let stress build up. If you recognize two or more of the following physical symptoms of stress, seek professional help from a mental health practitioner:

1. Changed eating habits.
2. Altered sleep patterns.
3. Upset digestive system.
4. Development of nervous habits.
5. Increased blood pressure.
6. Increased drinking or smoking.

Before Stress Becomes a Crisis

Pressures are building within you. Rather than wishing them to go away, it's important to understand exactly what is bothering you and determine what you can do about it. Here's a checklist to help you through a crisis:

Identify the symptoms:
- *What is your body saying to you?* Pain? Sick?
- *How are you acting?* Eating or drinking too much? Jumpy and nervous?

Figure out the cause:
- *What are you feeling?* Sad? Angry? Financial pressure? Too many things to do? Holiday frustrations?
- *What is causing you to feel this way?* Inner-office conflicts? New goal demands or policies? New boss? Family arriving?

Don't agonize! Do something!
- *Is it within your power to make changes?*
- *Where and how can you take charge of this situation?*
- *Will discussion relieve the problem?*

LIFESTYLE SKILLS

Healthy Lifestyle: Choosing Wellness

Wellness has become the operative word for describing a positive, proactive healthy lifestyle, one that both prevents disease and enhances the quality of your life. Wellness is defined as maximizing your potential—mentally, physically, and spiritually.

Reducing Health Risks

Harry was feeling pretty good. He was 38 years old, satisfied with his marriage, and had two fine kids. A consistently high sales performer, he had risen in his company to senior sales rep. He'd stopped smoking last year, seldom exercised except for the occasional golf game, and tried to keep his middle from getting too large. Except for the occasional backache, he had no health problems. Or so he thought.

Actually, Harry was a heart attack awaiting to happen. His blood pressure and cholesterol were abnormally high, and his lack of exercise and family history of heart disease put him at a high risk level.

Susan was also feeling pretty good. She was 32, also satisfied with her marriage, two fine kids, and outstanding sales performance. She prided herself on keeping thin. She rarely exercised, her smoking was up to half a pack a day, and she took birth control pills. Her mother had died of breast cancer at the age of 42, and her father of lung cancer at age 55. Susan was at high risk for cancer and for cardiovascular disease.

A big part of staying healthy involves knowing and reducing your risk factors. What's a *risk factor*? It's a condition or practice that increases the likelihood that you'll develop an illness. Some risk factors you can't control (age, gender, race); others (smoking, blood pressure, cholesterol) you can definitely do something about.

How do you find out about your risk factors? Just as there are warning lights on your car, there are "warning lights" for your physical health. If you are 5 feet 9 inches, weigh 250 pounds, and have a cholesterol level of 290, your warning lights are definitely on, and it's probably not just a loose fan belt!

Fill in the accompanying chart, discuss it with your doctor, and then keep it in your wallet as a reminder.

Risk Factor	Your Number	What It Should Be
Blood pressure		Under 140/90
Total cholesterol		Below 200
HDL (high density lipoproteins)		Over 50
LDL (low density lipoproteins)		Under 130
Triglycerides		Under 250

Body fat %	Women, 22%; Men, 15%
Ideal weight	Women: Count 100 pounds for your first 5 feet of height, then add 5 pounds for each additional inch.
	Men: Count 106 pounds for your first 5 feet of height, then add 6 pounds for each additional inch.
	Plus or minus 10 percent if large or small-framed body.
Cigarettes	None
Alcohol	No more than 2 drinks daily
Exercise, aerobic	20 minutes daily

Other risk factors to consider: age, race, gender, family history of diseases, response to stress, satisfaction with work and family life, oral contraceptive use, estrogen replacement therapy, dietary changes.

For more detailed information, call your local heart and cancer associations.

Check Your Lifestyle

Look at your current lifestyle and determine what necessary changes you can make to manage stress better. Turn to page 277 and examine your answers to "How do you currently manage stress?" Any item you marked "never," "hardly ever," or "sometimes" is an area for improvement. You can reduce your health risk and stress factors one at a time. Don't attempt to change everything overnight.

Look at your daily life. The following seven habits have been identified as promoting good health and longevity: (1) eating breakfast, (2) eating three meals a day, (3) keeping proper weight, (4) regular moderate exercise, (5) sleeping 7 to 8 hours, (6) no smoking, and (7) no more than one alcoholic drink per day.

Balancing Work and Personal Life

"Life after work?" said the single woman rep incredulously. Her married male colleague joined in, "I haven't seen my kid bat a home run in the entire season! And my wife has given up yelling about the paperwork." Or, "I'm a great mother and I'm great at my job, but I haven't had a moment for myself since 1988."

Sound familiar? Work seems to be eating up more and more time. Sales reps tend to be high-commitment, high-performance-driven individuals. Or they just don't last. And now tough market conditions are intensifying the pressures to perform. Most people sacrifice first themselves, then their relationships with their friends, then family without even realizing it. How are *you* doing?

Take Time for Yourself

Think about all the things you do in one week. What percentage of time do you estimate you spend on *yourself*, doing things that nourish, sustain, and enliven you as a human being? Do you need more time?

Achieving Balance

"We are body, mind, and spirit. We cannot stress one function of the self to the detriment of the others. When that happens we become unbalanced. Our lives become disrhythmic. The self suffers," writes George Sheehan in *Personal Best*.

Take this quick self-assessment to see how you are balancing your life.

Self-Assessment Rating Sheet

Rate each area below 1 to 5.   1 = outstanding, 5 = poor.

	Rating	*Actions to Achieve Balance*
Work	_____	_____
Relationships and love	_____	_____
Spouse or significant other	_____	_____
Family	_____	_____
Friends	_____	_____
Social	_____	_____
Financial	_____	_____
Intellectual	_____	_____
Cultural	_____	_____

Spiritual	_____	_____
Physical	_____	_____
Sex	_____	_____
Recreation and play	_____	_____
Exercise	_____	_____
Fun	_____	_____

You may wish the good fairy would wave a magic wand and give you 10 more hours a day. But 24 is all we get! *So what can you do?*

Step back. Consider your life. Stephen Covey says, "Begin with the end in mind." Look at the areas that you rated 3, 4, or 5. Then write down one or two actions in each area that you can do immediately (within the week) to improve the balance. Just in case your mind is blank, here are some actions other salespeople came up with during seminars, such as:

Social life: If you are not married or otherwise committed, go on a singles hike this weekend. Good for recreation and play, too!

Friends: Call an old friend for lunch; write two postcards to friends.

Work: Talk to colleagues about ways to streamline paperwork.

Financial: Make an appointment with a financial planner. Buy the insurance policy.

Intellectual: Go to a lecture at a museum, college, or school.

Sex: Buy something sexy and have a good time with a soulmate.

Schedule Self Time!

No one but you can balance your life. How much time during a day or a week do you spend meeting your needs and wants? You must nourish your own body, mind, and soul. As the proverb says, "Where the heart is willing, it will find a thousand ways, but where it is unwilling, it will find 1,000 excuses."

Shape Up for Success

"There is no question in my mind that an active lifestyle is linked to one's ability to perform."

James M. Rippe, MD, *Fit for Success*

Staying in shape and maintaining a regular exercise program is hard for anyone these days, but it's even harder for most salespeople. Reps report their biggest obstacles to fitness are being on the road 40 percent to 80 percent of the time in different locations, erratic schedules, and the ubiquitous excuse—no time.

Let's face it. When you're on the road, you have to be "on" all day and sometimes well into the night, if you have to entertain a client. Meetings are often scheduled for 7 AM. Paperwork faces you at 7 PM. The weather can be too hot or too cold. If you fly, your biological clock is often a wreck. If you drive, you're stuck on the road for long periods. You frequently find yourself in strange towns where you may feel disoriented (at best) or uncertain about your safety (at worst). You're stressed out, talked out, "meetinged" out; in a word, exhausted. The "couch potato workout"—lying on the bed watching TV—is understandably tempting.

The thing is, even though it's difficult for salespeople to maintain fitness while they're out there on the road, being fit is vitally important to your success and well-being. Take a look at top sales performers, the ones with the most energy, positive attitudes, and discipline. Sure, some look like they only exercise their arms lifting food to their mouths, but many take good care of themselves and that means being fit.

Fitness is a potent elixir. It helps reduce stress, high blood pressure, and obesity; improves self-esteem and personal appearance; and above all, increases energy. And energy, as any salesperson will tell you, pays off! Sales reps who regularly work out tell me that on average, they make 10 percent to 20 percent more sales calls per day. That's the bottom line: Being fit makes you able to handle your job and be more productive.

If you don't exercise regularly, the reason could be a variety of excuses. "I have to lose weight before I can exercise." "I need to lose 10 pounds first." "I'm too stressed to exercise." "First I have to get through this difficult period."

Well, if that is what you're thinking, you've put the cart before the horse. It's been proven that if you are going to change to a healthier lifestyle, beginning a program of regular exercise is the *first* thing you should do. Exercising helps make all those other changes you're talking about. It's a powerful way to decrease stress and increase energy. It is the only truly healthy way to lose weight.

It has been shown to be one of the prime components in any quit-smoking strategy. It improves your posture. It encourages you to eat more nutritiously. It helps you sleep. It gives you a more positive attitude. It makes you want to be healthy!

Your body was designed for movement. Use it or lose it.

If you are already an enthusiastic, regular exerciser, keep up the good work!

How Fit Are You?

Take this simple test to assess what kind of shape you are in.

Yes	No	
❏	❏	Can you touch your toes with your legs straight?
❏	❏	Can you walk 3 miles in 45 minutes without discomfort?
❏	❏	Is your weight within the recommended range?
❏	❏	Do you have confidence your body can play sports and perform activities you want to do?
❏	❏	Can you do 25 sit-ups and 25 modified (on your knees) push-ups?
❏	❏	Do you exercise aerobically 3 times a week for 30 minutes?
❏	❏	Do you have enough energy for your work and your personal life?

Fitness is the capacity of your body to perform. You need the following components for a balanced fitness program:

Aerobic exercise increases your stamina, improves your cardiovascular endurance, and gives you lots of energy. You must continuously move your large muscles for 20 to 30 minutes, three or four times a week. If you stick to it faithfully, you'll be hooked.

The thing to remember is that you do not have to be an athlete: you could walk 30 to 60 minutes, swim if water is your element, go for a bike ride, dance up a storm, or "do" the machines (skiing machines, stair climbers, stationary bikes, rowing machines, etc.). Whatever you choose to do, the best training guideline is to work hard enough to break a sweat, but not so hard that you're too short of breath to carry on a conversation.

Flexibility exercises keep the body supple and limber, increase the range of motion, and relieve stress. Do stretching exercises to limber all the joints at least four times a week for 20 minutes. Stretch in a relaxed, sustained way. Do not bounce or stretch to the point where you feel pain.

Strength and muscle tone measures the ability of a group of muscles to perform work for you. How much can you lift, push, and carry? To build strength, you can use weight lifting equipment or calisthenics: push-ups, sit-ups, and leg raises. Either way, you firm up stomach, arm, chest, and leg muscles. Do strengthening exercises two or three times a week.

Good posture is standing erect, with straight vertical alignment, equal heights of shoulders, hips, and knees, and at the same time maintaining the three natural curves of your lower, middle, and upper back. Strengthening and flexibility exercises create good posture.

Weight management is maintained by balancing proper nutrition and aerobic exercise. Depending on your frame size, age, and genetic disposition, you need to stay within a recommended range for good health.

Coordination is the ability of your body to execute movements and sports in a harmonious way.

Agility is the ability to move in a quick and easy way. It's very important in sports such as tennis, basketball, volleyball.

Relaxation is the ability of your body to be free of tension. (See page 304.)

Planning Your Fitness Program

Becoming fit is like making a sale because you must listen to yourself, determine what your needs are, your goals, obstacles, features, and benefits. Research the possibilities. Make an action plan. Be flexible. And know your bottom line.

What is the right exercise program for you? Discover what your body needs at this time in your life. Start with your goals, and then answer the following questions:

❑ Lose weight   ❑ Gain weight   ❑ Stay the same
❑ Increase endurance
❑ Tone and strengthen muscles
❑ Build bulk
❑ Lose inches
❑ Reduce tension, stress, and anxiety

What physical restrictions, due to health problems, do you have?

1._____

What exercises do you like to do?

1._____

2._____

3. _____

What exercises do you do to compensate for a physical problem?

1. _____
2. _____
3. _____

How do you prefer to exercise?

❑ Group exercise
❑ Work out alone
❑ Work out at home
❑ Join a gym or health club

How much time do you have available?

_____ per day   _____ per week

What is your exercise budget? _____

What are your major obstacles to achieving your fitness goals?

1. _____
2. _____
3. _____

How are you going to overcome these obstacles?

1. _____
2. _____
3. _____

How will you benefit from getting into shape?

1. _____
2. _____
3. _____

List your three major goals:

1. _____
2. _____
3. _____

State what exercise you will do and when you will do it to achieve your goals:

	Exercise	*When*
1.		
2.		
3.		

Simple Exercises to Do on the Job

At your desk, at home, or on the road:[1] (1) use a comfortable, supportive chair, (2) use a headset if you're on the phone a lot, (3) set

---

[1]Sandra Fisher, *Sandra Fisher's Fitness Breaks* © 1988.

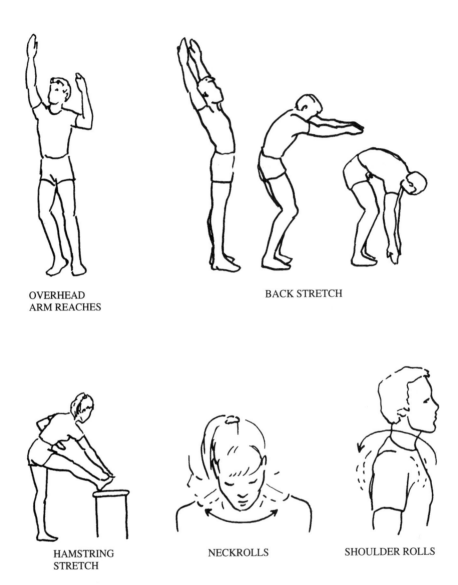

OVERHEAD
ARM REACHES

BACK STRETCH

HAMSTRING
STRETCH

NECKROLLS

SHOULDER ROLLS

desk, chair, and computer at proper height, so you are not straining,
(4) ensure good lighting.

1. *Overhead arm reaches.* In a standing position, alternatively
   stretch arms above your head, hold for four seconds, repeat
   four times, relax.

2. *Back stretch.* Bend over forward, bending knees slightly, touch hands to the floor, relaxing neck and head. Remain for four seconds and roll up to standing position. Do four times.

3. *Hamstring stretch.* Stand up, place one leg on top of chair, keeping knee straight, bend over from waist, try to touch your toes, hold for 10 seconds. If necessary, hold onto chair for balance. Do each leg four times.

4. *Neck rolls.* In a sitting position, drop chin to chest and roll the head slowly from side to side, four times in each direction, relax.

5. *Shoulder rolls.* In a sitting position, lift both shoulders and roll them back, and forward, four times back, four times forward, relax.

The car is a great place to unkink and get rid of tension.[2] Place hands in 10 and 2 o'clock position on the steering wheel.

1. *Shoulder rolls.* Same as above.

2. *Shoulder shrugs.* Inhale and raise shoulders to ears, hold for two seconds, exhale and drop them. Repeat eight times.

3. *Shoulder twists.* Twist right shoulder toward middle of wheel, hold for two seconds, and return to place. Repeat four times each side.

HIGH-ENERGY, NUTRITIOUS DIET

Eat Healthy: The Choice is Yours!

You're driving down the highway, it's 2 PM and you're starving. That last sales call took longer than you expected. Which fast-food place will it be today? Which has the shortest line? "Gimme a burger, fries, and shake, please." Gotta get to that 2:30 PM meeting.

Sound familiar? Maintaining a balanced diet is difficult for anyone. But for salespeople, the difficulties are compounded by the demands of the profession. What with the erratic, long hours; the time spent on planes, trains, and in the car; the need to entertain clients, often by entertaining them in fancy restaurants where temp-

---

[2]Exercises are from Sandra Fisher's *Workout While U Drive* audiotape. See bibliography at the end of the chapter for order information.

tation abounds; not to mention attendance at sales and trade show meetings where coffee and doughnuts are too frequently the standard fare, making the effort to eat healthily can seem like a Herculean task.

The Notorious Salesperson's Diet

Sales profession folklore has it that the typical salesperson's four basic food groups are caffeine, sugar, grease, and booze. Unfortunately for the already overly stressed salesperson, these foods undermine one's ability to think clearly and be consistently energetic. They contribute to tension headaches, gastrointestinal upset, "hyperness," inability to concentrate, anxiety, and a host of other ailments. That's exactly what a salesperson *doesn't* need to win clients!

The Unhealthy American Diet

What's wrong with the American diet? The same thing that's wrong with the salesperson's diet—too much fat, sugar, salt, and alcohol, and not enough fruits, vegetables, and grains (complex carbohydrates). Our 40 plus percent fat intake is making us larger, but not healthier. According to studies, two-thirds of all calories in the average American diet have little nutritional value: 42 percent from fat, 24 percent from sugar, 5 percent from alcohol. Fifty percent of us eat more protein than recommended, and the average person consumes 128 pounds of sugar a year!

At any one time, over 35 percent of people report being on a diet. (Are you one of the 35 percent?) But within one year, 90 percent of dieters regain at least two-thirds of the weight they lost.

The old adage "You are what you eat" proves true. Scientists are reporting the myriad links between poor nutrition and a wide range of mental and physical ailments, ranging from depression and anxiety to heart disease, hypertension, stroke, diabetes, and cancer.

With all this working against you, what's a nutrition-starved salesperson to do?

---

[3]Additional free copies of the pyramid are available from the US Department of Agriculture, Washington, DC 20250.

The Food Guide Pyramid

A Guide to Daily Food Choices

KEY

⬤ **Fat** (naturally occurring and added)

▽ **Sugars** (added)

These symbols show fat and added sugars in foods

Fats, Oils, & Sweets
USE SPARINGLY

Milk, Yogurt, & Cheese Group
2-3 SERVINGS

Meat, Poultry, Fish, Dry Beans, Eggs, & Nuts Group
2-3 SERVINGS

Vegetable Group
3-5 SERVINGS

Fruit Group
2-4 SERVINGS

Bread, Cereal, Rice, & Pasta Group
6-11 SERVINGS

Choose the New American Diet— The Food Guide Pyramid[3]

The food guide pyramid helps you plan a well-balanced, nutritious diet to provide the nutrients, vitamins, and minerals you need. The smaller the section, the less of that type of food you should eat.

How Much Is a Serving?

A serving is one cup of milk or yogurt, one egg, a piece of meat or fish about 3 by 4 inches, one cup of vegetables, one medium piece of fruit, $1/2$ cup of juice, one slice of bread, or $1/2$ cup of cooked grains or pasta.

General Guidelines for a Healthy Diet

Make sure to consider your age, frame size, activity level, and any special health conditions when making food choices.

Enjoy your food!   Take time to plan the meal, whether it's selecting a restaurant or making it at home. Eat in a calm atmosphere in an unhurried, pleasurable manner. (Yes, it can be done!)

Eat a variety of foods.   Capture all the nutrients, vitamins, and minerals you need. To reduce the risk of cancer, make sure to include foods rich in vitamins A and C, cruciferous (cabbage-family) foods, and to help you deal with stress, eat foods with B vitamins (grains). The more color the better in your vegetable and fruit selections.

Maintain proper weight.   Too many extra pounds may be risky, but at the same time, don't starve yourself. It's best to keep weight under control. Diets low in fat and high in fiber help keep the unnecessary fat off.

Eat breakfast.   Even though health professionals tout breakfast as the most important meal of the day, less than 50 percent of Americans eat it. But by skipping breakfast and not fueling your body, you become ravenous later in the day, and energy levels drop precipitously. Reps report eating dinner, then searching for snacks, and uncontrollably shoveling in pretzels, cookies, chips, and so on all evening while plopped in front of the TV. And this all starts with not eating right at the beginning of the day.

Don't skip meals.   Have you noticed how cranky you get when you get too hungry? No patience to listen to a prospect! That's because your blood sugar level is dropping and signaling your body that it needs energy. Food is energy and essential to maintain consistent blood sugar levels. Eat at each mealtime, and depending on your body and needs, keep fueled up on light snacks.

Avoid fats.   Make fat 20 to 30 percent of your diet. Use lean meat, fish, and poultry, and limit butter and margarine, egg yolks, fried food.

Eat less sugar. The average American consumes more than 120 pounds of sugar a year. Too much.

Eat less salt. Salt contributes to hypertension and water retention.

Drink less alcohol. Up to one drink a day is recommended in the health guidelines.

Reduce caffeine. One or two cups of coffee or tea, or one caffeinated soda a day are acceptable. If you're feeling wound up, don't add another stimulant to your diet.

Eat more whole grains, fruits, and vegetables. These offer most of the nutrients your body needs.

Take vitamin and mineral supplements. A reasonable program might include a multivitamin plus 1000 mg of vitamin C, or a balanced "stress formula" of vitamins A, E, D, C, and the B complex. Consult a nutritionist or read books for in-depth information.

Eat for Energy: Peak-Performance versus Anti-Peak-Performance Foods

What you really want is to go out there and *sell, sell, sell,* and this takes energy and stamina. A vice president of sales confessed sheepishly that between his big belly and being out of shape, his 46-year-old body wouldn't be able to keep up the pace required of his successful sales reps. And a rep from another company reported that a sales manager, along on a sales call, fell asleep as he was making the presentation.

To eat for energy, first become aware of which foods will enhance your ability to perform and which will inhibit it. Maybe your diet simply makes you feel jittery or constantly fatigued. The next time you pop something into your mouth, think about its effect on you. Does it:

- Give you energy or make you sleepy?
- Pick you up and then make you crash?
- Relax you or turn you into a motormouth?

Then make healthier decisions about what you eat. Here are some suggestions:

Dos:

Breakfast: fresh fruit or fruit juice, low-fat yogurt, unsweetened cereal and low-fat or skim milk, bagel and jelly, one egg, cottage cheese, whole grain toast or roll, English muffin.

Lunch: salads, noncreamy low-fat dressing, fish, chicken, or lean meat, noncream soups, unbuttered veggies, potato or rice, yogurt, cottage cheese, pasta without cream sauces, lots of water.

Late afternoon: 1 to 2 ounces of fruit or even a couple (not 10!) cookies to benefit from the focusing and calming effects of carbohydrates.

Dinner: grilled or poached fish, chicken, vegetables, grains or starches.

Don'ts:

Breakfast: sausage, bacon, home fries, french fries, cream cheese, butter, pancakes with butter and syrup, pastries, croissants, greasy muffins, excessive amounts of coffee.

Lunch: high-fat meats, such as hamburgers, fried foods, high-fat cheeses, creamy salad dressings, mayonnaise, pasta with cream sauce, butter, rich desserts, alcohol, shakes.

Late afternoon: sodas, cookies, chips, ice cream.

Dinner: fat-laden food, too many alcoholic drinks.

Rate Your Diet

Do you:

❑ Eat 3–4 servings of fruit daily?
❑ Eat 3–5 servings of vegetables daily?
❑ Choose lower fat milk and dairy products?
❑ Eat low-fat fish and chicken more often than high-fat meat products?
❑ Eat less than four high-sugar foods each week?
❑ Eat home-cooked meals more often than fatty processed food?

The more checks you have, the more likely it is you are eating nutritiously.

Your Nutrition Profile

List foods that you eat on a typical workday in the left-hand column. Next to any foods that you consider to be less than healthy, list alternative, healthy foods that you can eat instead.

Breakfast _____   _____

               _____   _____

               _____   _____

               _____   _____

               _____   _____

Lunch _____   _____

               _____   _____

               _____   _____

               _____   _____

               _____   _____

Dinner _____   _____

               _____   _____

               _____   _____

               _____   _____

               _____   _____

Snacks _____   _____

               _____   _____

               _____   _____

               _____   _____

               _____   _____

Number of glasses of water per day_____   _____

Indicate your body composition:

❏ Too much fat
❏ Just right
❏ Too little fat

Number of pounds you need to lose or gain? _____

List the foods you will add to or remove from your diet: _____

_____

_____

_____

Recommended Daily Dietary Guidelines (For Moderately Active Women of
120 Pounds and Men of 170 Pounds)

	Women	Men
Calories	1,800	2,500
Fat/grams	<60 grams	<80 grams
Fat/percent	<30%	<30%
Cholesterol	<300 mg	<300 mg
Sodium	<2400 mg	<2400 mg

RELAXATION SKILLS

Relax, slow down, and take it easy are common admonitions. But
do you know what relaxation actually means? Do you think that
playing golf or tennis is relaxation? Or reading a book? If you
answered yes, you're wrong. They are recreation.

Relaxation is the opposite of the stress response. It is when you
turn off all stimuli so the mind and body are at rest—deep rest.
When your heart rate slows down, your breathing becomes slow
and deep, your blood pressure drops, your muscles let go of tension, your mind is calm, and you feel at peace—that's relaxation.

Total relaxation is difficult to achieve. Telling yourself not to get
excited in the midst of an aggravating situation rarely helps. Usually, your muscles tighten into a nagging neck pain.

Try this quick way to experience how tight muscles produce
pain: Make a fist, and contract all the muscles in your arm. Hold it.
Notice how your hand and arm feel, especially as you continue
holding. Note the white knuckles. Feeling pain yet? Release and
shake your arm and fingers. See how good it feels. Be aware of the
contrast. That's what happens every time you are under stress and
your muscles tighten.

Now you will be able to learn relaxation techniques. These skills
require practice until they become automatic. Think of it as if you
were learning any other new skill, such as skiing or operating a
computer. It takes five to six weeks to learn a new neuromuscular
skill. *The goal is to enable you to relax anywhere, in any situation.*

By incorporating relaxation into your daily life, you reduce the
buildup of stress and tension, and allow the immune system to

regenerate itself and heal again. Recent research on treating heart disease has shown that along with diet and regular aerobic exercise, the daily practice of a relaxation technique can reverse arterio-sclerosis, or buildup of plaque in the arteries.

Techniques to Aid You in Eliciting the Relaxation Response

First, you have to become aware of when you are tense. Once you become conscious of being tense, whether from sore muscles, holding your breath, or clenching your teeth, you can do something about it. *You can change your breathing, do some stretching exercises, and mentally refocus your thoughts.* To learn the techniques, you need to practice in a quiet room. Turn off the phone, the kids, and make yourself comfortable. Don't go to sleep. You should remain alert to your experience, without analyzing it. Keep external stimuli to a minimum. Ideally for maximum health benefits, you should spend 20 to 30 minutes a day performing one of these relaxation techniques.

Instant relaxation. Do this anywhere, anytime. Let your mind go blank. Slowly take a deep breath and exhale. Say to yourself, "I feel calm and at peace." Repeat twice or more.

Breathing. Focus your mind on your breath, how it comes in and how it goes out of your body. Slow it down. Consciously inhale for four seconds, hold breath for two seconds, exhale for four. Take your time.

Meditation. Meditation is an ancient practice used by eastern cultures during which you try to focus your mind on one thought, or object, excluding all other thoughts. If your thoughts drift, consciously return your awareness to the single thought. Studies show that meditational practice can bring about major physiological changes for deep relaxation. You need to be comfortable, in a quiet environment, and remain passive. This clears your mind and body of tension. Increasingly, meditation techniques are being adapted by Western cultures and serve as the basis of the following techniques:

Progressive relaxation. This technique combines deep breathing with contracting and releasing muscles. Sit or lie down in a comfortable position. Focus on your right leg. Inhale and contract all the leg's muscles. Hold it for three seconds, then exhale and release, "letting go." Shake it gently. Turn your attention to the left leg. Continue this way, going to the buttocks, abdomen, back, shoulders, right arm, left arm, neck, face, and end with a total body contraction. Take two deep breaths and lie peacefully for two to five minutes.

Visualization. Visualize a peaceful, safe, and restful image, such as a tranquil lake, a beautiful garden, a sunrise, or a sunset.

Autogenics. Autogenics trains your body and mind to respond to internal verbal commands to relax and return to a balanced, normal state. Begin with 30 seconds to 1 1/2 minutes of training and repeat five to eight times a day. Gradually increase to 20 minutes.

Take a few deep breaths. Focus your attention on each part of your body, starting with your feet; progress to arms, back, shoulders, face. Say, "I feel heavy and warm. My legs feel heavy and warm. My arms feel heavy and warm. My face feels cool. My body is warm and heavy. I am calm and peaceful." Other thoughts are: "I feel quiet. My mind is quiet."

Which relaxation techniques appeal to you to use?

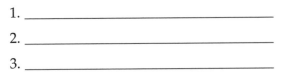

1. _____

2. _____

3. _____

Describe how you can use any of these techniques during a typical stressful sales situation: _____

_____

And in your lifestyle? _____

_____

Your Personal Stress Reduction Plan

Manage stress or it will manage you! You've learned a lot about stress. You can't change the wind, but you can adjust the sails. You can change the way you think about things and the way you act. Now what are you going to do about it?

What actions do I need to take to consistently reduce my stress levels?

1. _____

2. _____

3. _____

4. _____

This is what I commit to doing: (Be specific: how often, where, and when?)

1. _____

2. _____

3. _____

4. _____

5. _____

These are the results I expect:

1. _____

2. _____

3. _____

4. _____

This is how I will evaluate my progress:

1. _____

2. _____

3. _____

4. _____

These are the benefits I will get:

1. _____

2. _____

3. _____

4. _____

Good luck! Go for it!

Bibliography

Books

Bailey, Covert. *The New Fit or Fat.* Boston: Houghton Mifflin, 1991.

Benson, Herbert. *The Relaxation Response.* New York: Morrow, 1975.

Borysenko, Joan, PhD. *Minding the Body, Mending the Mind.* New York: Bantam, 1987.

Davis, Martha, PhD, Elizabeth Robbins Eshelman MSW, and Matthew McKay, PhD. *The Relaxation & Stress Reduction Workbook.* Oakland, CA: New Harbinger Publications, 1988.

Gawain, Shakti. *Reflections in the Light: Daily Thoughts and Affirmations.* San Rafael, CA: New World Library, 1988.

Moyers, Bill. *Healing and the Mind.* New York: Doubleday, 1993.

Ornish, Dean, MD. *Dr. Dean Ornish's Program for Reversing Heart Disease.* New York: Random House, 1990.

Rippe, James, MD. *Fit for Success.* Englewood Cliffs, NJ: Prentice Hall, 1989.

Sheehan, George, MD. *Personal Best.* Emmaus, PA: Rodale Press, 1989.

Audio and Videotapes

Workout While U Drive by Sandra Fisher. Fitness by Fisher, PO Box 596, New York, NY 10028, 212-744-5900.

Guided Relaxations by Sri Swami Satchidananda. Integral Yoga Center, Route 1, Box 1720, Buckingham, VA 23921, 800-262-1008.

The Complete Guide to Exercise Videos. Distributor for 250+ exercise videos. Collage Video, 5390 Main Street NE, Minneapolis, MN 55421. For free guide, call 800-433-6769.

Chapter Twelve

How to Sell in Tough Times to Difficult People Without Cutting Your Price

Alan Cimberg

Let us turn the calendar back to October 1969. I, Alan Cimberg, salesperson, am about to get into my car to make a first-time sales call on a purchasing agent of a large company. I have been told that if I can sell him, he can purchase more of my products than any other three companies put together. Obviously, it is a very important sales call. Why don't you ride along with me. Get your seat belt on. Are you comfortable? Good! Here we go—and if you remain perfectly quiet, you may hear what I am saying to myself on this ride.

"Alan Cimberg, this is your big chance. You can be a hero. All you have to do is to load this prospect with as much of your products as you can jam into his warehouse. But, then again, there just isn't any fooling these big buyers. I can just see it now. I am but a few minutes into my presentation and he shows little interest. Shortly he says, 'What I am purchasing now is far superior to these. Their packaging is much better than what I see here. And your prices are a little bit too high; there is nothing here of interest to me.'"

And I continue my mutterings with, *"The company I work for stinks. They simply do not have it when it comes to programs, products, policies, prices—nothing. Oh well, I've got to fill out a report on this call. I may as well get it over with."*

We arrive at the prospect's place of business. I ask you to wait for me in the car. I go in and return 25 minutes later. And my question to you is, "Did I or did I not get an order in there?" You are right. I didn't. He knew by the look in my eye. He knew by the sound of my voice. He knew by every move I made that I did not expect him to give me an order and he wasn't going to disappoint me by *giving me one*.

ACHIEVING BALANCE

The determining factor here was I programmed myself for failure by the negative picture I played in my mind. There is a Latin word for what had transpired; it is called *homeostasis,* balance. The mind visualized my failing and, as a result, the body had to achieve a balance with the mind. Psychologists refer to it as "the self-fulfilling prophecy." There's a comedian on TV who expresses it much better. He says, "What you see is what you get." Because our subconscious cannot distinguish between a real and a vividly imagined experience, it will react to mentally created stimuli in the same manner as to actual events.

Is it not therefore logical to assume a mental picture of a *successful* sale would be the stepping-stone to achieving it?

Does this sound difficult? It isn't. You have already used a less directed form of visualization every day of your life. Each time you daydream or recall an event, you probably rely on imagery to help you along.

Visualization does something incredibly powerful. It "programs" the visual, creative, intuitive, right side of your brain to understand where you're heading. Your goal is now quickly acceptable for review by a glance at your picture or by simply calling up its mental image. Vivid mental pictures are used to provoke goal achievement and personal success.

The process goes by many names—visualization, guided imagery, inner pictures, movies of the mind. But no matter what it's called, this amazing technique has proven just how potent the directed mind can become. Also, if you can "see" where you want to go, you can probably figure out how to get there.

Golfer Jack Nicklaus "goes to the movies" inside his mind. When he crouches low to check the distance between the ball and the cup, he sees himself making the proper putt and also visualizes the ball dropping into the cup. The sales process can be diagrammed as a

baseball playing field. This book shows how salespeople can tag all the bases. Do not overlook the importance of the player in the kneeling position. At this very moment he visualizes successfully getting on base. Rick Wallheuter, the Olympic pole vaulting star, exclaimed, "I not only see myself going over the bar, but I tell myself, 'Rick, go over that bar.' "

The successful formula then is:

Visualize whatever it is you want to achieve.
Verbalize—tell yourself exactly what you are going to make happen.
Vitalize—make it happen.

THE POSITIVE ATTITUDE

The failure of our mission when we rode together was due to my negative attitude. It is practically impossible to achieve anything without *positive* expectations.

Those of us who have children know the concept. The child comes to us and says, "I can't do it." The very first thing we say to that child is, "Yes, you can." Actually, we do not really know whether the child can or cannot do it. But this much we do know—we have to remove the negative picture and replace it with a positive one.

A positive attitude enables us to summon up our most powerful resources at will.

From the very important standpoint of health, it is generally agreed that negative emotions suppress the immune system and cause illness, while positive feelings promote healing. New studies strongly indicate every illness that can befall the body, from the common cold to cancer and heart disease, can be influenced positively or negatively by a person's mental state.

It is well to remember that, of all the factors that separate top performers from everyone else, *a positive attitude* is the most important, the simplest to acquire, and the most fun.

THE SALE BEFORE THE SALE

Unlike my attitude during the ride, as a salesperson you must first make "the sale before the sale." You must sell yourself on:

1. Yourself.
2. Your company.
3. Your product or service.
4. Your prices.

The absence of these is the reason, in my opinion, more than 50 percent of sales calls are doomed to failure *before the actual sales interview*. Where did I actually lose that sale? Before I got out of the car, of course. And it explains why for such a long time I found each call a painful experience.

Here are my suggestions for selling ourselves on these four points.

Selling Yourself

Many years ago, we needed a new home. We walked into a real estate office. The sales agent asked us a few simple questions: In what area are you seeking? How many rooms? How much down payment can you afford? How much mortgage money will be available? And then we got into her car. For the next five hours, we went on what appeared to be a safari. In one house and out the other, in one and out another. By 5 o'clock, I didn't get rid of her; she got rid of me. She said, "Mr. Cimberg, do you know what the problem is?" "No," I said, "what is the problem?" She said, "You don't know what you want." That wasn't the problem. *She* didn't know what I wanted.

The next day we went to another real estate office. This one greeted us, had us sit down comfortably, and then asked, "Tell me, Mr. and Mrs. Cimberg, *what* type of house are you looking for? *What* area would you prefer to locate? *What* kind of house are you living in now? *What* do you wish your present house had? Exactly *what* are you looking for in a house? *Where* would you want this house to be? *Where* have you already been viewing some homes? *When* did you move into your present house? *How* do you expect to pay for this house? *Why* did you select that particular area? *What* are the school ages of your children? *Who* exactly would be occupying the house?"

Why did she ask me these questions? Obviously, because the reasons I will buy any home she shows me are in *my* head and she's got to get those reasons out. If we will only get out of our mind how can we *sell* this person and replace it with the word *help*, we can triple our sales.

I therefore suggest a selling philosophy of **stop selling and start helping.** Selling is doing something *to* them. Helping is doing something *for* them. (Who would *you* buy from?) My philosophy in effect says, "Sure I'm here to sell you, but first I'm going to help you, because that is the only way I can get what is good for both of us."

Remember, the sale moves forward when the *prospect* is talking. Find prospects' problems by asking what, where, when, how, why, and who. Selling is a problem-solving situation. And the problem is the difference between what they want or need and what they have. *Wants* and *needs* are not necessarily the same. I might *need* castor oil, but *I wouldn't want it.* Equally, I *want* a color television set, but I don't *need* it.

Do not wait for customers to come to you with problems. Go to them with solutions after you have learned as much as you can about their business. When it comes down to it, we have complicated the selling process. It has been "me against him," which doesn't pay.

Encourage prospects to give you as much additional information as possible by your saying:

"That sounds interesting . . . Why do you say that?"

"Good question . . . Why do you ask that?"

The simple two-letter word *oh* said with an upward inflection will reveal a lot, too. And then you should listen and listen hard. We have two ears and one mouth; we should listen twice as much as we talk. As a matter of fact, we should listen with *three* ears: What the prospect is saying, what the prospect is trying to say, and what it is the prospect really means. And don't interrupt. But be interruptible. When you are talking, watch their faces for signs they want to cut in with some more information. Stop in midsentence if you have to. When I conducted a six-hour sales session in Taiwan, I learned something about listening at its best. It's embracing the speaker with your eyes. Above all, be a sharp listener, not a fast talker. You can *listen* your way into a sale. All of this results in your building the most precious thing you can get, and that is a trust relationship. There's a very strong need for it, because we have to offset the negative image of the salesperson.

That image is reflected in a survey of 1,564 people, which was taken by the Gallup organization. The question was, "How would you rate the honesty and ethics of the 24 occupations listed?" On top were clergymen; second was pharmacists; followed by dentists and medical doctors. Would you like to know who came out on the bottom? *Salespeople!*

And if that isn't enough, look up the word *sell* in any dictionary, and depending on its size, you will find one or more of the following definitions:

To exchange something for money or its equivalent. (That's a fair definition in itself, but we have to list all the meanings the dictionary gives.)

To get rid of something.

To betray a trust.

Hoax.

Hard sell.

Dupe.

High pressure.

Cheat.

Trick.

To do something dishonorable.

To give up one's honor for a profit.

It's shocking, isn't it? But here's the next one, and this definition can be found in *Webster's New World Dictionary*, 20th Century Edition: "to exchange one's services for a *price*, especially for a dishonorable purpose as for . . . *prostitution*."

Because of this poor image, buyers are alert for our first untruth—exaggeration or even puffery—at which point we are dead.

In connection with our need for getting prospect input, let me tell you of an all-day sales training session I had with some insurance people a few years ago. The day went well. At the end of the session, a man came toward me and he had stars in his eyes. He said, "Alan Cimberg, it was a great day that I was here to listen to your presentation." And then he showed me a slip of paper on which he had printed in beautiful letters my exact words, which were, "You should never again make a presentation on insurance until you first find out for what possible reasons your prospect might be interested in insurance." And he continued with, "Before I make any presentation, I'm going to read this note carefully so that I never forget it."

And then he asked if he could drive me to the airport. We got to the airport. We were in the lounge, and I was having my usual ginger ale. He cleared his throat and I sensed it. He was going to try to sell me life insurance. I did not mind; it takes one to know one. And then—listen carefully to his opening statement to me—he said, "Mr. Cimberg, you look to me like the kind of man to whom it is very important that he build an estate for his children."

Dear reader, I want you to know that Mrs. Cimberg and I agree that leaving money to children deprives them of the motivation to make it on their own. Now, with that opening statement, how much insurance am I ready to buy? None, of course, because he wasn't finding out what my needs are or the possible reasons I would buy insurance.

I could just picture it. He gets back to the office and his sales manager asks how he made out on his interview with me. I can just hear his reply: "I couldn't get Alan Cimberg to sign on the dotted line."

That comment would have been a joke because not only didn't he get me to sign on the dotted line, but he also wasn't even on first base.

I saw myself making that very same mistake countless times, when I rushed into my presentation without the necessary input. And then I wondered why I was being turned down.

Now, just suppose he followed the advice on the piece of paper and he asked, "Let's assume you were going to buy some life insurance. For what possible reason would you buy it?" I might reply something like, "Since you asked me to pretend, I would say it would be for this (pointing to my throat), my voice box. I have a fear that someday something happens to it and, as a sales trainer, I'm out of business." Now he has something to deal with that would be of interest to me. But he doesn't go rushing into his presentation, because he is aware that the *more* he knows about my wants or needs, the easier it is to close the sale. So he would follow up with, "That sounds very interesting. Is there any other reason that would prompt you to consider buying life insurance?" My answer would be, "Yes, my wife, Freda. She has been a wonderful mother and wife, and I have a fear that someday if something happens to me or because of some sharp rise in inflation, there may not be enough money for her to live in the manner in which she is entitled."

No, I am not going to tell you that if he dealt with me in that manner, I would have said, "Give me that order pad. Where do I sign?" What I am saying is, now he's got my attention and interest. He has a solid platform on which to build his sales presentation. (See diagram of sales process on page 311.)

Selling Your Company

In my training of salespeople, I've had the opportunity of getting close to them. And often they would share with me the many gripes they had about the companies for which they worked. What was startling to me was that these gripes were *identical* to the ones I had when I was selling. Here is a list of them, and see if any of them are familiar to you.

The communications in this company are atrocious.

This company doesn't really care about me as a person.

The changes—there are constantly so many changes in management and procedures.

I'm overworked.

I'm underpaid.

I do not get the proper help.

I do not get the proper recognition.

The paperwork is tremendous.

I do not get the help I need.

We're supposed to be a quality house. We should be arrested for some of the stuff we turn out.

And deliveries! There are late deliveries . . . mixed up deliveries . . . and sometimes *no* deliveries at all.

And the equipment in our plant . . . much of it is outdated.

As for my territory . . . they should give it back to the Indians.

Does any of this sound familiar to you? If you're anything like the great majority of salespeople I train, the answer is undoubtedly yes. Of the many thousands of salespeople I have trained, it was rare for someone to deny having a poor impression of his or her company.

Obviously, these gripes are universal with salespeople, so if you should take a new job elsewhere, you will be carrying this list along with you wherever you go. The grass is not greener on the other side. There is just as much crabgrass there.

We communicate in many ways: verbally, by body language, and by the vibrations we give off. And when we come face to face with a prospect, don't we reveal how we really feel about the company we represent? Then, under those circumstances, is there any wonder why we walked out without an order?

If you must say something negative about your company, whether to a customer or someone else, follow it up with two positive things.

Let's get back for a moment to the complaint about changes. It's almost to the point that if our company is doing the very same things it did at this time last year, something is amiss. In this ever-changing world, changes are a must, not for the sake of change, but because we have to keep up with outside situations that are changing daily. Changes are prevalent in every company. It got to the point in one company that a sales manager was leaving the office for lunch. He turned to his secretary and said, "Martha, if my boss calls, get his name."

Selling Your Product/Services

I went into a drugstore recently to buy a new electric shaver. I saw two shavers on display, one with a $50 price tag and one with a $40 price tag. I asked the owner to explain the difference between the two. His answer was, "$10". I went to the next store and saw the same two shavers and the same two price tags. I asked the same question: What's the difference? This time the clerk said, "You see that $50 shaver? It has 384 cutting edges and those cutters are made from case-hardened steel. There's a very thin shaving screen above the cutters; then there are two roller combs on each end, and the entire thing is powered by high-energy cells." And I didn't buy. Why? Because he was talking about the shaver. Who should he be talking about? Me, the customer, Alan Cimberg.

I went to the next drugstore, saw the same two shavers with the same two price tags and asked the same question. This time the clerk said to me, "This $50 shaver has 384 cutting edges, so that they will cut every one of your whiskers. And those cutters are made of high case-hardened carbon steel so that you'll get a cool shave and it won't burn your face. And notice the two roller combs on each end so that you won't feel a pull or pinch. You'll get a closer shave.

And the whole thing is powered by high-energy cells. That means electricity or not, you're never without a shave."

This clerk was not only talking about the features, but also the corresponding *benefits* to me, the customer. People don't buy things for what they are. People buy things for what they will *do* for them. According to *Hardware* magazine, last year more $1/4$-inch drills were sold than ever before, and not one person wanted a drill. What did they want? You're right. Holes—$1/4$-inch holes.

One apocryphal story goes like this: In one of the wars a great many years ago, all the soldiers were given a free insurance policy against being captured by the enemy. They were covered to the extent of $50,000. To make the offer sweeter, they sold supplementary insurance for a very small sum. In no time, a colonel in the South sold more of this supplementary insurance than anyone else. His supervisors were amazed and they decided to stay in the back room to listen to his pitch. This is what they heard: "OK, you guys, now listen to this. If you go into battle and are captured, your family receives $50,000. On the other hand, if you take out supplementary insurance for a very small fee, and you are captured, the army has to shell out *$100,000.* Now on the basis of that, who do you think they are going to send into battle *first?*"

The heart and soul of our presentation is in the benefits. And the extent to which we have fully determined the prospect's needs and wants and covered them with the appropriate benefits is the extent to which we will be successful in the sale.

Selling Your Price

We all know there are seminars that improve the skills of salespeople and teach them how to deal specifically with purchasing agents. But did you know there are seminars attended by purchasing agents that help *them* handle salespeople? They really do exist; I've been to them.

While attending on one of these seminars, I overheard some purchasing agents talking about you, the salespeople who call on them. What I heard spoke volumes about the weakness of salespeople through the ages. One purchasing agent said, "I could take the most confident salesperson in the world and reduce that person to a stuttering, blubbering idiot with five simple words."

You know what those words are: "Your price is too high." You've heard it. You've felt its impact. It stopped me in my path many times just when I thought the sale was going smoothly.

Why is this objection constantly thrown at us? Why do purchasing agents use it so often? The first and most obvious reason is it may be true. Your price may be too high. More often than not, however, your price is not too high. After all, companies stay in business only by remaining competitive.

The primary reason purchasing agents claim your price is too high is they are looking for a better deal. That's their job. They have to test you to see if there is a better price to be had, and they often get it when you cave in.

When you hear the words, "Your price is too high," you are being told you have failed in one essential aspect of the sales process; that is, you have failed to justify your price. You do that by creating *value*.

What is occurring in the buyer's mind is a weighing process. What you have said about features and benefits versus the price you have quoted is being evaluated. If the scale tilts too far in the price direction, the objection is, "Your price is too high." If the scale tilts toward the value, you've made a sale.

The Benefit of Benefits

Quite often, salespeople fail to emphasize the perceived value of their product. Hence, when the evaluation process occurs, they lose. It is essential to give your customers all the benefits relevant to your product or service. This requires *product* knowledge on your part. (I need not dwell on the importance of product knowledge. If we do not have it, how can we sell it?) Be sure to include and emphasize those benefits that are relevant to the needs and wants. This requires *customer* knowledge.

Cutting Your Price

Except in extreme cases, I strongly suggest you do not cut a quoted price. And if you will role-play with me, I will give you my reasons.
Me: "OK, I'll cut the price by $500."
Would you agree that:

1. You will always wonder how much less I would have accepted.
2. On all future calls, you will never accept my first quote no matter what it is.
3. But here is the greatest loss on my part. I have lost the most precious thing I have and that is my *integrity.* You think I am dishonest or else why did I quote a higher price in the first place?

So I suggest again, except in extreme cases, do not cut the quoted price. You may, when you first quote the price, advise the buyer that you are reducing it by *x* number of dollars for such and such a reason.

And while I advocate not cutting the price, *you may alter your price by altering the conditions.*

1. You may ask the buyer to pick up the shipment at your loading dock.
2. You might ask the buyer to pay the freight.
3. You might suggest the shipment be deferred until such time as your trucks are in the buyer's area.
4. You might suggest bulk instead of packaged products.

5. You may ask if the order could be doubled.

Think of other valid reasons you may give for cutting prices.

If you have run out of options and the conversation is getting nowhere, you might remind the buyer, "You get what you pay for." Or else say, "Let us set the matter of price aside for a few minutes and let's talk about . . . ", and guess what you talk about—the benefits, benefits, benefits that are important to the buyer.

Another instance of the importance of our making *relevant* presentations was forcibly brought back to mind the other day when I went to a local automobile showroom and was greeted by a man who didn't even bother to get up from his desk. He said, "May I help you, sir?" Now *there's* a great opener for an automobile salesman. I felt like saying, "Yes, I came in to buy a tie. Have you got something in brown to match my eyes?"

When I revealed the startling fact that I had come in to buy a car, he took me over to a sedan and lifted the hood. He pointed proudly to the engine and said, "Look." I looked, but didn't see what he wanted me to see. I know *nothing* about engines and care even less. Then he took me to the trunk. He opened it and pointed to the roomy compartment. "That will hold five pieces of luggage," he said. Well, that disqualified me immediately. I own only two pieces of luggage, and I wasn't about to go out and buy three more pieces just because the trunk could hold them.

Let's look at what was happening in that interaction. Did the car salesman give a hoot about me? Of course not. He was interested in only one thing—making the sale. He didn't care about uncovering what I was looking for in a car, and he probably would not listen when I volunteered information. He didn't care about adding value to the sale.

Suppose, just suppose, after I explained my interest in the car, he had said to me, "Tell me, Mr. Cimberg, what's important to you in a car?" Who does he want me to talk about? Me, Alan Cimberg. Contrary to what a lot of people think, the Alan Cimbergs of this world want to talk about themselves. They want to talk about their hopes, their wishes, and their fears. I know what you're thinking now—that it's extremely difficult to get prospects to open up. That is because they do not feel they are in a safe space. Once they get the feeling that you're out to help them in addition to selling them, the stage is yours.

I would have said to him, "What's important to me in a car? When I'm out driving, if I hear a rattle, if I hear as much as a squeak, I get nervous." With that piece of information, here is what he could very well say to me. "Mr. Cimberg, I'm not going to tell you that when you drive this car you'll never hear a squeak or a rattle. What I am saying is when it does happen, it isn't your problem—it's ours to take care of." With that assurance, am I not ready to pay more for the car than any other quote I may have received?

If my next-door neighbor Mr. Albert came into the showroom, that is an entirely different story. That salesman should get the hood up as quickly as possible and talk about the engine, its torque and all those other things that are beyond me. Mr. Albert's hobby is taking things apart and putting them back together.

Another neighbor, Mr. Harmon, trades his car in every year. Need I tell you what you talk to him about?

Mr. Lewis, down the block, likes having the most attractive car in town. You talk to him about interior styling, the sculpted graceful curves, leather seats, and everything else that would give him what *he* needs.

Mr. Ross will bore you to death talking about the miles per gallon that he gets on his car. You know what he wants.

Mr. Fogel, his wife, and his two children are, shall we say, rather heavy-set. With them, you talk about all the things that will give them comfort.

Mr. Vossons narrowly escaped death as a result of an accident. You talk to him about the safety features designed to provide peace of mind for everyone who rides in the car.

There is nothing that will diffuse in the buyer's mind the importance of a high price as quickly as relevant benefits. It fully answers the important question on a prospect's mind—"What's in it for me?" And with different people, there are different answers to that question pertaining to the very same product, as we have just described with the automobile.

If you wonder whether the matter of benefits has withstood the test of time, I quote from the good book:

> In the Garden of Eden the serpent said to Eve, "As soon as you eat of the apple your eyes will be opened and you will be like divine beings." When Eve saw that the tree was desirable as a source of wisdom she took of its fruit and ate.

Jack Lacey, an eminent sales trainer, refers to the major benefit as "the hot button." Our job is to find it.

There are several other possible reasons for being told a price is too high. You might hear someone say, "Well, you're asking $5,000 and I only have $4,500 in my budget." That's one of the easiest objections to handle. Notice that the price is not too high, but the customer just doesn't have the money. Your job now is to work with your prospect to find a way to make the sale possible—help him find financing; sell him a less expensive product; or show him that his budget is unrealistic for what he needs and maybe he'll find more money.

When asked to elaborate on his objection, another customer may say, "Your price is too high because the competition charges $100 less." This happens most often when the salesperson is coerced into giving a price before presenting a complete picture of the *relevant* benefits. When this happens, it is too easy for the prospect to dismiss your product with an unfair comparison to your competition.

We have all met prospects who were so busy they just wanted to know the bottom line: price. It's easy to cave in and give them what they want, but don't do it. It would be unfair to both of you. A price is meaningless without a value attached to it—and that is the salesperson's job, to convey value. So be polite, but insist on telling your prospects what they are getting for their money.

Why would a comparison based solely on price be unfair? Most often the comparison is between apples and oranges. Be sure to point out the differences to your prospects. Those differences should be described in terms of features that will be benefits to them in relation to their *specific needs*.

It is important to have done your homework on your competition before a comparison is made. If you have, you will be able to answer this objection quickly and realistically. Part of a realistic comparison is the discussion of the bottom-line cost that purchasing agents understand so well as return on investment. Although a competitor's price may be lower, in the long run your product may cost less. For example, you may be able to add value to the sale by throwing in a service contract or paying for shipping.

Remember this: When comparing prices, you have to justify only the *difference* in price, not your total price. If you charge $500 and the competition charges $450, you should only address the $50 difference. If all else fails, you can "reduce it to the ridiculous:" "$50, when amortized over the 20-year life of this product, is only $2.50 per year, less than a penny per day . . . "

BE A PITCHER, NOT A CATCHER

As a last word, here's some advice on handling objections in general. Don't answer an objection and then pause, waiting for the next one to be hurled at you. That's being a catcher of objections. Instead, move on with your presentation or, better yet, *ask for the order!*

COMMITMENT

And now, I will give you a big chunk out of my life. It was the early days of my job as a salesman. I was no great shakes at it. I did it by what I called "selling by the numbers." That is, on an average, I found I could make one sale after four calls. Mathematics was never my strongest suit, but I knew that if I wanted the earnings two sales would yield, well, you know the rest.

At that time, I lived in a small three-room apartment. It consisted of a small eat-in kitchen (I had to stand and push my chair aside to open the refrigerator door), a medium-size bedroom shared by my 12-year-old daughter and 9-year-old son, and a folding bed made famous by Mr. Castro's little girl in the living room where Mom and I slept. It was time that we looked for a home of our own. We could have continued to manage with a small kitchen and the extra effort required to convert the sofa into a bed, but a 12-year-old girl shouldn't be sharing a room with a 9-year-old boy, brother or not. It just wasn't right. So it was time to purchase our own home.

Off we went (with the real estate agent you read about earlier). I inherited my parents' creed of living within my means. So we made it very clear to the agent what we could afford as a down payment and monthly mortgage money after that. The homes we saw did not exactly grab us. Only one of them had the picket fence that we felt was a must, and that was in need of repair and painting.

When we thought we had finished for the day, we happened to come across a dream house, even judging only from the outside. It had been built recently. There certainly was no point in investigating it. It was obviously much too much beyond my means. But my wife had to use the bathroom so she went in alone. She came

326 Chapter 12 / How to Sell in Tough Times to Difficult People Without Cutting Your Price

out and said five words to me that I will never forget. "Daddy, buy me this house." Do not ask me why. I don't know. But Daddy did buy her the house, and Daddy got sick over it immediately. (I remember the day we moved in. She called out to me to come look out the window at a beautiful rosebush. I could not do it.) I started to calculate the very minimum I would have to make to pay off the mortgage. I did not go very far in doing so. My head began to spin.

My father, from whom I didn't ask one red cent, did not speak to me for six months because he said, "You had no business buying that house." (We would not have been talking for a longer period except that my daughter was unhappy about the estrangement and asked if I would please go straighten it out.) My mother-in-law, who always thought I was an idiot, was now sure of it.

Get ready now, because here comes the $64,000 question. Did I or did I not make the monthly payments? Of course, you know that I did.

Why? The reasons were:

1. I merely started to do those things I knew all along I should be doing and I stopped doing those things I knew I should not be doing. You know what they are as well as I do.
2. I remembered what psychologists said—that we do not use 15 percent of our talents. And I started to stretch my mind and my leg muscles (much more of the former than the latter).
3. Last and most important, I was *committed* to getting it done.

Alexander Graham Bell wrote, "What this power is, I cannot say. All I know is that it exists. And it becomes available only when you are in that state of mind in which you know exactly what you want and are fully determined *not to quit until you get it.*"

Be aware that there is a danger of quitting when the going gets tough. That is why you should tie your project to something you fervently desire. It will motivate you from the inside to hang on and to move forward. As it most often happens, your difficulty will be solved and dissolve. You are on the way to becoming stronger than ever. Your commitment becomes achievement. Bet on it!

My fervent desire was paying off the mortgage. Yours might be a beautiful home with a car to match. Or to be manager, vice president, and yes, president, too. Why not? Others have done it. You can, too.

You have now learned the secret of how today's entrepreneurs achieve the remarkable things they do.

Remember, selling need not be solemn. Relax, smile, laugh, have a sense of humor, poke fun at yourself.

I wish you good selling.

Index

A

Accomplishments, tracking, 138
Accountability, 139–40
Accountants, 255
Account Blueprint, 12–19
  case studies, 22–26
  competitive information in, 15
  creating, 19–22
  revised, 17–19
Acknowledging, 71–72
Action plans, 120, 128, 140
Active voice in writing, 224
Adrenal glands, 275
Advertising, 36
Aerobic exercise, 293
Agility, 294
Alcohol, 301
Aligning, 72
Alternatives
  in close, 111
  in negotiations, 179–81
Anatomy of sale, 1, 2
Anger in negotiations, 194–95
Apostrophes, 226
Appointments by phone, 38–59
  pre-call preparation, 53–54
  rejection in, 56–59
  requesting, 48–49
  script for, 45–51
  secretary screening, 54–55
ARC method for meeting objectives, 51
Assembly line operation, phone prospecting as, 58
Assertiveness, 250, 284–85
Associations, prospecting in, 34
Assumptions
  and communication problems, 167
  false, 198–99
Assumptive close, 111
Attainable goals, 126–27
Attention getters
  in negotiations, 196
  in presentations, 80
Attitudes of successful people, 124
Audience
  assumptions about, 199
  establishing rapport with, 84–85
  gaining attention of, 80
  organizing writing for, 215

Audience—*Cont.*
  for presentations, 81
  when planning writing, 205
Audiocassettes, in prospecting, 37
Audiovisual equipment, for presentations, 82–84, 90–92
Autogenics, 306

B

Balance, 290–91, 310–11
  positive attitude and, 311–12
  work and personal life, 289–90
Behavioral effects of stress, 279
Belief in self, 124
Benefits of product, 319, 322–24
  versus features, 51
Blanchard, Ken, 125
Blessing-White Company, 129
Body language, 104, 163
  during presentations, 87–88
Bootlegging, 250
Brainstorming, and writing, 212–15
Breakfast, 300, 302
Breathing to relax, 305
Broadcast fax, 37
Brochures, 11
Business directories, 182–83
Business letters, salutation, 227
Business line, prospecting by, 33
Business relationships; *see* Relationships
Buying decisions; *see* Purchasing decisions
Buying signals, 108–9

C

Caffeine, 301
Calendar of events close, 111
Career goals, 132
Center of influence, 44
Change, 167
  within company, 317
  openness to, 184–85
Character ethics, 253
Chemistry, in sales call, 10, 16

328

Clarity in negotiations, 176–78
Closing, 105–12
 fears in, 112
 for objections, 99, 103–4
 process, 110–11
 questions about, 108–9
 timing for, 108
Coaches, 139
Code of ethics, 239
Cold calling, 37; *see also* Appointments by phone
Colons, 227
Columbia University, 234
Comfort Zone, 74
Comma splice, 228
Commas in writing, 225–26
Commitment, 169, 325–27
 in negotiations, 181–83
 to relationship, 191
Committees, 45
Communications; *see also* Listening
 anger and, 194
 avoiding breakdowns, 174
 elements in process, 152
 problems from assumptions, 167
 two-way, 156–58, 168, 173
Company, selling, 316–17
Competition
 information in Account Blueprint, 15
 pricing, 324
Computer monitor, projecting image for presenta-
 tion, 84, 91–92
Computers, for data storage on prospects, 5, 56
Concern, 96
Conclusion
 to memos, 209
 to presentations, 86–87
Confidentiality of information, 236
Conflict, 190
Conflict of interest, 256
Conflict resolution skills, in ethical issues, 252
Confrontations, 94
Conscience, 247
Consultant, becoming, 64–66
Consultative sales approach to selling, 63
Consumers, invasion of privacy, 238
Contract, time management, 145
Coordination, 294
Coping skills for stress management, 282–84
Corporate functions, responsibilities of, 81–82
Corporate knowledge, 8
Corporate social responsibility, 237, 238
Covey, Stephen, 253–54
 The 7 Habits of Highly Effective People, 129
Credibility, 44, 169, 192
Credit profile, of prospect, 8
Customers
 awareness of, 9–10
 behavior and personality, 16
 goals for relationships with, 73–74
 needs, 12, 15–16
 as new business source, 35, 36
 role in ethical issues, 254–57
 state of mind, 72–73

Customers—*Cont.*
 writing to, 205
Cut-and-paste approach to writing, 204

D

Deadlines for goals, 128
Dead Poets Society, 124
Decision implementer, 44
Decision influencer, 44
Decisions; *see also* Closing *and* Purchasing decisions
Dejection, 96
Delays, planning for, 141
Delegating tasks, 141
Desire, 123–28
Diet, 297–304
 American, 298
 and energy levels, 301–2
 food guide pyramid, 299
 nutrition profile, 303
Dinner, 302
Direct mail, 36
 mailing lists, 238
Directories, 182–83
Durkheim, Emile, 254
Discipline, 117
Dress, 66
 for success, 11

E

Edison, Thomas, 122–23
Ego, versus empathy, 67–68
Ego drive, versus empathy drive, 68–70
Emotional effects of stress, 279
Empathy, 99–100
 ego versus, 67–68
Empathy drive, versus ego drive, 68–70
Employees, versus manager on job goals, 127–28
Energy, foods for, 301–2
Enrollment body language, 88
Enthusiasm, 97
Entrapment, 250
Ethical issues, 233–64
 in business relationships, 234
 conflict resolution skills in, 252
 conscience or self-interest, 247–48
 customer's role, 254–57
 developing boundaries, 252–53
 education programs, 234
 knowledge influencing, 246
 legal limits, 122–23
 mail-in survey, 266–68
 management issues, 236–238
 personal, 239–46
 speaking up, 257–58
 spotting patterns, 249–52
 Truth or Consequences Case, 240–46
Ethics, defining, 235–36

Ethics checklist, 241
Exercise (fitness), 291–93, 295–97
    aerobic, 293
    flexibility, 293
Existing customers, as new business source, 34
Eye contact, during presentations, 88

F

Failure
    fear of, 122, 138
    programming for, 310
Family goals, 130
Fats in diet, 300
Fax, broadcast, 37
Fear
    in closing, 112
    of failure, 122, 138
    of presenting, 79
    of rejection, 112, 122
Features of product, versus benefits, 51
"Fight or flight" response, 271
Financial goals, 131–32
First impressions, 66–67
Fitness, 291–93
    planning program, 294–95
    testing, 293–94
Flexibility, in negotiations, 181
Flexibility exercise, 293
Flip charts, 83, 90
Focus, 118
    lack of, 117
Food guide pyramid, 299
Former customers, 36
Free samples, 37
Free trials, 37

G

Gallup organization, 120
    poll on honesty, 314
Gestures, during presentations, 88
Goals, 117–46
    congruency with values, 129
    customer relationships, 73–74
    defining, 118–23
    desire to achieve, 123–24
    inventory exercises, 130–34
    learning to, 121
    measurable, 125–26, 138
    for prospecting, 39, 57
    reasons for, 118
    reasons for not setting, 121–22
    reviewing, 138
    SMART, 125–29
    time frames for, 128, 136–37
    written, 119, 120
Good, Bill, *Prospecting Your Way to Sales Success,* 30
Guided imagery, 310

H

Handouts, for presentations, 82
Harvard Business School, 234
Harvard University, motivation study, 118–20
Health
    mental state and, 312
    reducing risks, 288–89
    stress and, 275–77
    wellness, 287
Helping, versus selling, 313
High-pressure gimmicks, and resistance, 110
Hill, Napoleon, *Think and Grow Rich,* 136
Holtz, Lou, 135
Homeostatis, 310
Honesty, with customers, 254
Hostility, 96
Hot buttons, 16
Human resources professionals, 258
Humor, and stress management, 286
Hyphens, 226–27

I

Indifference, 97
Industry knowledge, 9
Influence, 100
Information
    confidentiality, 236
    on prospects, 4
Initiative, 185
Integrity, 193, 321
Intentions, 70–71
Interruptions, planning for, 141
Invasion of privacy, 238

J

Jargon, 224
Job interviews, 162–64
Jobs, goals for, 127

K

Key word, 207–8, 209, 212
KISS principle, 118

L

Lacey, Jack, 324
Language, 172
    definition, 150
Laughter, 286
LCD panel, 84, 91–92
Learning

Learning—*Cont.*
  goal setting, 121
  from mistakes, 123
Library, of product knowledge, 7
Listening, 149–74, 314
  criteria, 152
  importance of, 152–55, 171
  in negotiations, 184–88
  to prospects, 152–54
  and relationship development, 70, 158–61
  as selling skill, 11
  and success, 154–57, 172
Lunch, 302

M

MacKenzie, Alec, *The Time Trap,* 142
Magazines, as prospecting source, 35
Manager, versus employee on job goals, 127–28
Market identification, 30–31
Marketing, 255–56
  problem solving approach, 28, 30
Meals, skipping, 300
Measurable goals, 125–26, 138
Meditation, 305–6
Memo
  conclusion to, 209
  sample, 207
Mental effects of stress, 279
Mental state, and health, 312
Mineral supplements, 301
Mistakes, learning from, 123
Morality, 247
Motivation
  from goals, 126
  study on, 118–20
Movies, desire portrayed in, 124
Muscle tone, 294

N

Negativity, 122
  coping with, 97–99
Negotiations, 175–202
  anger in, 194–95
  attention getters, 196
  commitments, 181–83
  effective requests in, 196–98
  false assumptions, 198–99
  flexibility in, 181
  listening in, 184–88
  to maintain relationships, 183–84
  objectives of, 178
  options, 179–81
  preparation for, 176–77, 200
  by teams, 189–92, 201
  time frame for, 178
Networking, 34, 35–36
Newsletters, 36

Newspapers, as prospecting source, 35
Niche marketing, 33
"No whining" form, 137–38, 146
Nutrition; *see* Diet

O

Objection handling, 93–105
  coping with negativity, 98
  handbook for, 51–53
  pause in, 104
  resistance forms, 95–97
  response, 99–104
  in telephone prospecting, 49
Objectives, of negotiations, 178
Obstacles, overcoming, 136
Office etiquette, 66
Opinions, and conflict, 190
Optimism, 124
Organizational effects of stress, 279–80
Outline, 216–21
  use in postwriting checklist, 220–21
Overhead projectors, 83–84, 91

P

Paperwork, 141
Pareto's principle, 30
Passive voice in writing, 224
Pause in objection handling, 104
Payoff matrix, 248–49
Peers, writing to, 205
Perfectionism, 141
Persistence, in prospecting, 55, 57
Personal appearance, for sales call, 10–11
Personal issues in ethics, 239–46
Personality
  learning about, 159
  in sales call, 10
Personality ethics, 253
Personal life, 170
  balancing with work, 289–90
Personal stress reduction plan, 307–8
Personal time, 290, 291
Pharmaceutical business, 255
Phone presentation, 50
Physical effects, of stress, 279
Planning; *see also* Pre-call planning
  fitness program, 294–95
  presentations, 84–87
  and time management, 140
  writing, 204–9
Platform speakers, 164
Politics, 252
Positive attitude, 66–67
Post card mailer decks, 37
Poster boarding, 136
Posture, 294
Power, empathy and, 100

Practice, of sales skills, 11
Pre-call planning, 1–26
Presentations, 79–92
    audience for, 81
    body of, 86
    body language during, 87–88
    conclusions of, 86–87
    materials and audiovisuals for, 82–84
    planning, 84–87
    practicing skills, 190
    purpose, 80–81
Pressure, fear of applying, 112
Price
    of competition, 324
    cutting, 321–25
    selling, 319–20
    structure for, 6
Priorities, for presentations, 80
Privacy invasion, 238
Probing, 99, 100–102
Productivity goals, 132
Products
    knowledge of, 6–8
    selling, 318–19
Progressive relaxation, 306
Promises, 192
Promotion of service industries, 256
Prospecting, 27–59
    as assembly line operation, 58
    awareness development, 28
    discipline for, 29–30
    goals for, 39, 57
    market identification, 30–35
    rationale, 27
    record keeping for, 55–56
    rejection in, 56–59
    schedule for, 40, 43
    script for, 45–51
    sources, 32–38
    ultimate objectives, 74
Prospecting Your Way to Sales Success (Good), 30
Prospects, 3
    file system for information, 4–5
    information from, 313, 316
    negative feelings of, 97–98
    qualifying, 3, 47–48
    right to object, 94–95
    source information about, 4
    sources, 3–4
Public relations, 36
Punctuation, 225–29
Puppy dog technique, 37
Purchasing decisions
    learning reasons for, 161
    persons involved in, 43–45, 47–48
    process, 61–62

Q

Qualifying prospect, 47–48
    criteria, 3

Questions
    to clarify prospects' objections, 100–101
    about closing, 108–11
    during presentations, 87
Quotas, 126
    and stress, 280
Quotes, punctuation with, 226

R

Rapport, 70
    building in telephone presentation, 47
Recommended daily dietary guidelines, 304
Record keeping, for prospecting, 55–56
Recreation, 304
Referrals, 1, 32–33
Regret, 117
Rejection
    fear of, 112, 122
    in prospecting, 56–59
Relationship building, 61–77
    by becoming consultant, 64–66
    empathy skills in, 70–71
    first impressions, 66–67
Relationships, 1, 3
    commitment to, 191
    ethics in, 234
    negotiations to maintain, 183–84
Relaxation, 294
    skills for, 304–8
Relaxation response, 274
Relevant goals, 127
Repair department, for prospecting
    sources, 38
Requests, effective in negotiations, 196–98
Resistance
    forms of, 95–97
    high-pressure gimmicks and, 110
Responsibilities, of corporate functions, 81–82
Risks
    list of, 187
    reducing health, 288–89
    from unethical conduct, 257
Rocky 3, 124
Run-on sentences, 228

S

Sales calls; see also Pre-call planning
    handling stress on, 273–74
    objectives for, 12–19
    personal appearance for, 10–11
Sales objective, in Account Blueprint, 15
Sales planner, Account Blueprint as, 12–19
Sales practices, unethical, 237; see also
    Ethical issues
Sales strategy, 28, 29
Salt, 301
Salutation of business letter, 227

Scheduling; *see* Time frame
Script, for prospecting, 45–51
Secretary screening, 54–55
Secular issues, 246
Selective perception, 28
Self, belief in, 124
Self-fulfillment prophecy, 310
Self-preservation, 235
Self-talk, negative or positive, 274, 285
Self time, 290, 291
Selling
    company, 316–17
    definitions, 314
    evaluating skills, 11
    versus helping, 313
    price, 319–20
    products or services, 318–19
    yourself, 312–16
Semicolons, 227
Seminars, 35
Sentence structure, 223, 228
Service business, 255
Service department, for prospecting sources, 38
Services, selling, 318–19
Serving, in diet plan, 299
The 7 Habits of Highly Effective People
    (Covey), 129
Skepticism, 95–96
Slides, 84, 90–91
SMART goals, 125–29
Social responsibility of business, 237, 238
Software, bootlegging, 250–51
Specialization, 31
Specificity in goals, 125
Standards of conduct, 247
Stand and Deliver, 124
Statement close, 110
State of mind of customer, 72–73
Strategic alliances, 37
Strength and muscle tone, 294
Stress
    defining, 270–71
    determining current, 278–79
    and health, 275–77
    impact of, 269–70, 279
    sources of, 243–45
Stress management, 269–308
    assertiveness, 284–85
    coping skills, 282–84
    current procedures, 277–78
    humor and, 286
    lifestyle skills, 287–97
    reduction techniques, 282–87
    support systems, 285–86
    time management in, 284
Stress response, 271–73
Style of writing, 222–30
    personal or impersonal, 225
    punctuation, 225–29
Subliminal messages, 235
Success, 121
    listening and, 154–57, 172
    personal attitudes and, 124

Sugar, 301
Summary of benefits close, 110
Support systems in stress management,
    285–86
Surveys, 38
Suspects, 3
Synchographics, 238
System organizer, 140

T

Teaching, prospecting sources from, 38
Teams, negotiations by, 189–92, 201
Technical language, 224
Testimonials, 111
Thesis sentence, 206–9, 217
Think and Grow Rich (Hill), 136
Time frames
    for goals, 128, 136–37
    for negotiations, 178
    for prospecting, 40, 43
Time management, 140–41, 284
    contract, 145
The Time Trap (MacKenzie), 142
Timing for closing, 108
To-do list, 137
Topic sentence, 208–9
Top management
    as role model in ethics, 237
    writing to, 205
Trackable goals, 128
Trade secrets, 236, 256
Trade shows, 35
Trial close, 105, 110
Trust relationship, 188, 191, 314
Two-way communications, 156–58, 168, 173

U

Unethical behavior; *see also* Ethical issues
    condoning, 235
    risks from, 257
    in sales practices, 237

V

Value added, 324
Values, 129
Vertical prospecting, 33
Videos
    bootlegging, 250–51
    in prospecting, 37
Visual aids, 11
Visualization, 306, 310
Vitamin supplements, 301
Voice mail, and telephone prospecting, 51
Voice resonance, during presentations, 88

W

Weight management, 294
Wellness, 287
Win-win conclusion to negotiations, 200
    commitment to, 182
Women, ethical stance, 250
Wordiness, 223–24
Work, balancing with personal life, 289–90
Writing, 203–31
    back-door approach, 209–11
    brainstorming and, 212–15
    current usage style, 224–25
    format for, 206
    organizing, 211–22
    outline for, 216–21
    planning, 204–9

Writing—*Cont.*
    plunging-in approach, 203–4
    postwriting checklist, 220–21, 229–30
    purpose of, 205–6
    ranking components in, 215–16
    style, 222–30
    thesis sentence for, 206–9
Written goals, 119, 120
    importance, 124–29
    statement of, 134–35
Written plan, for pre-call planning, 19

Y

Yale University, motivation study, 118–20

DATE DUE
